The Adaptable South

The Adaptable South

Essays in Honor of George Brown Tindall

Edited by

Elizabeth Jacoway

Dan T. Carter

Lester C. Lamon

Robert C. McMath, Jr.

Louisiana State University Press • Baton Rouge and London

Copyright © 1991 by Louisiana State University Press
All rights reserved
Manufactured in the United States of America
First printing
00 99 98 97 96 95 94 93 92 91   5 4 3 2 1

Designer: Rebecca Lloyd Lemna
Typeface: Palatino
Typesetter: Graphic Composition, Inc.
Printer and binder: Thomson-Shore, Inc.

Library of Congress Cataloging-in-Publication Data

The Adaptable South : essays in honor of George Brown Tindall / edited
    by Elizabeth Jacoway . . . [et al.].
        p. cm.
    Includes bibliographical references and index.
    ISBN 0-8071-1678-5 (cloth)
        1. Southern States—History—1865–1951. 2. Southern States–
    –History—1951– 3. Tindall, George Brown. I. Tindall, George
    Brown. II. Jacoway, Elizabeth, 1944–   .
    F215.A33   1991
    975'.04—dc20   91-10468
                                                                    CIP

for George Brown Tindall
Gentleman, Scholar, Teacher, Friend

C O N T E N T S

Preface   ix

Introduction: The Adaptable South   1
  Dan T. Carter

The Church That Forgot: Southern Presbyterians Adapt to the
New South   18
  Jack Maddex

God, Cotton Mills, and New South Myths: A New Perspective
on Salisbury, North Carolina, 1887–1888   44
  Gary R. Freeze

Ignoring the Color Line: Maryville College, 1868–1901   64
  Lester C. Lamon

New Negroes for a New Century: Adaptability on Display   90
  Walter B. Weare

New Woman, Old Family: Passion, Gender, and Place in the
Virginia Fiction of Amélie Rives   124
  Wayne Mixon

Toward a Marriage of True Minds: The Federal Writers' Project and the Writing of Southern History   148
Jerrold Hirsch

Frank Graham and the Politics of the New South   176
Julian Pleasants

From Shotguns to Umbrellas: The Civil Rights Movement in Lowndes County, Alabama   212
Charles W. Eagles

Jimmy Carter: A Southerner in the White House?   237
Robert C. McMath, Jr.

Interview with George Brown Tindall   264
Conducted by Elizabeth Jacoway, Dan T. Carter, and Robert C. McMath, Jr.

The Principal Writings of George Brown Tindall   291

Contributors   295

Index   297

PREFACE

In the fall of 1966, I walked into George Tindall's seminar and my
life changed. With no background in southern studies, I had never
heard of William Archibald Dunning or reflected much on racism,
all of which was immediately apparent to George Brown Tindall.
Within a matter of weeks, the elegant gentleman with the wry wit
and the bow ties had led me into a world of new concerns, deeper
meanings, and higher callings, and in his gentle way he encouraged me to see that this could be my world, too.

My experience was not atypical. Though surely not as backward as I, all of George Tindall's graduate students have been sustained by his warmth, challenged by his example, lifted by his encouragement, and chastened by his high standards. All have had
their lives changed by him, and all have wanted to be involved in
this effort to honor him.

Festschrift was a word I heard first in that dazzling Tindall
seminar, and I wondered then who would do the volume honoring
George Tindall. Little did I dream that it would be me and my contemporaries at Chapel Hill at that time. The idea for this project
emerged over dinner at the Southern Historical Association convention in Louisville in 1985. The four of us—Dan Carter, Les Lamon, Bob McMath, and I—constituted ourselves as a self-styled
"editorial board," anointed me editor in chief, and set about the
business of selecting a theme, locating and contacting potential
contributors, soliciting proposals and critiquing them, commis-
sioning papers and critiquing them, calling for revisions and cri-

tiquing them. There have been more delays and missed deadlines in this project than in a space launch; but there have also been delightful planning sessions and celebrations at fine restaurants and hotels across the South. All of this planning and effort and celebrating goes back to the fact that George Tindall took a group of fresh-faced and naive southern youngsters, treated us with respect, set a standard of excellence and showed us with his own life how to achieve it, and turned us into very different people. It is our hope that what he finds here will please him and that it will honor him before his profession.

This effort has been directed from a private study in Newport, Arkansas, often with the needs and concerns of two little boys interjecting themselves forcefully into the process. Dan, Les, and Bob have been very patient with me, and I am grateful. I am grateful, too, to the other contributors, who labored heroically to bring their essays into line with the theme of adaptability, who persevered through the tedium of numerous revisions, and who were unfailingly cheerful, if not always prompt, in their responses. Special thanks are in order for Beverly Jarrett, whose encouragement emboldened us to initiate the project and whose steady hand guided us through the process of acceptance by LSU Press; for Bill Powell, whose careful sleuthing yielded the initial list of Tindall Ph.D.'s; for Betty Brandon, who compiled the Tindall bibliography; for Margaret Dalrymple and John Easterly, who piloted the project through the shoals of publication; and for Gerry Anders, whose superb copy-editing saved us from more errors than I care to confess. Finally, I am grateful to my children, Timothy and Todd Watson, for their patience in sharing their mother with this project, and to my husband, Tim Watson, for his gracious and generous and unfailing support.

Elizabeth Jacoway

The Adaptable South

Introduction

The Adaptable South

Dan T. Carter

In significant ways, the American South's distinctiveness within the larger national culture stems from its Janus-like orientation toward the past as well as the future. In his 1974 Fleming lectures at Louisiana State University, George Brown Tindall spoke of the "persistent tradition in New South politics," a tradition that precluded any complete transformation in southern affairs. This tension between a devotion to the past and a realization of the necessity for change has characterized the complex (and sometimes contradictory) behavior of southern individuals and communities as southerners have sought to wrestle with the profound changes in southern life engendered by military defeat, economic devastation, and emancipation, and then by the economic and social upheavals of the twentieth century. In the essays that follow, several of George Tindall's former students trace the processes of change in the postwar South, and each of them suggests ways in which individuals and groups retained key elements of the old order even as they accommodated themselves to the new.

Few historians have captured this ambivalence more subtly than George Tindall, whose career has been devoted to understanding what David Potter called the "sphinx" of southern history. Tindall's career began in the spring of 1946 when he arrived at the University of North Carolina in Chapel Hill, part of that first wave of World War II veterans who would reshape American colleges and universities in the 1950s and 1960s. Having majored in English at Furman University (where he met his wife, Blossom McGarrity), Tindall made a brief detour through the English department's graduate program. But at the encouragement of his lifelong friend Isaac Copeland, he switched to history and enrolled in the Southern History seminar of Fletcher Green, the dominant figure in the training of southern historians in the years before and after the Second World War.

In the intervening four decades of a distinguished career of teaching and research in the field of southern history, Tindall has assumed something of the role Green played for an earlier generation in the training of southern historians. At the same time, in his books, articles, and lectures he has shaped much of the framework for historical writing on the late nineteenth- and twentieth-century South.

Tindall's first published work showed him, at the outset of his career, wrestling with the historical dilemmas of race, that most fundamental of southern themes. His research paper in Green's seminar, a description and analysis of South Carolina's disfranchisement convention of 1895, became the basis for his M.A. thesis. Later he published a revised version in the *Journal of Southern History* as "The Campaign for the Disfranchisement of Negroes in South Carolina." In this first scholarly publication, Tindall's distinctive voice already could be heard. Always the careful, even-handed scholar, the young historian described with unusual subtlety the differences between the Negrophobic Tillman "reform" disfranchisers and the Conservative heirs of Wade Hampton, for whom the best that could be said was that they wanted to let sleeping dogs lie. At the same time, the twenty-eight-year-old South Carolinian made it clear that he had little use for the shibboleths of the traditional white South, dismissing the myths of Reconstruction as stories of black domination that had been "rehearsed in more and more macabre shapes with the passage of time."[1]

His dissertation, published three years later as *South Carolina Negroes, 1877–1900*, was marked by that same fairness as well as by a willingness to confront the fundamental realities of black oppression in the Palmetto State. *South Carolina Negroes* became one of those works destined to have a significance far beyond the bounds of the topic itself. Along with Vernon Lane Wharton's study of race relations in Mississippi, Tindall's monograph would have a major impact upon the emergence of a new generation of historians writing in the field, an impact generously acknowledged by C. Vann Woodward in his 1974 edition of *The Strange Career of Jim Crow*.[2]

In this first monograph, Tindall exposed the bad faith and the fraudulent intentions of the disfranchisers, and in his sober conclusion he pointed toward the ways in which racism had come to dominate southern politics. After 1895, he wrote, the "great fear of the Negro vote palsied those who had liberal or progressive tendencies," and "direct appeals to racial prejudice" often became the convenient path by which white Democrats gained election. Segregation, Tindall concluded, had simply replaced slavery as the "instrument of maintaining the subordination of the Negro by a caste system based on race."[3]

Tindall's early religious training and the influence of several

1. George B. Tindall, "The Campaign for the Disfranchisement of Negroes in South Carolina," *Journal of Southern History,* XV (1949), 224. The centrality of race was a theme to which Tindall returned in the following decade, exploring both the continuing validity and the limitations of U. B. Phillips' notion of race as the central theme of southern history. Tindall, "The Central Theme Revisited," in *The Southerner as American,* ed. Charles G. Sellers (Chapel Hill, 1960), 104–29.

2. August Meier and Elliott Rudwick briefly discuss Tindall's early views on race in their study *Black History and the Historical Profession, 1915–1980* (Urbana, Ill., 1986), 147.

3. George B. Tindall, *South Carolina Negroes, 1877–1900* (Columbia, S.C., 1952), 302.

of his teachers in his native up-country South Carolina led him away from the traditional racial assumptions of most southern whites. Although the specific sources of that change were difficult to recall, Tindall suspects that "either a social gospel message, or simply a foundation of values, filtered through a conventional religious upbringing, however backslidden a Baptist I may have become since." Half a century later he would still remember an elementary school teacher as she described to his class an incident in which white children had shoved black children off the sidewalks of Greenville in a youthful assertion of white supremacy. The parents of those black children, Laura Butler gently lectured her fourth graders, were citizens "and subject to taxes like our own parents. They had as much right to the sidewalks, therefore, as anybody else." Seven years later, for his high school term paper, Tindall wrote on the inadequacies of black education. ("So far as I know," he later recalled, "time has mercifully left no copy of that paper in existence.")[4]

Like other southerners of his generation, Tindall returned from the war eager to take part in the construction of a new and racially more humane South. As an active member of the Chapel Hill branch of the American Veteran's Committee, Tindall supported the chapter's call for the integration of the University of North Carolina. Such an aberration from southern norms might be blamed on mere youthfulness in the late 1940s; however, George and Blossom Tindall could offer no such excuse for joining the non-segregated Chapel Hill Community Church when they returned to the university a decade later. Throughout the 1950s and 1960s, in his personal life and in his professional role, Tindall made clear his opposition to racial discrimination, an opposition that hardly endeared him to one University of North Carolina alumnus. "I am glad I studied history under Dr. De Roulhac Hamilton and R. D. W. Conner, and not you," wrote a member of the university's

4. George B. Tindall, "Jumping Jim Crow" (Paper delivered at the annual meeting of the American Historical Association, Chicago, December, 1986, copy of typescript in possession of author), 3, 7.

class of 1935. "I feel sorry for the kids who have to study history under a liberal." Biology, he warned Tindall with an unmistakable reference to the race issue, "does not lend itself to liberalism."[5]

After an interview with Tindall in the late 1950s, civil rights activist Virginia Durr worried that Tindall was too much the even-handed scholar for her single-minded tastes. Still, she recalled, "you knew where he stood, and you knew that he didn't have any use for a racial system that had kept blacks down for generations."[6] Virginia Durr was correct on both counts. Tindall was the careful scholar who was always uneasy at the way in which ideological zealotry could lead scholars to twist their evidence to match a priori conclusions. And he warned that historians should always be ready to embrace knowledge for its own sake since they could "never know for sure when the seemingly irrelevant might suddenly speak to our needs." Still, he recognized that he wrote from a particular frame of reference, and he readily confessed his fondness for history that was relevant "in the sense of something which speaks to our concerns today."[7]

If his book on South Carolina's Negroes introduced Tindall as a major scholar in southern history—and in the emerging field of Afro-American history—the publication of *The Emergence of the New South* established him as the preeminent scholar of twentieth-century southern history. Rupert Vance, the eminent Chapel Hill sociologist-historian, had been commissioned to write the tenth volume in Louisiana State University Press's History of the South series. In 1956, however, Vance decided he would never finish the volume, and the Littlefield Fund's advisory board turned to Tindall, then a young assistant professor at Louisiana State University. By the time Tindall returned to Chapel Hill as an associate professor in 1958, he was well into the research on the project.

5. J. Stephens to George Tindall, "Sunday," 1968, in Box 2, George Brown Tindall Papers, Southern Historical Collection, University of North Carolina, Chapel Hill.

6. Author's interview with Virginia Durr, September 12, 1988.

7. George B. Tindall, "Bookfest" (Paper delivered at the Southern Book Festival, Nashville, September, 1989, copy of typescript in possession of author), 4.

It was a daunting task for any scholar. Tindall's assignment required him to write a work describing the "major political, social, cultural, and economic developments" of the South from the beginning of World War I to the end of World War II. This was a period into which historians had only recently begun to make limited forays. Despite the existence of significant monographs in some areas, there were great historiographical lacunae that required Tindall to plunge into basic research in the primary sources. Moreover, as David Potter noted, it was doubtful if "any of Tindall's predecessors . . . had to cope with change at as many levels as he . . . encountered."[8] In many ways, the challenge Tindall faced was similar to that of C. Vann Woodward when the latter wrote *Origins of the New South*. But Woodward at least had the advantage of nearly half a century's perspective on much of his material. Tindall, writing in the early and mid-1960s, had to bring the story up to 1945 and describe events still directly connected to the issues of his day.

Through twenty chapters, 2,700 footnotes, and 731 pages of text, Tindall sought to capture the complexity of the upheavals in southern society during and between the two world wars. Chapter after chapter amounted to minimonographs, whether devoted to a subtle discussion of the relationship between conservative and progressive impulses in the "business progressivism" of the 1920s or to a thoughtful survey of the impact of the New Deal on southern society. Chapter after chapter broke ground in research, analysis, and interpretation, challenging a new generation of scholars. In the end, said David Potter, Tindall placed his "stamp upon a segment of Southern history which embraces one-sixth of the period since the founding of the Republic." No one, said Potter, had succeeded in capturing such "multiplicity of significant developments and such immeasurable sweep of change."[9]

8. David M. Potter, *"The Emergence of the New South:* An Essay Review," *Journal of Southern History*, XXXIV (1968), 420.

9. *Ibid.*, 424. Tindall's *Emergence of the New South* won four awards: the Jules F. Landry Prize of LSU Press; the Southern Historical Association's Sydnor Award; the

In a series of important essays and books in the 1970s, Tindall developed many of the themes he first had traced in *Emergence of the New South*. In his Lamar lectures delivered at Mercer University in 1970 (and published two years later), he explored the historical continuities and parallels of southern politics since the Civil War. Through three graceful essays he sketched the forces that have inhibited the creation of the Republican party as a political alternative in the region, and he pointed toward the many ironies of a past almost forgotten by contemporary Democrats and emerging Republicans.[10]

Three years later he placed these developments in a larger perspective when he gave the Fleming lectures at LSU, constructing his own down-home version of a political dialectic that saw a thread of continuity running through the transition from Bourbonism to Populism to Progressivism. "The Bourbons," he said, "had achieved the ultimate success of all durable conservative movements, the reconciliation of tradition with innovation. While inventing a New South they kept alive the vision of a traditional organic community. The Populists challenged that vision, or so at least the Bourbons thought, and thus had to be put down by fair means or foul. The Progressives, finally, while they took over certain 'populistic' ideas of a more active government, were the legitimate heirs of the Bourbons. Built into their synthesis was the persistent tradition in the South."[11]

If the Lamar and Fleming lectures reflected Tindall's growing strength as a synthesizer of southern history, they also revealed to those who did not know him a dry, often self-deprecating humor. As he began his exploration of his tripartite dialectic of Bourbon, Populist, and Progressive, he mockingly suggested that this

---

Lillian Smith Award of the Southern Regional Council; and the Mayflower Cup of the North Carolina Society of Mayflower Descendants.

10. George B. Tindall, *The Disruption of the Solid South* (Athens, Ga., 1972).

11. George B. Tindall, *The Persistent Tradition in New South Politics* (Baton Rouge, 1975), xii.

and other "triangular patterns" in Western culture (Father, Son, and Holy Ghost, the Hegelian trinity, and the human qualities of body, mind, and soul) might simply be conceits. Even the Fleming lectures, he noted with mock seriousness, were divided—like Gaul—into three parts.

That quality of playfully purposeful humor made his 1973 presidential address before the Southern Historical Association in Atlanta a refreshing send-up of scholars' attempts to achieve respectability through pomposity. There in the "new Babylon on the Chattahoochee" Tindall looked back over a decade in which riots, racial conflict, and bitter ethnic partisanship had undermined David Potter's notions of national consensus. Rather than simply accepting the notion that southerners were quaintly irrelevant to the rediscovery of ethnicity, Tindall suggested that they formed their own part of the ethnic and cultural tableaux. South of the Mason and Dixon line, white southerners with names like "Kruttschnitt, Kolb, DeBardeleben, Huger, Lanneau, Toledano, Moise, Jastremski, or Cheros got melted down and poured back out in the mold of good old boys and girls." Who, after all, could "be more WASPish than Scarlett O'Hara"?[12]

And side by side with southern whites, "ethnic" black southerners emerged from their even greater African diversity toward a common Afro-American culture. Although Tindall was too scrupulous a historian to suggest that these two ethnic groups had blended, he insisted that by viewing black and white "ethnic subcultures" one might better understand the fundamental bonds that maintained black and white southern identity in the face of the massive forces of national homogenization. Perhaps, he suggested almost wistfully, white and black southerners might learn that they ultimately share a "common heritage, indeed a common tragedy, and often speak a common language, however seldom they may acknowledge it."[13] This was all vintage Tindall: alternatively play-

12. George B. Tindall, "Beyond the Mainstream: The Ethnic Southerners," *Journal of Southern History*, XL (1974), 8.

13. *Ibid.*, 10, 17.

ful and dead serious, always understated and wry, and always with an insightful turn that took his work beyond the conventional.

Tindall himself well represents the contradictions of his subject matter. Although hardly an intellectual traditionalist, he has always cast a skeptical eye on the enthusiasms of the age. As late as the 1960s he was still uncertain about the absolute soundness of the aeronautical principles of flight, rejecting an invitation to give a speech some distance from Chapel Hill. "I am not persuaded that the airplane has been perfected," he explained, "and this somewhat restricts my radius."[14] And who else would wear bow ties bravely through the 1960s and into the 1970s before the fashion wheel finally turned back in his favor? Perhaps that same free-spirited willingness to push against the grain made it easier for him not only to question the racial conventions of his youth, but also to challenge some of the more exaggerated claims of methodological innovations within the historian's profession.

In 1984 Tindall eloquently set forth his views on the writing of history in an article in the American Historical Association's *Perspectives*. He pleaded with his fellow historians to avoid the discipline's retreat into a world of pseudo–social science with its mandarinic jargon and its subordination of observation to theory.[15] Tindall's "History and the English Language" reflected his lifelong skepticism of theoretical frameworks that substitute ideology and doctrine for careful research and that cloak commonplace observations in pretentious jargon—"sesquipedalian bafflegab," as he has called it. Normally the kindest of individuals, Tindall has always

14. George Tindall to Thomas H. Taylor, October 22, 1969, in Box 2, Tindall Papers. Actually, his uneasiness over air travel, now long since put aside, stemmed less from theoretical objections than from a hair-raising flight back from Hawaii he endured at the end of World War II.

15. George B. Tindall, "History and the English Language," *Perspectives*, XXII (July, 1984), 7–8, 10–11. "My personal reaction [to a statistically elaborate manuscript]," he wrote to one publisher in the late 1960s, "is that this particular study is much ado about demonstrating the obvious."

been at his most acerbic when confronting some scholarly neologism. "What do you get if you cross a Mafioso with a deconstructionist?" he asked his students, and answered himself sardonically: "Somebody who will make you an offer you can't understand." Theory and abstraction are useful, he once confided, but when they take precedence over observation, they become an "academic disease."[16]

Tindall's essay was not an attack on newer methodologies, for he has consistently welcomed the contributions of cliometricians, the *Annalistes,* and the new social historians, incorporating their work into his graduate seminars and three National Endowment for the Humanities summer seminars. At the same time his own work on ethnicity and his provocative forays into mythology hardly suggested a nostalgic attempt to re-create the historical narrative of nineteenth-century historians.[17] Rather, "History and the English Language" reflected Tindall's career-long commitment to the importance of writing that is clear, accurate, and even elegant. Historians need to get away from the notion that there is "something . . . naughty about good writing," Tindall observed, quoting Walter Prescott Webb. Nor, he argued, are literary felicity and a compelling narrative framework incompatible with the new social history or with innovative methodologies. "It would perhaps help to recast the issue as a question of style or clarity in the use of language, whatever approach one is taking." History, he reminded his readers, is an art as well as a social science.[18]

16. George Tindall to author, June 25, 1987; copy in possession of author.

17. George B. Tindall, "Mythology: A New Frontier in Southern History," in *The Idea of the South: Pursuit of a Central Theme,* ed. Frank E. Vandiver (Chicago, 1964), 1–15; George B. Tindall, "The Benighted South: Origins of a Modern Image," *Virginia Quarterly Review,* LX (1964), 281–94.

18. Tindall, "History and the English Language," 11. Fortunately, Tindall's wife Blossom also stands guard with sharpened blue pencil to help him fend off stylistic heresies. As his editor for the Fleming lectures concluded after reviewing his manuscript, "I have searched far and wide for the kinds of infelicities that justify my salary—without success." Beverly Jarrett to George Tindall, August 17, 1974, in Box 3, Tindall Papers.

Tindall's work and his training of students have always reflected a commitment to blending innovative approaches with the best scholarly traditions of literary excellence. That commitment is vividly demonstrated in "Clio's Decalogue," a list of commandments for historical writing distributed to his graduate seminar. These "Commandments of the Muse" stress the importance of basic elements of composition, from the use of the active voice to the crafting of a vigorous and readable narrative that will appeal to general readers as well as to professional historians. As he says in his first commandment, "Thou shalt smite thy reader hip and thigh with thy first sentence." [19]

Tindall's faith in the importance of good narrative writing has borne fruit in significant work, including his textbook *America: A Narrative History.*[20] At a time when most historians rushed toward multiauthored "social history" textbooks, Tindall held the line with this single-author work, incorporating the insights of a new generation of historians but placing them in the context of a readable narrative that emphasizes the centrality of culture, religion, and politics.

Perhaps that inner respect for tradition—along with a careful attention to his sources—has strengthened Tindall's skepticism when confronted with historians' glib conclusions that the changes within the South have led to its "disappearance." As he suggested in his 1973 presidential address to the Southern Historical Association, scholars have often misread that process. We learn "time and time again from the southern past and the history of others that to change is not necessarily to disappear" or to "lose one's identity." Far from losing one's identity, in fact, to change "sometimes is to find it."[21]

In the essays in this volume, nine of George Tindall's former

19. As Tindall always notes, his decalogue is derived from a longer list first prepared by the late William B. Hesseltine, a southern historian at the University of Wisconsin who shared Tindall's commitment to good writing.

20. George B. Tindall, *America: A Narrative History* (New York, 1984).

21. George B. Tindall, *The Ethnic Southerners* (Baton Rouge, 1976), 21.

students have examined some of the ways that southerners and their region have maintained their identity—sometimes because of, sometimes in spite of, but always in the midst of change. Sensitive to and in large part shaped by Tindall's understanding that the past continues to interact with and shape the present, the authors of these essays focus on the processes by which the South has accommodated itself to the ineluctable necessity of change. The careful reader will find here ample evidence for both continuity and change in the history of the New South: the concept that all the authors have employed to encompass the inevitable tension between the twin forces of continuity and change is "adaptability." In this view, to *adapt* is to retain significant portions of the old while incorporating elements of the new; to be *transformed* is largely to transcend the past. These essays focus on the processes of adaptation that have changed the South at the very moment that they have forged links of continuity with the past.

It was the Civil War, of course, that first forced the white South to turn, however reluctantly, away from that comfortable past. As Jack Maddex shows, with the destruction of their dream of a "consecrated slaveholding nation," the first postwar generation of Southern Presbyterians found themselves no longer inhibited by the rigorous intellectual demands of the antebellum comprehensive theology/ideology; gradually they turned from the Old South hesitantly toward the New, jettisoned their defense of slavery, embraced the paternal supervision of blacks as a transition process, and eventually came to terms with total black separation and independence. Maddex concludes that as Southern Presbyterians gradually abandoned the prewar basis for their southern identity, they accepted "decentralization" and "racial separation" as hallmarks of their church life, a process remarkably parallel to the way in which conservative southerners had come to terms with the larger society. By 1900, the Presbyterian church formed in the heat of the Civil War, the former bulwark of Old South values, had revised its collective memory and forgotten the earthly Jerusalem it had loved.

12

This hardly meant that the church was simply a passive reflection of the evolution of southern society after the war. In his essay on the community crusade for cotton mills in post–Civil War Salisbury, North Carolina, Gary Freeze argues that although religion was not the "causative agent of industrialization," it played more than a rhetorical role in the community's transition from an agricultural market town to an increasingly industrial urban culture.

The linkage of benevolent religious paternalism and the pursuit of profits was not unique to the postwar South; in five relatively small antebellum factories along the Deep River near Salisbury, predominantly Methodist factory owners had articulated notions of "evangelical stewardship" in their enterprises. Religious paternalism, however, played an even larger role after the war. In Salisbury's new "communal ethos" of benevolence and profit, the owners' insistence upon order, piety, restraint, and hierarchical control drew upon long-standing agrarian evangelical traditions.

Lester Lamon's account of Maryville College also describes the links between Old South and New, but it is a reminder that change does not always flow in the same direction. From a twentieth-century perspective, the cautiously prudent decision of Tennessee Presbyterians to open their struggling college to blacks seems an uninspiring mixture of decency, timidity, and economic calculation, whereas their ultimate decision to exclude blacks shows the narrow limits of change. In a world in which segregation was the norm, Maryville's tenuous commitment to racial egalitarianism suggests the limited range of abandoned alternatives in race relations.

As traditional paternal interracial relationships faded and political marginalization, disfranchisement, and legal segregation spread throughout the region, black southerners struggled to find strategies for survival. In Walter Weare's view, the emerging exposition movement showed how the region's small black bourgeoisie sought to use for its own ends a "black New South creed, with its emphasis on progress, modernization, materialism, racial solidarity, business enterprise, scientific agriculture, self-help, and public relations." Confronted with a conflict between the equally American ideologies of racism and progress, the promoters of Afro-American expositions sought to adapt to the new age by launching an "accommodative counterattack, preaching a gospel of progress, proselytizing the premodern black masses, and seizing every opportunity to testify before skeptical whites."

There were, of course, profound ironies in black southerners' embracing a movement that emphasized a synthesized, pseudoscientific ideology of progress *and* white supremacy. As Weare notes, however, the real raw materials of cultural autonomy belonged to the black bourgeoisie's "poorer brothers and sisters," and they were hardly the model sought for the new century. Survival—adaptability—had its price.

The Virginia novelist Amélie Rives struggled against constraints that were more subtle than those facing blacks, but equally powerful: the constraints of convention that bound women to rigid gender roles. Although much of Rives's work seems to be a rejection of the past in what Wayne Mixon describes as an "iconoclastic treatment of the themes of passion and gender," Mixon demonstrates nonetheless the extent to which Rives firmly rooted her novels in her commitment to what she considered the best of the southern past. Her own sense of noblesse oblige toward the poor evinces more than a passing resemblance to the traditions of Old South paternalism. And in such novels as *World's-End* she made it clear that, for her at least, peace and contentment could be found only in her home in the foothills of the Blue Ridge Mountains. As Mixon concludes, "Through her writing Rives encouraged the growth of an indigenous southern feminism, urging the region she loved so deeply to adapt to change that would make possible a fuller life for half of its population."

Amélie Rives's attempts to reconcile change and tradition were not unique. Jerrold Hirsch's study of the Federal Writers' Project and the writing of southern "folk history" reflects the profound ambivalence of many southerners in the 1930s. In the act of defining what was (and what was not) southern folklore, southerners revealed their deepest assumptions about the past and the future of southern society. How did one define the canon of southern folklore? Was folklore simply the remnants of an archaic and obsolete set of quaint customs? Or was it a reflection of a changing but still dynamic popular culture? Hirsch notes that B. A. Botkin, folklore editor of the Federal Writers' Project, grappled with these issues as he sought to unite the writing of folklore and traditional "history." Ultimately, the ways in which both writers and readers of the project's guidebooks responded to these questions reflect the processes of adaptation under consideration here.

Julian Pleasants demonstrates that North Carolina's Frank Porter Graham sought to reconcile past and future in a state and region he loved. Pleasants argues that Graham's life "mirrored a South in transition." According to Pleasants, Graham did not question the need for economic transformation in the South; he was never a nostalgic defender of the rural past. But he did believe that southerners should work to maintain what he saw as the more humane values of the traditional South, particularly those rooted in a Christian community that balanced material and human values.

In some respects, Graham appeared to be an aberration in southern society. In a region dominated by social and political conservatism and a skepticism of any taint of "radicalism," he championed (almost indiscriminately) radical and liberal causes. In the end, deep-seated white racial fears and hatreds destroyed Graham in his 1950 campaign for the United States Senate, revealing some of the limits to southern adaptability. Yet one of the reasons Graham survived as long as he did was the fact that he was so rooted in southern tradition.

White fears and hatreds have shaped racial and economic relationships in Lowndes County, Alabama, for much of its history. Most Americans first came to know of this Black Belt county because of the brutal 1965 murders of white civil rights activists Viola Liuzzo and Jonathan Daniels (and the reluctance of local white juries to convict the white murderers). As Charles Eagles shows, however, the Liuzzo and Daniels murders were simply the culmination of a century of violence and white oppression in which blacks were regularly reminded of the unrestrained power of the white minority.

Politically, that structure of oppression shifted rapidly in the mid-1960s as local black Lowndes County residents threw off the fears of generations and fought back with voter registration drives and political organization. Only five years after the deaths of Liuzzo and Daniels, John Hulett, one of the earliest leaders of the black movement, won election as sheriff. That election signaled a "new pattern in race relations." Blacks now voted, served on juries, and freely entered all public facilities. Despite predictions of white flight from the county (or worse), most whites adapted to the new order, and they did so much more quickly than many observers, North or South, would have dreamed possible.

Robert McMath's examination of Jimmy Carter gives us a different lens for viewing southern adaptability. If Carter's political appeals often seemed contradictory, they nevertheless represented with some authenticity the complex blend of Carter's own historical past. As McMath notes, Carter's family represented all three strands of the southern political tradition Tindall described: Bourbons, Populists, and Progressives. And Carter's political career, both as governor of Georgia and as president, showed the ways in which he sat squarely in the tradition of southern "business progressivism" that Tindall described as the synthesis of southern Populist and Bourbon traditions. Thus, even Jimmy Carter, the living symbol of the New South, reflected that blending of past and present that has allowed the South to maintain its identity through a century and a quarter of upheaval.

In sum, we have sought in this volume to illuminate the ongoing tension between southern past and southern present by suggesting that a persistent regional conservatism has led usually to adaptation rather than transformation in southern society. Reflecting many of the themes that have shaped George Tindall's career as a historian of the New South, these essays underline his central understanding of the continuing tension between the forces of continuity and change in southern life. Following the example of Tindall's work, we have tried to ground our generalizations in precise observations in specific historical settings rather than to base our work upon borrowed theories. To the extent that we have succeeded in all of these things, we honor George Tindall.

The Church That Forgot

Southern Presbyterians Adapt to the New South

Jack Maddex

W hen the Presbyterian Church in the United States (PCUS—informally "the Southern Presbyterian church") reunited in 1983 with its "Northern" counterpart, observers recognized its decision as an instance of southern adaptation. Previously, the reunion question had divided cosmopolitan "liberals" from regional "conservatives," and the church had made a gradual adjustment from southern traditions to modern norms.[1] Some observers contrasted the PCUS ethos of 1983 with the conservative sectionalism of the PCUS in 1883. In noting that contrast, they overlooked an even more decisive adaptation in Southern Presbyterian history. Southern and conservative though they were, the Southern Presbyterians of 1883 had experienced a deeper change in southern life than their successors would face a century later. Adapting their church life belatedly and sometimes reluctantly, they fashioned a new "Southern Presbyterian" synthesis for effective ministry in the New South.

1. Jean Caffey Lyles, "A Kairos Moment in Milledgeville," *Christian Century,* March 16, 1983, pp. 235–36; Flynn Long, "Who Are the Southern Presbyterians?" *A.D.,* XI (June, 1982), 12–14. That adjustment is the dominant theme of Ernest Trice Thompson, *Presbyterians in the South* (3 vols.; Richmond, Va., 1963–73), III.

A hundred thousand Presbyterians lived in the Confederate South in 1861—90,000 members of the strict confessionalist "Old School" denomination, and 10,000 of the more liberal, decentralized "New School."[2] Those Presbyterians were very much at home in the slaveholding South. Most of their ministers owned slaves, and many of their lay leaders were owners of considerable numbers of slaves. Presbyterians were concentrated in stable, long-settled plantation districts. South Carolina had more Presbyterians per capita than any other southern state, among them a group of especially influential theologians. West of the Appalachians, Presbyterians were fewer but were concentrated in plantation areas and in cities. As a disproportionately upper-class and informed group, Presbyterians exerted influence in their communities. Their educational standards and comprehensive Calvinist belief-system suited them to intellectual leadership and made their leaders valued champions of the causes they espoused. Ministers usually spoke for the church, but what they said both reflected and influenced the continual informal discourse among Presbyterians at large.

Church leaders naturally formed ideas about the South in which they lived and worked. Until the 1820s, many of them conceptualized the South as a spiritual frontier, conspicuously in need of their gifts of piety, education, and gentility. Most of them took slavery for granted, but few discussed it at length. Some, believing it was part of the southern problem, professed a mild and ineffective manumissionism. After the 1820s, however, Southern Presbyterian leaders became increasingly conscious of their South as a slaveholding society and dedicated themselves to a ministry that would relate to its social structures. The conditioning influence of master-slave relations in their everyday lives, along with their paternalistic conception of social responsibility, disposed these leaders to a hierarchical, proslavery consciousness. Abolitionist discussion of the morality of slavery contributed to this development, but so did the leaders' impression that they were succeeding in civil-

2. On the "Schools" see Jack P. Maddex, Jr., "Old School / New School," in *Encyclopedia of Religion in the South,* ed. Samuel S. Hill (Macon, Ga., 1984), 570–72.

izing and Christianizing a South in which slavery continued to flourish.

By the 1850s slavery held a prominent place in the Presbyterian leaders' conception of southern life. "Slavery is implicated in every fibre of Southern society," the Synod of South Carolina pointed out.[3] Slavery, the New Orleans pastor Benjamin M. Palmer observed, "underlies and supports our material interests"; it "is interwoven with our entire social fabric" and "has fashioned our modes of life, and determined all our habits of thought and feeling, and moulded the very type of our civilization."[4] In the Free-Soil controversy the South Carolina theologian James H. Thornwell identified the individual rights of southerners with the status of slavery. "The geography is only an accident in this matter," he explained. "The Southern man, politically, is the slaveholder. . . . The rights of the South are the rights of the South as slaveholding. . . . This is what makes the real difference betwixt the two sections."[5] Identification of the South with slavery undergirded an emerging proslavery Christian consciousness.

The consciousness found one expression in the Presbyterian leaders' ethical defense of slavery against northern criticism. Reading the Bible in a world of masters and slaves, theologians found positive assurance that their system was morally acceptable. They went further than northern conservatives who granted that God would tolerate slaveholding temporarily. "Slavery," the Virginia theologian Robert L. Dabney wrote, "*is morally right.* Slavery is a righteous, a just institution." It was, he reiterated, "a relation which may be absolutely innocent and not merely excusable because of circumstances." "Like every human arrangement," Thornwell stated in 1860, slavery was "liable to abuse; but in its idea, and

3. James H. Thornwell, "Relation of the Church to Slavery," in Thornwell, *Collected Writings*, ed. John B. Adger and John L. Girardeau (4 vols.; Richmond, Va., 1871–73), IV, 396.

4. Benjamin M. Palmer, Thanksgiving sermon, November 29, 1860, in T. Cary Johnson, *The Life and Letters of Benjamin M. Palmer* (Richmond, Va., 1906), 210.

5. James H. Thornwell, "The State of the Country," in Benjamin M. Palmer, *The Life and Letters of James Henley Thornwell* (Richmond, Va., 1875), 602.

in its ultimate influence upon the social system, it is wise and beneficent."[6] Opposing individual-rights theories, theologians appealed to prescriptive, divine authorization of the master-slave relation. Since they rejected contemporary libertarian norms, they did not rely heavily on racial arguments that blacks were an exception to those norms.

As an inseparable corollary to their defense of slavery, Southern Presbyterian thinkers insisted that masters had a duty to govern slaves benevolently and educate them in Christianity. Slaves were "not like the poor in Ireland, having claims on all the world," missionary John B. Adger reminded Charlestonians. Rather, "the claim of these is on us, for we claim them as ours. . . . *They belong to us. We, also, belong to them.*"[7] Because slavery was morally legitimate, it was capable of reform; indeed, proslavery Christian morality *required* its reform. With a sense of destiny, ministers increased their service to slaves. One showcase of their work was the interdenominational ministry of Charles Colcock Jones to slaves in Liberty County, Georgia. Another was Zion Presbyterian Church in Charleston, where in 1860 John L. Girardeau preached to 431 black and 61 white members.[8] In church as well as society, slaves were visibly subordinate to masters.

In 1857 the New School Presbyterians in the South left their northern-dominated denomination, declaring that they held slaves "from principle," not from extenuating circumstances, "believing it to be according to Bible right."[9] In the Old School church, proslavery southerners and conservative northerners had long united

6. Robert L. Dabney ["Chorepiscopus"], in Richmond *Enquirer*, April 29, 1851, pp. 1, 4; James H. Thornwell, "Sermon on National Sins," in Thornwell, *Collected Writings*, IV, 541.

7. John B. Adger, *The Religious Instruction of the Colored Population: A Sermon Preached . . . in the Second Presbyterian Church, Charleston, S.C., May 9, 1847* (Charleston, 1847), 6, 13.

8. Erskine Clark, *Wrestlin' Jacob: A Portrait of Religion in the Old South* (Atlanta, 1979), describes the Jones and Girardeau ministries.

9. Robert M. Morrison at General Assembly, Presbyterian Church in the United States of America (New School), 1856, quoted in *Presbyterian Witness* (Knoxville), June 16, 1857, p. 1.

against abolitionists. Increasingly, however, they discovered their differences: southern theologians did not consider legitimate slaveholding to be exceptional or temporary, and they rejected northerners' expectations of eventual manumission.[10] The secession crisis exposed conflicting loyalties. In 1861 the Old School's General Assembly recognized the Union government's claims and ruled that an 1818 antislavery pronouncement was still in force. The presbyteries in the new Confederacy then formed the Presbyterian Church in the Confederate States of America (PCCSA), recognizing southern independence and asserting the moral legitimacy of slavery.[11]

Inspired by Christian proslavery principles as well as civil loyalty, Confederate Presbyterians threw themselves into their nation's struggle. With a sometimes millennial vision of God's purpose for the Confederacy and the PCCSA, they looked forward to a Christianized slaveholding nation after victory. It was in that spirit that the PCCSA General Assembly suggested in 1864 "that it is the peculiar mission of the Southern Church to conserve the institution of slavery, and make it a blessing both to master and [to] slave."[12] Uniting the Old and New Schools in the Confederacy, the PCCSA rapidly acquired a denominational tradition. Its building blocks included the patriotic writings of the dying Thornwell, the work of chaplains in Confederate army revivals, the fighting piety of Stonewall Jackson, and the goodwill mission to Britain by the Richmond minister Moses Drury Hoge.

When the Confederacy fell, Southern Presbyterians turned from their millennial visions to survey the smoldering ruins of their

10. See the debate between George D. Armstrong and Cortland Van Rensselaer in *Presbyterian Magazine*, VIII (1858), 8–26, 65–85, 151–68, 346–74, 481–99, 529–54.

11. *Minutes of the General Assembly, of the Presbyterian Church of the United States of America, 1862* [PCUSA, Old School] (Philadelphia, 1862), 162–63, 166; James H. Thornwell, "Address to All the Churches of Jesus Christ Throughout the World," in Thornwell, *Collected Writings*, IV, 447–55.

12. *Minutes of the General Assembly of the Presbyterian Church in the Confederate States of America, 1864* [PCCSA] (Richmond, 1864), 293.

homeland. "The Confederate government was the only human government that I ever loved," Professor James Woodrow told his students at Columbia Seminary in South Carolina. "There was lamentation," Girardeau later remembered, "deep, heartfelt, indescribable, over the loss of a country."[13] Some felt "dead" in the prime of age, extinguished with the society that had structured their lives. Ministers who had been quoting biblical calls to arms now took up texts from the Babylonian Exile. The debacle, they found, had actually shaken the faith of thousands.[14] Liberated blacks left the paternalist "courts of the Lord" to form their own churches, plantation-belt presbyteries reported catastrophic membership losses, and economic devastation paralyzed denominational institutions.

Acquiescing in what it regarded as the decree of Providence, a Southern General Assembly in 1865 renamed the PCCSA "the Presbyterian Church in the United States." The embittered commissioners joked that their church was "*in,* not of, the United States."[15] The survival of the former PCCSA surprised northerners, but its founding experiences had given it a very special claim on its members' loyalty. Their wartime "trials," a Mississippi Presbyterian pointed out, had served "to render us eminently a united and homogeneous body."[16] "We have had, besides sorrowful recollections, little left us on earth," the young theologian William E. Boggs later reflected, "save our family ties and the Church of our Lord." Leaders called on southerners who had lost their social institutions

13. Marion W. Woodrow, ed., *Dr. James Woodrow, as Seen by His Friends* (Columbia, S.C., 1909), 82; John L. Girardeau, "The Suffering Seaboard of South Carolina," *Southern Presbyterian Review,* XXVII (1876), 213.

14. Richard McIlwaine, *Memories of Three Score Years and Ten* (New York, 1908), 212; Synod and presbytery reports in *Southern Presbyterian* (Columbia, S.C.), December 28, 1865, p. 1, and in Thompson, *Presbyterians in the South,* II, 106–107; *Southern Presbyterian,* May 3, 1866, p. 2.

15. McIlwaine, *Memories,* 242.

16. Tombeckbee [pseud.] in *Southern Presbyterian,* August 29, 1867, p. 2.

on earth to build up the institution that linked them to eternal society. For many, the PCUS commanded intense loyalty as the institutional survivor of, and surrogate for, the South they had lost. "If needs be, we would all die for her," Adger told a South Carolina presbytery.[17]

Some church leaders summoned members to carry on the struggle by a "war of ideas." At first, they meant a real continuation of the sectional conflict. Some hoped that some form of bound-labor system would yet prevail in the South.[18] Dabney carried on the contest by revising a wartime proslavery manuscript and publishing it in 1866. The PCUS Assembly of 1865, conceding that the civil conflict might be decided, insisted that the ideological one was still raging. The idea that slavery was sinful was "one of the most pernicious heresies of modern times," and true Christians had to separate from antislavery churches.[19] The continuing enemy was the libertarian ideology that had produced abolitionism. As missionaries of the "Northern" Presbyterian Church in the United States of America (PCUSA) organized Unionist constituencies in the South, PCUS leaders came to target that church as their surrogate enemy in what would in time become a surrogate war.

The most substantial battle of the redefined conflict was the contest for the church loyalty of the freed people. At first, PCUS bodies deplored the departure of their black members and reiterated the exhortation to minister to blacks in the antebellum ways. Girardeau, who was fortunate in retaining a significant black congregation, drafted an admonition to "give, as heretofore, the gos-

17. William E. Boggs, "Church and State in Their Reciprocal Relations and Fundamental Contrast," *Southern Presbyterian Review*, XXXV (1884), 177; John B. Adger, "Church Power," *ibid.*, XXV (1874), 500.

18. John L. Girardeau, "Our Ecclesiastical Relations to the Freedmen," *ibid.*, XVIII (1867), 9; "The Sources of the Nile," *ibid.*, 472; John B. Adger and G. J. A. Coulsen, "The Future of the Freedmen," *ibid.*, XIX (1868), 290–93.

19. Robert L. Dabney, *A Defence of Virginia (and Through Her, of the South) in Recent and Pending Contests Against the Sectional Party* (New York, 1867); *Minutes of the General Assembly of the Presbyterian Church in the United States, 1865* (Richmond, 1866), 385 [hereinafter the minutes of annual PCUS General Assemblies will be cited as *Minutes of the General Assembly*, PCUS, (year)].

pel to these people." He still told white patriarchs to teach and govern well "the freed people in their households," but he could offer presbyteries no specific policy guidance.[20] Even the PCUS Assembly, in adopting his document in 1866, deleted some of its unrealistic seigneurial ideas. By 1868 Girardeau admitted that since emancipation "the peculiar duty of the people of the South to furnish religious instruction to the negroes while they were slaves . . . exists no longer."[21] Only the general responsibility to them as fellow human beings remained.

Finding only a few family retainers left in their slave galleries, ministers groped for ways to respond. Most of them quietly gave up. A few in North Carolina joined the PCUSA to continue a credible ministry to blacks. In 1866 a PCUS presbytery in Georgia bravely ordained three blacks as ministers—but when it ruled that they could participate only in deliberations about blacks, the three joined the PCUSA. Others proposed halfway measures to recognize black leadership within the PCUS. Dabney condemned all the proposals for "Ecclesiastical Equality of Negroes," but most church leaders knew it would have to be part of any practical ministry to the blacks, and they still believed that such a ministry was their duty.[22] As a compromise between paternalism and equality, the PCUS Assembly in 1869 authorized a "gradual maturing process" for black congregations and elders under white control. In 1874, when its black membership was almost extinct, the PCUS finally adopted a plan to organize separate black presbyteries. Most proponents hoped that the policy would lead eventually to an autonomous black denomination.[23]

20. Girardeau, "Our Ecclesiastical Relations," 15–17.

21. *Minutes of the General Assembly*, PCUS, 1866, pp. 35–36; John L. Girardeau, "The Past and Present Relations of Our Church to the Work of Foreign Missions," *Missionary*, II (1868), 74.

22. *Southern Presbyterian*, May 3, 1866, p. 2; June 14, 1866, p. 3; June 21, 1866, p. 3; October 18, 1866, p. 3; Thompson, *Presbyterians in the South*, II, 216; Robert L. Dabney, "Ecclesiastical Equality of Negroes," in Dabney, *Discussions by Robert L. Dabney*, ed. Clement R. Vaughan (4 vols.; Richmond, Va., 1890–97), II, 199–217.

23. *Minutes of the General Assembly*, PCUS, 1869, pp. 388–89; *ibid.*, 1874, pp. 516–18.

The new separatist policy marked a change in Southern Presbyterians' ideas about race relations. Gradually and with misgivings, they were giving up a model of hierarchical attachment for one of racial separatism. In their postbellum South the races, like the world, no longer seemed to hold together. In 1861 Palmer had told the PCCSA Assembly that Christ's cross, "the great magnet of the earth," was progressively unifying the peoples whom sin had separated. By 1872 he had reversed the portrayal: it was sin that impelled peoples to seek unity, he now taught, and God who separated them in order to limit the evil they could do. While other church leaders deplored the loss of black members, Palmer was secretly pleased by it. If the blacks had remained, he imagined, civil rights laws might have required black leadership in congregations.[24]

After some of the postbellum changes became fixed conditions, the "war of ideas" assumed an ideal and mythic character. Church leaders still memorialized the Confederate cause on suitable occasions, but they increasingly redefined the cause and, consequently, the basis of southern identity. They deemphasized slavery and emphasized "constitutional liberty."[25] Their enemy was still libertarian radicalism, but chiefly in its more abstract and extreme forms. Relaxing their animus against northerners and (eventually) against Republicans, they remained in conflict with northern churches as centers of radicalism. In Southern Presbyterian publications, the "war" against northern ideas appeared mainly in the form of an adversarial relationship with the relatively conservative PCUSA. The interchurch conflict became a surrogate for the sectional conflict—without, however, the latter's political and social character.

24. Benjamin M. Palmer, Sermon to General Assembly, PCCSA, 1861, in Johnson, *Palmer*, 258–59; Palmer, Speech at Washington and Lee University, 1872, *ibid.*, 355; Benjamin M. Palmer to Robert L. Dabney, December 30, 1872, in Robert L. Dabney Papers, Union Theological Seminary, Richmond, Virginia (hereinafter cited as Dabney Papers, UTSVa).

25. See, for example, John L. Girardeau, Address in *Confederate Memorial Day at Charleston, S.C.: Re-interment of the Confederate Dead from Gettysburg* (Charleston, 1871), 6–22.

The PCUS's divorce from sectional politics was part of a pietistic divorce from *all* politics. Church members who had lost their commonwealth on earth became disillusioned with civil religion. When northerners attacked their church as proslavery and pro-Confederate, they defended it by questioning those identifications. In that apolitical stance they soon found experienced allies. During the war the Kentucky minister Stuart Robinson had led many Border States Presbyterians to deny the legitimacy of church pronouncements on political issues. Expelled from the PCUSA in 1866, those Presbyterians moved toward the PCUS, but they made endorsement of "the non-secular character of the church" their condition for affiliation. The PCUS General Assembly of 1867 concurred "substantially" in a Kentucky manifesto on the subject, and the 1870 Assembly made it the main issue of contention with the PCUSA.[26]

Increasingly, therefore, PCUS apologists attacked PCUSA wartime policies for having been generically "political," not for having been specifically Unionist. Their defense of the PCCSA's record did not depend on defense of slavery or secession. Attributing Robinson's doctrine to Thornwell, they interpreted PCCSA policies as nonsecular. At the PCUS Assembly in 1870, the militant Dabney rebuked his colleagues. The church, he insisted, should denounce the Union conquest and declare that the Confederate cause had been right. Many assembly members sympathized with Dabney's feelings, but they nonetheless followed the "nonsecular" policy.[27] In the 1870s and 1880s, PCUS bodies avoided political pronouncements. Almost all the members were southern conservatives, but the church did not officially espouse their causes as it had during the war. Even the PCUS press was sparing in comment about Reconstruction politics. The "war of ideas," unable to restore

26. *Minutes of the General Assembly*, PCUS, 1867, pp. 144–45, 178–93; 1870, pp. 529, 538–39. See Jack P. Maddex, Jr., "From Theocracy to Spirituality: The Southern Presbyterian Reversal on Church and State," *Journal of Presbyterian History*, LIV (1976), 438–57.

27. Edward M. Green and Robert L. Dabney, reminiscences in T. Cary Johnson, *The Life and Letters of Robert L. Dabney* (Richmond, Va., 1903), 351–55.

Old South society, became redirected to otherworldly objectives. Ironically, this shift led to ecclesiastical nonbelligerency in sectional politics and to the surrogate interchurch conflict.

Behind the postbellum changes in church policy a deeper change of outlook was occurring. Before 1865 the theologians, especially in their scholarly *Southern Presbyterian Review*, had applied their hierarchical, organic Calvinist perspective to the whole range of intellectual inquiry. After 1865 their vision grew more diffuse. They saw the world no longer as coherent and progressing, but as fragmented and deteriorating. They no longer expected human history to lead to the millennium. Losing interest in secular topics, the *Review* emphasized spirituality and church government. Internecine debate replaced ideological consensus. The writers now perceived secular scholarship as the enemy, not the handmaiden, of revelation.

Thornwell, who had been a comprehensive theologian, became in death the mythic patron of a narrowly focused denominational intelligentsia. A minister noted that "no discussion of any question in the Southern church . . . can be regarded as complete, until the authority of Dr. Thornwell has been quoted on one side or the other, or both."[28] Controversialists quoted tendentiously, reading Thornwell within their postbellum context rather than his own. His theories of church government dominated their interest, and hierarchical social theology gave way to ecclesiastical constitutional law. Suspicion of central power, prominent in Reconstruction-era conservative politics, became an obsession in church government as well. In 1867 this obsession assured the rejection of the centralized church constitution that a PCCSA committee had prepared. Successive revisions turned the document into a decentralized constitution by the time of its adoption in 1879.[29]

28. Fair Play [pseud.] in *South-Western Presbyterian* (New Orleans), May 5, 1881, p. 1.

29. The successive draft proposals, from 1867 to 1879, were all printed under the title *The Book of Church Order of the Presbyterian Church in the United States*. See Jack P. Maddex, Jr., "Presbyterians in the South, Centralization, and the *Book of Church Or-*

In the first years after the South's surrender, the course of Southern Presbyterianism showed more evidence of destruction of old commitments than of adaptive reconstruction of those commitments. Proslavery consciousness was fading because the social realities to which it applied had been uprooted, but Presbyterian leaders seemed slower than many other southerners to embrace a new outlook. In the ideological hiatus, many could see God's place for them in heaven or in church institutions, but not in a fluctuating and confusing New South. Ostensibly, in those first years such leaders did little positive adapting. The erosion of their old commitments, however, was clearing the way for them to redefine the basis of the southern identity they longed to maintain. Slavery and hierarchical social philosophy, close to the core of the southern church's definition in the 1850s, became expendable for the postbellum denominational community (although not for all of its members). Without those twin pillars to lean on, Southern Presbyterians could adapt only by redefining their Southern Presbyterianism.

Interchurch relations provided the main occasions for official redefinition. In 1861 the PCCSA General Assembly, in its "Address to All the Churches" of the world, expressed willingness to lose communion with churches that denied the morality of slavery. By 1867 that declaration appeared prophetic. The PCUS then appointed a commission to establish relations with British and European churches, but the commissioners never sailed. Hoge learned from his foreign contacts that the emissaries would meet universal rejection because of their church's proslavery history.[30] For many years Southern Presbyterians felt the sting of that ecumenical ostracism.

der, 1861–1879," *American Presbyterians / Journal of Presbyterian History*, LXVIII (Spring, 1990), 24–25.

30. Thornwell, "Address to All the Churches," in Thornwell, *Collected Writings*, IV, 459, 462–63; Peyton Harrison Hoge, *Moses Drury Hoge: Life and Letters* (Richmond, Va., 1899), 247; E. Thompson Baird, Speech printed in *South-Western Presbyterian*, July 17, 1873, p. 1.

Ostracism declined as other churches discovered that the PCUS was a permanent reality. In 1870 the PCUSA sent commissioners to the PCUS Assembly to propose exchange of fraternal delegates. The PCUSA's leaders desired eventual church union, but southern church leaders understood that a step toward union would cause "the general abandonment" of the PCUS "by the people."[31] These same leaders, however, differed about how to respond to the PCUSA initiative because they held differing conceptions of the basis of Southern Presbyterian distinctiveness. Taking a middle course, the Assembly defined four great obstacles to fraternal relations: the wartime "political utterances" of the PCUSA, its alleged doctrinal laxity, its 1866 action against the Border State dissenters, and its official accusations that the PCCSA had been formed to promote rebellion and slavery. In this action and in a subsequent official compendium of its pronouncements, the PCUS minimized the extent of its past Confederate commitment.[32]

The church leaders were redefining, as other southerners were, the enduring basis of their southern identity. After 1870 they avoided explicit identification with slavery and the Confederacy. They defined the PCUS primarily as a nonsecular and strictly orthodox Presbyterian church. This church continued to be identified with the geographic South. Its scope was never officially defined as regional, but except for a short-lived presbytery in Ohio there was no attempt to establish a presence in the northern states.[33] The PCUS leadership made decentralization and racial separation "southern" hallmarks of church life at a time when conservative southerners were seeking to institutionalize them in government and society. In its demand for retraction and apology from the PCUSA, also, the PCUS showed an ardent, enduring sense of

31. "The General Assembly of 1870," *Southern Presbyterian Review,* XXI (1870), 455.

32. *Minutes of the General Assembly,* PCUS, 1870, pp. 529–30, 537–42; *The Distinctive Principles of the Presbyterian Church in the United States, Commonly Called the Southern Presbyterian Church . . .* (Richmond, Va., 1870), i–x.

33. On the Central Ohio Presbytery, see Harold M. Parker, Jr., *Studies in Southern Presbyterian History* (Gunnison, Colo., 1979), 19–20, 197.

southern honor. Southern Presbyterianism was staying southern by redefining its southern content.

In 1870 the redefinition of Southern Presbyterianism was still rudimentary, imprecise, and tentative, but it was sufficient to enable the PCUS to adapt and develop with the New South in the following years. The Southern Presbyterian membership constituency was itself changing. The "nonsecular" Presbyterians in the Border States were becoming members of the PCUS—a Maryland presbytery in 1866, the Kentucky synod in 1869, and the Missouri synod in 1874. Most of these new members had been conservative Unionists or neutrals rather than Confederate sympathizers, and they had criticized Confederate as well as Unionist civil religion. Robinson hoped to turn the PCUS into a national church, and the Missourians long hoped to reunite the PCUSA and PCUS on their "nonsecular" platform.[34] After the war the PCUS depended heavily on financial aid from the Border State conservatives, and the new members acquired great influence in its councils. Of the twenty general assemblies between 1868 and 1887, six met in cities the Confederacy had never governed and six elected moderators who had never been Confederates.

Social and demographic changes also shifted the Presbyterian center of gravity within the Confederate South. The onetime master-and-slave churches in the Low Country languished, Presbyterians migrated to centers of economic growth, and a growing urban middle class found Presbyterianism congenial. Many of the Northern Presbyterians who moved to the South joined PCUS congregations. By the 1880s the PCUS was growing rapidly, but the coastal presbyteries of South Carolina still reported fewer members than they had had in 1860. Churches in the Virginia tobacco country and the old cotton areas of Georgia grew slowly. In contrast,

34. "The General Assembly of 1867," *Southern Presbyterian Review,* XIX (1868), 120; Stuart Robinson to Samuel J. Baird, October 20, 1868, in Samuel J. Baird Papers, Library of Congress; *Old School Presbyterian* editorial reprinted in *South-Western Presbyterian,* March 12, 1874, p. 3.

PCUS membership multiplied rapidly in western Texas, the Florida peninsula, and the larger cities and their environs. It also showed impressive growth in the Virginia mountains, the industrializing mineral region of Alabama, and western Arkansas. Presbyterianism was following the currents of prosperity and population from old plantation locales to New South growth areas.[35]

Institutional influence in the church followed the same currents. In 1861 the PCCSA had divided its agency headquarters among regional centers of plantation production and trade: Columbia, Richmond, Memphis, and New Orleans. By 1875 the locus of PCUS agency locations moved northward. Two were in Baltimore, one in Richmond, and one in Memphis—all supervised by committees of local residents. After the war Columbia Seminary suffered financially and on occasion had to be closed down entirely. Union Seminary in Virginia overtook it as the principal PCUS theological school, largely because Professor Benjamin M. Smith, a sectional moderate, was able to secure funds from northern philanthropists.[36] As the PCUS base of support expanded and the events of 1861 became less central to denominational tradition, the generational balance of leadership also changed. Younger, less-known commissioners spoke out more in general assemblies and deferred less to the denominational patriarchs.[37]

Even in the early years of Reconstruction a few Presbyterian intellectuals adopted a New South agenda. Chancellor John N. Waddel of the University of Mississippi hoped that the decline of the plantations would end the custom of "gentlemanly indolence" and teach southerners that "all honest labor is royal and noble."

35. These conclusions are based on my analysis of annual church statistics in *Minutes of the General Assembly,* PCUS, 1866–90.

36. Francis R. Flournoy, *Benjamin Mosby Smith, 1811–1893* (Richmond, Va., 1947), 85–87, 98–102.

37. John B. Adger, "The General Assembly at Savannah," *Southern Presbyterian Review,* XXVII (1876), 540–41; Adger, "The General Assembly at New Orleans," *ibid.,* XXVIII (1877), 534–35; Adger, "The General Assembly at Louisville," *ibid.,* XXX (1879), 550; Joseph B. Stratton, *Extracts from an Elder's Diary* (Richmond, Va., 1896), 102–103; *Christian Observer* (Louisville), May 24, 1882, p. 4.

Although the North Carolina minister Charles Phillips opposed the Republican administration of Governor W. W. Holden, he promoted progressive social views that some of his colleagues considered "rank Holdenism." His sister Cornelia Phillips Spencer used her column in the *North Carolina Presbyterian* to encourage economic development and new roles for women. In Virginia a progressive minister, William Henry Ruffner, became superintendent of public instruction and campaigned for public schools against Dabney's vociferous opposition.[38]

More conventional Southern Presbyterians drifted into new currents of opinion gradually. In 1875 and 1876 prominent elders urged their fellow General Assembly commissioners to follow "the watchword of the day" and move with "progressive times." By 1880 appeals for "improvement" often appeared in PCUS publications. At a veterans' reunion Boggs urged his Confederate comrades to be patient and peaceful in political action, show benevolence to blacks, build up the southern economy, and maintain model southern homes.[39] Post-1865 pessimism gave way to expectations of progress, and theologians again foresaw "a good time coming" within human history. Andrew F. Dickson, the superintendent of the PCUS seminary for black ministers, won a Boston essay contest for his optimistic rebuttal to doubts about the progress of Christianity.[40]

38. John N. Waddel, "The Works of Dr. Philip Lindsley," *Southern Presbyterian Review,* XVIII (1867), 204; Drury Lacy to Bessie Lacy Dewey, March 14, 1867, in Drury Lacy Papers, University of North Carolina, Chapel Hill; Charles Phillips in *North Carolina Presbyterian* (Fayetteville, N.C.), January 4, 1871, p. 1, January 18, 1871, p. 1; Cornelia Phillips Spencer, *Selected Papers,* ed. Louis Round Wilson (Chapel Hill, 1953), 158–203; William Henry Ruffner, *The Public Free School System: Dr. Dabney Answered by Mr. Ruffner* (N.p., [1876]).

39. Speeches quoted in John B. Adger, "The General Assembly at St. Louis," *Southern Presbyterian Review,* XXVI (1875), 659; Adger, "General Assembly at Savannah," 590; William E. Boggs, "The South Vindicated from the Charge of Treason and Rebellion," *Southern Presbyterian Review,* XXXII (1881), 788–96.

40. Edward Martin, "The Conversion and Restoration of the Jews," *Southern Presbyterian Review,* XXXI (1880), 70–92; Henry F. Hoyt, "The Middle Advent," *ibid.,* 675–90; Edward P. Davis, "The Regal Character of Christ: An Argument for Foreign Mis-

Along with their optimism, Southern Presbyterians recovered a sense of American patriotism. In 1869 Dabney had warned that southerners probably would not support the United States in a foreign war. In 1878 his seminary colleague Thomas E. Peck declared that southerners still had "no country in the sense in wh[ich] we had one before the war between the States,—i. e. no country that we can *love*."[41] By then, however, many Southern Presbyterians were of, as well as in, the United States. William S. Plumer, ousted from a northern position for wartime conservatism, brought American national pride with him to a professorship at Columbia Seminary. While a few ministers still perceived the nation as despotic, others came to praise it as constitutional. Robert Q. Mallard, an Atlanta pastor, eventually concluded that the war had "only intensified the feeling of patriotism" and "issued in the solidarity of a great nation."[42]

In the late 1860s Hoge and Dabney were of one mind in bewailing the ruin of Virginia and denouncing the northern conquerors. After a period of stress and an apparent breakdown, Hoge came to a conciliatory and cosmopolitan outlook. Enjoying nationwide recognition, he sought "to urge such devotion to the common weal as to bring all the people, North, South, East, and West, into harmonious relations with each other."[43] At the 1882 commencement at Hampden-Sydney College, Dabney delivered an impas-

---

sions," *ibid.*, XXXIV (1883), 561–88; Andrew F. Dickson, *The Light: Is It Waning? Why? How Much? And What Shall We Do?* (Boston, 1879), 5, 13–51.

41. Robert L. Dabney, "The United States as a Military Nation," in Dabney, *Discussions . . .* (Mexico, Mo., 1897), IV, 148; Thomas E. Peck, Sermon on Jeremiah 29:7, September 1, 1878 (MS in Alexander Sprunt Papers, Presbyterian Study Center, Montreat, N.C.). For a sidelight on the volume of Dabney's work cited here, see n. 70 below.

42. William S. Plumer, *Hints and Helps in Pastoral Theology* (New York, 1874), 327–37; Robert Q. Mallard, *Montevideo-Maybank: Some Memories of a Southern Christian Household in the Olden Times* (Richmond, Va., 1898), 65.

43. Moses Drury Hoge, Address on the death of Jefferson Davis, December 11, 1889, in Peyton Harrison Hoge, *Moses Drury Hoge*, 464.

sioned diatribe against the New South. In his own speech the next day, Hoge artfully wove the most appealing images from Dabney's address into a pro–New South exhortation. Recalling the same Confederate memorial occasion, he redirected the audience from the dead to the living South and to the future that the graduates might achieve for the latter.[44] Both speakers won the hearts of Southern Presbyterians, but by his visionary strategy Hoge also guided their feet in a direction that Dabney would not take.

In the same adaptive spirit Southern Presbyterian writers preserved a positive and sometimes defensive memory of the Old South but sloughed off proslavery social theology. They remembered Christian paternalism fondly and attributed southern slavery to Providence, but they now depicted emancipation as an equally clear step forward in God's plan. In 1885 a Virginia minister, although insisting that the master's discipline had elevated the slave, conceded that slavery "might be very wrong." It may have been the master's duty "to set the slave free and elevate him by other methods."[45] Even the Old South myth could dispense with proslavery ideology.

Concerning the present, church leaders gradually internalized new presuppositions. In 1867 Palmer still considered servitude a divine arrangement that enabled the leisure class to promote "refinement and civilization." In 1872 he was coming to accept "the new condition of things" which called for "a personal devotion to labor, rather than a mere superintendency of it as wrought by others." In 1891, opposing the Louisiana Lottery, he invoked the divine "law" that "each unit in society lives by his individual and personal labor."[46] If the recalcitrant Palmer could forget proslavery axioms, it was possible for the post-Confederate generation not to

44. Peyton Harrison Hoge, *Moses Drury Hoge,* 464.

45. Robert C. Reed, "The Southern Presbyterian Church and the Freedmen," *Southern Presbyterian Review,* XXXVI (1885), 96–97.

46. Benjamin M. Palmer, *The Family in Its Civil and Churchly Aspects* (Richmond, Va., 1867), 124–25; Palmer, Speech at Washington and Lee University, 1872, in Johnson, *Palmer,* 357; Palmer, Speech on Louisiana Lottery, 1891, *ibid.,* 554.

learn them. In student debates at PCUS colleges and seminaries in the 1870s, some students argued conscientiously against divine authorization of slavery and other tenets of Confederate apologetics. In 1884 college president Richard McIlwaine found his students at Hampden-Sydney inclined to agree with the antislavery content of their ethics textbook.[47] They had not received proslavery norms as part of their southern and Presbyterian upbringing.

Dabney, as an unreconstructed Rebel, monitored subtle changes in the consciousness of his Presbyterian friends and neighbors. In 1869 he was surprised to hear them say that Reconstruction was "not so bad as we fancied" during the war. "The only difference I can see," he concluded after serious reflection, "is, that we did not realize then how rapidly we should be degraded to the level of our oppressions." It was their own adaptation that had made his neighbors feel complacent.[48] In later years Dabney confirmed his impression that "subjugation" was changing the consciousness of southerners. By 1881 he could remark that "all the Confederates are staunch adherents of a set of dogmas, every one of which in 1861–65 they 'resisted unto blood.' " The final result of the northerners' victory was that "they have made us like themselves."[49] His adaptive fellow southerners had made themselves "at home" in a slaveless South that was still alien to Dabney.

It was in foreign missions that Southern Presbyterians again encountered slavery as a living system. After 1865 a considerable number of church leaders thought of emigrating to slaveholding Brazil, and a few did settle in Campinas province. It was concern

47. Johnson, *Dabney,* 334–35; Eumenean Society (Davidson College) Minutes, January 16, 1874, in *The Papers of Woodrow Wilson,* ed. Arthur S. Link (68 vols. to date; Princeton, N.J., 1966–), I, 39; J. Gray McAllister, *The Life and Letters of Walter W. Moore* . . . (Richmond, Va., 1939), 55–56; McIlwaine, *Memories,* 340–41.

48. Robert L. Dabney to Moses Drury Hoge, January 23, 1869, in Johnson, *Dabney,* 301–302.

49. Robert L. Dabney, "Politics and Parties in the United States" (MS in Dabney Family Papers, University of Virginia, Charlottesville), 39; Robert L. Dabney, "The Rise and Fall of the Confederate Government," *Southern Presbyterian Review,* XXXIII (1882), 304.

for them that led the Synod of South Carolina, in 1866, to suggest establishing a PCUS mission field there.[50] The first PCUS missionaries to Brazil, G. Nash Morton and Edward Lane, had been inspired by Dabney's personal interest in emigration, and they began their work by visiting the colonists at Santa Barbara. At first, the colony and the mission were closely associated. Emigrants and missionaries joined to form a PCUS presbytery in 1872, and the missionaries founded an academy at Campinas partly to serve the educational needs of emigrant families.[51]

Although mission and colony grew apart, Southern Presbyterians were again organizing churches that included masters and slaves. The devout mistress and the faithful servant reappeared as pillars of the church.[52] In time, however, the missionaries from the Reconstruction South could look into plantation society as outsiders, with critical eyes. Morton was amused when a fat and wealthy planter with four slave boys waiting on him asked whether Protestantism would be cheaper to practice than Catholicism. The southern missionaries increasingly allied with liberal elements in Brazilian culture. By 1888 they welcomed the abolition of slavery as a progressive step that would assist their work.[53] A mission that had originated in proslavery persistence had come to represent emancipationist interests.

In interchurch relations—a crucial arena for PCUS self-definition—a paradoxical situation developed after 1870. The PCUS had declined fraternal relations with the PCUSA for reasons mostly rooted in the recent sectional conflict. In 1871, however,

50. *Minutes of the General Assembly,* PCUS, 1866, p. 19.

51. G. Nash Morton in *Missionary,* II (1869), 24; Edward Lane, *ibid.,* III (1870), 3, 100; Presbytery of Sao Paulo Minutes, January 13, 1872, *ibid.,* V (1872), 40–41; Edward Lane to Robert L. Dabney, August 26, 1869, December 18, 1869, and May 14, 1870, all in Dabney Papers, UTSVa.

52. Edward Lane in *Missionary,* VIII (1875), 106; G. Nash Morton, *ibid.,* 256; Nannie Henderson, *ibid.,* XXI (1888), 422.

53. G. Nash Morton in *Missionary,* V (1872), 20; W. C. Porter, *ibid.,* XXI (1888), 311; Nannie Henderson, *ibid.,* 354; Samuel R. Gammon, "Some Facts About Brazil," *Union Seminary Magazine,* I (1890), 300–305.

PCUS leaders responded differently to an overture from the Reformed Church in America (RCA), a Dutch Reformed body in the North. They immediately began fraternal relations with the RCA, and many proposed outright union with it.[54] Even PCUS critics of the union proposal did not discuss the RCA record on slavery. In 1855 the RCA had declined, because of slavery, to admit a group of churches in North Carolina. It had gone further than the PCUSA in endorsing the Union war effort, and had officially described slavery as evil and oppressive. Remarks offensive to southerners often appeared in its *Christian Intelligencer.*[55] Beyond the special problem of relations with the PCUSA, evidently, the PCUS could overlook the wartime lines of division.

It continued to do so in relations with other churches. In 1873 the PCUS declined official representation at the Evangelical Alliance conference, but it expressed positive regards for the Alliance, whose antislavery history was well known.[56] In 1873 and 1874 it exchanged fraternal greetings with two Scottish churches whose antislavery communications in the 1850s had led the "Old School" church to suspend relations with them. In 1876, after protracted controversy, the PCUS decided to join the new World Alliance of Reformed Churches. Opponents of affiliation criticized the WARC as a centralizing device, a theologically latitudinarian coalition, and a back door to fraternity with the PCUSA. Dabney was

54. Thomas R. Welch, Speech quoted in John B. Adger, "The General Assembly of 1872," *Southern Presbyterian Review,* XXIII (1872), 476; Joseph Ruggles Wilson and John S. Grasty, Speeches quoted in Samuel S. Laws, *A Letter . . . to the Synod of Missouri (O. S.) . . .* (St. Louis, 1872), 91, 96–97.

55. *Southern Presbyterian Review,* IX (1856), 471; *Acts and Proceedings of the Reformed Protestant Dutch Church in North America,* 1861, pp. 35, 101; 1862, pp. 143, 210–11; 1863, pp. 356–58; 1864, pp. 503–504; 1865, pp. 648–49; *North Carolina Presbyterian,* January 31, 1866, p. 2; May 23, 1866, p. 2; *Central Presbyterian* (Richmond, Va.), August 25, 1869, p. 2; St. Louis *Presbyterian,* February 24, 1882, p. 4.

56. *Minutes of the General Assembly,* PCUS, 1873, p. 333; Philip D. Jordan, *The Evangelical Alliance of the United States of America, 1847–1900: Ecumenism, Identity, and the Religion of the Republic* (New York, 1982), 49–52, 64–65, 70–72.

almost alone in stressing the antislavery records of member churches as a barrier to affiliation.[57]

The surrogate conflict with the PCUSA occasioned disagreements within the PCUS. Some PCUS leaders had longer bills of grievances against the PCUSA than others. The more conciliatory group regretted the harsh tone of the 1870 action, attributing it to pro-Confederate revanchist feelings. The more hostile group continued to regard the slavery and war questions as issues between the two churches. A middle group defended PCUS policy but interpreted the issues fairly narrowly and disclaimed revanchism. After the PCUSA addressed some of the PCUS criticisms, the PCUS agreed to a new discussion of the issues. In 1875 PCUS and PCUSA representatives exchanged position papers and responses in a Baltimore church. Agreeing that most of their differences would not preclude official relations, the PCUS committee demanded satisfaction only for the wartime accusations against the PCCSA and for unresolved church-property conflicts in the Border States. The PCUS General Assembly went further, promising to exchange delegates if the PCUSA would officially apologize for the accusations.[58] It reduced the issue to the honor of the southern church, not the cause of the slaveholding South. However, the nature of the accusations still enabled hostile leaders to bring up the cause in their polemics.

While demanding retraction from the PCUSA, PCUS apologists were satisfied with their own church's record. They interpreted PCCSA General Assembly statements as nonsecular and disregarded other expressions of Confederate Presbyterian opinion. Historical doubts about the accuracy of their interpretation persisted, especially among the Missourians who joined the PCUS in 1874. In a new study in 1876, the General Assembly interpreted

57. *Minutes of the General Assembly,* PCUS, 1873, p. 324; 1874, p. 515; Robert L. Dabney, "The Pan-Presbyterian Alliance," *Southern Presbyterian Review,* XXVII (1876), 77–78, 88–89.

58. *Minutes of the General Assembly,* PCUS, 1875, pp. 17, 75–102.

most PCCSA statements as being compatible with the nonsecular policy, but admitted that some were not. It officially disavowed the latter and annulled the 1864 statement of intent to "conserve slavery." The combination of reinterpretations and disavowals reduced the church's support of slavery and the Confederacy to the level of de facto recognition.[59]

At that point it was open to question whether the PCUS retained any distinctive policy about slavery. Disturbed by the implications of recent actions, Dabney sought reassurance on the subject. At the 1878 General Assembly he introduced a motion to interpret the admission of the PCUS to the WARC as a recantation by member churches of their past antislavery pronouncements. Dabney was challenging the PCUS to reaffirm the morality of slavery, but most commissioners did not intend to permit a debate on that subject. By sixty-nine votes to forty-one, they tabled the motion as soon as Dabney presented it. The minority again invited discussion by filing a formal protest, but the majority again avoided it by replying only to the parliamentary objections. In 1879 the PCUS Assembly did state, albeit ambiguously, that WARC membership did not negate any prior church pronouncements.[60]

After 1875 many PCUS leaders sought a way to remove the "accusations" obstacle to relations with the PCUSA. The PCUS and PCUSA assemblies exchanged cordial telegrams, encouraged communication between their overlapping synods, and denied that their past actions impugned one another's Christian character. In 1882 the PCUS Assembly devised a formula to initiate fraternal relations. Each Assembly, "while receding from no principle," expressed "regret for and withdrawal of" whatever past pronouncements "may be regarded as reflecting on, or offensive to" the other.[61] Critics complained that "Young America" and the New

59. *Ibid.*, 1876, pp. 232–34, 285–98.

60. *Ibid.*, 1878, pp. 641, 655–63; 1879, p. 19; "The General Assembly," *Southern Presbyterian Review*, XXIX (1878), 600–602; *Central Presbyterian*, July 24, 1878, p. 1.

61. *Minutes of the General Assembly*, PCUS, 1882, pp. 530, 541, 552–53.

South had taken over the PCUS Assembly;[62] nevertheless, the churches exchanged delegates in 1883 and went on to adopt a mutual cooperation agreement in 1889. The withdrawal of unspecified pronouncements upheld the honor of the PCUS without defining its relation to the proslavery ideas of the Old South.

That relation remained an issue for the severe critics of reconciliation with the PCUSA, although not for the PCUS as a whole. Most of the critics—including Palmer, Dabney, Girardeau, and Adger—had played important roles in the conflict of the 1860s. They saw the PCUSA accusations as being inseparable from the PCUSA endorsement of Union and emancipation, and considered that endorsement the real issue.[63] Dabney saw fraternal relations as a "betrayal" of the PCUS "righteous testimony" against abolitionism.[64] "Brute force has compelled the abrogation of slavery," Girardeau told the 1882 Assembly. "But are we prepared to give up this principle and confess that we affiliate with the Northern view on this subject?" Conceding that "the Confederacy is dead," he asked: "But is our Church dead? Is the cause of our Church a lost cause?" The next day Girardeau repeated the argument in another unsuccessful battle, telling commissioners that by ruling that black ministers had equal voting rights in PCUS presbyteries "you condemn the whole history of our Church."[65] During the Reconstruction years Girardeau's conception of "the cause of our Church" had become obsolete. Some churchmen would continue into the 1890s to consider the acceptability of slavery a permanent part of true

62. Charles A. Stillman to James Woodrow, [June 14, 1882], in James Woodrow Papers, South Caroliniana Collection, University of South Carolina, Columbia; Robert L. Dabney to Charles W. Dabney, June 20, 1882, in Charles W. Dabney Papers, Southern Historical Collection, University of North Carolina, Chapel Hill.

63. John L. Girardeau at General Assembly, quoted in *Christian Observer*, May 31, 1882, p. 3; Robert L. Dabney, "The Atlanta Assembly and Fraternal Relations," in Dabney, *Discussions*, II, 514–18; Benjamin M. Palmer, "Fraternal Relations," *Southern Presbyterian Review*, XXXIV (1883), 324–26.

64. Dabney, "Atlanta Assembly," 525.

65. Girardeau at General Assembly, 3, 5.

doctrine—but by then, PCUS missionaries in Brazil were welcoming emancipation and PCUS missionaries in the Congo were harboring fugitive slaves.[66]

The opponents of fraternal relations, seeing their conception of PCUS principles rejected, imagined that organic union with the PCUSA would soon occur. Under that impression Dabney left Union Seminary for a new career at the University of Texas. In fact, the majority of the PCUS did not pursue union. Their adaptation of Southern Presbyterianism provided for a southern church with its own policies on political pronouncements, doctrinal strictness, race relations in the church, and features of church government.[67] The definition of "Southern" Presbyterianism now centered on those points, not on slavery or southern nationalism.

As they redefined their southernness and adapted to be southern in a New South, the Southern Presbyterians also revised their denominational memory. When members of the 1861 Assembly had adopted their address to the world's churches, they had read it as a proslavery and pro-Confederate manifesto. When later PCUS assemblies quoted it, they interpreted it as nonsecular and neutral on the sectional issues.[68] PCUS hagiography continued the revision of memory. The editors of one minister's writings excised disunionist remarks he had written in 1853. The editors of another's *Complete Works* could not cut those works any shorter than eight thousand pages, yet managed to omit almost all of the

66. John B. Adger, *My Life and Times* (Richmond, Va., 1899), 199–200; Robert L. Dabney, *The Practical Philosophy* . . . (Mexico, Mo., 1897), 403–404; Stanley Shaloff, *Reform in Leopold's Congo* (Richmond, Va., 1970), 131–32. See also the sources cited in n. 53 above.

67. Robert L. Dabney to Charles W. Dabney, June 20, 1882, in Charles W. Dabney Papers; *Minutes of the General Assembly*, PCUS, 1882, p. 567; *ibid.*, 1888, pp. 458–60.

68. Synopsis of "Address" in David E. Frierson, "The First General Assembly of the Confederate States of America" (MS in David E. Frierson Papers, South Caroliniana Collection, University of South Carolina, Columbia), 2; *Minutes of the General Assembly*, PCUS, 1865, pp. 384–85; 1866, p. 37; 1870, p. 538; 1876, pp. 233–34, 285–87, 289.

author's writings about slavery and the Confederacy.[69] The denominational press, in publishing Dabney's short writings, rejected a whole volume as "secular."[70] After haggling over particular items, Dabney accused the press of "trimming a man, whose life and work you would perpetuate, to suit your notions, and then handing the resultant down as if it were real."[71] Improbable claims that Thornwell had favored emancipation in 1860, and Dabney in 1863, became enshrined in their biographies.[72]

Early in the twentieth century, the scholarly South Carolina minister William S. Bean was amazed when he perused his synod's sources for the 1850s and 1860s. The denominational tradition he had imbibed had not prepared him to find the church in the front ranks of a proslavery crusade.[73] In the adaptive process the "usable past" of Southern Presbyterianism lost much that had been eminently usable to the PCCSA in 1861, but it preserved, reshaped, and reapplied what was still useful in the New South. The PCUS of 1883 suffered from its provincial limitations, but it belonged to the New South instead of the Old. Outliving the South that had given it its original identity, it was well prepared for ministry to the next generations of southerners.

69. John H. Bocock, *Selections from the Religious and Literary Writings* . . . (Richmond, Va., 1891), 236. Cf. Bocock, "Our Ecclesiastical Literature," *Southern Presbyterian Review,* VI (1853), 411. The eight-thousand-page opus is Thomas Smyth, *Complete Works,* ed. J. William Flinn and Jean Adger Flinn (10 vols.; Charleston, 1908–12).

70. Admirers published Volume IV of Dabney's *Discussions* independently.

71. Quoted in Johnson, *Dabney,* v.

72. Palmer, *Thornwell,* 482–83; Robert L. Dabney to William N. Pendleton, July 20, 1874, in Charles W. Dabney Papers; Johnson, *Dabney,* 282–83.

73. Frank D. Jones and William H. Mills, eds., *History of the Presbyterian Church in South Carolina Since 1850* (Columbia, S.C., 1926), 59.

God, Cotton Mills, and New South Myths

A New Perspective on Salisbury, North Carolina, 1887–1888

Gary R. Freeze

I n 1887 the people of Salisbury got religion, then faithfully built a cotton mill. Local tradition holds that the North Carolina community first industrialized after an itinerant evangelist challenged leaders to build the mill to employ the poor in their midst. The local elites, agreeing that "what Salisbury needs, next to religion, is a cotton mill," raised the necessary capital. By late 1888, the Salisbury Manufacturing Company had commenced operations, and the town became one of many in the South to espouse the regenerative nature of cotton mills. The mill's role in Salisbury's postbellum recovery was testament to the phoenixlike rise of the New South.[1]

Years after the revival, Salisbury's community crusade also became important in the early historiography of southern textiles. The episode became an integral part of Broadus Mitchell's 1921 contention that the rise of the cotton mills in the South was a "moral movement" aimed at the uplift of communities and the

---

1. James S. Brawley, *The Rowan Story, 1753–1953: A Narrative History of Rowan County, North Carolina* (Salisbury, N.C., 1953), 220–24.

poor whites within them. To Mitchell, the benevolent religiosity that transformed Salisbury exemplified a regional "impulse to furnish work." Mitchell found that "all the circumstances for the founding of this factory were singularly in keeping with the philanthropic prompting."[2] The crusades that produced other mills, although not as dramatic, were said to have come from the same impulse.

Mitchell's thesis long remained the model for southern textile studies. In recent decades, however, students of the New South have uncovered numerous anomalies. Beginning with C. Vann Woodward, scholars have pointed out that profit mattered more than philanthropy to most of the early manufacturers. Moreover, according to Paul D. Escott and others, the rhetoric of philanthropy did not lead to much action.[3] Although labor relations were sometimes personal in the earliest factories, these scholars submit, a sense of social obligation seldom developed before corporate welfare work was introduced during the Progressive decades. Southern manufacturers built mills to make money for investors; only incidentally were the fortunes of labor a factor. Religious values had little to do with the process, although much to do with the rhetoric.

Even Mitchell's fabled crusade has fallen to the dictates of revisionism. "The tale of the Salisbury cotton mill reveals much about industrialization in the piedmont, but the real story is very different from Broadus Mitchell's myth," Escott argued, citing evidence that a long-term commercial campaign was the real impulse for founding the mill. The benevolent thrust of the revival was simply one of many ploys used by the commercial crusaders.

2. Broadus Mitchell, *The Rise of the Cotton Mills in the South* (Baltimore, 1921), 134–35.

3. See C. Vann Woodward, *Origins of the New South, 1877–1913* (Baton Rouge, 1951), 222–24; Paul D. Escott, *Many Excellent People: Power and Privilege in North Carolina, 1850–1900* (Chapel Hill, 1985), 210–20; and Jacquelyn Dowd Hall *et al., Like a Family: The Making of a Southern Cotton Mill World* (Chapel Hill, 1987), 24–31. Escott covers the Salisbury crusade on pp. 213–16. Hall *et al.* do not mention it.

"Helping the poor," Escott found, "was one among many arguments pulled out to convince the people to give their support."[4]

In showing that the businessman and not the evangelist first broached the idea of a mill, Escott contributed to a growing tendency to neglect the extent to which Southern religion interacted with regional industrialization. Revisionists have stressed that economic and class interests led the New South down a "Prussian Road" of modernization that retained the essential agrarian values of the Old South. This is in contrast to the Woodward thesis that the region began to transform itself on the way to postbellum reunion by adopting both the commercial and cultural creeds of a Whiggish southern minority. The continuity-versus-change debaters, long the animators of New South historiography, have seldom used postbellum developments in religious culture as a way to synthesize the strengths of the two positions. Change in the dominant values of a traditionally agrarian society may also be explained as the acceptance and application of the cultural values of a particular group whose identity is as tied to evangelical as to economic goals. This process, as suggested by Anthony F. C. Wallace for northern industrialization, can be demonstrated for the New South by reading religion back into the Salisbury crusade, thus giving a fuller and more balanced reappraisal of the episode.[5]

Both Mitchell and Escott produced myths about the Salisbury episode. Although religion was not the causative agent of industrialization, it was an important element in the process of change. A new perspective on the crusade can demonstrate that a traditional but revitalized religious ethic was a powerful agent in the acculturation of the Salisbury community into the New South's

4. Escott, *Many Excellent People*, 213.

5. See Anthony F. C. Wallace, "Paradigmatic Processes in Cultural Change," *American Anthropologist*, LXXIV (1972), 467–78, and *Rockdale: The Growth of an American Village in the Early Industrial Revolution* (New York, 1978), 477–85. The "Prussian Road" model for southern textiles is advanced in Dwight B. Billings, Jr., *Planters and the Making of a "New South": Class, Politics, and Development in North Carolina, 1865–1900* (Chapel Hill, 1979).

emerging industrial order. The cotton-mill paternalism espoused as a community ethos had its roots in a protoindustrial past, yet it became a tool for adapting to the needs of the time. The believers in faith and factory in Salisbury took from the past the elements needed for a new future.

In the days when the New South burst at the seams with the energy of growth and change, Salisbury slumbered. Vice-President Adlai E. Stevenson, visiting Salisbury in 1893, thought the town was "one of the oldest places" he had seen in the United States. In certain ways the community had not changed since Stevenson's colonial ancestors came to the wilderness of Rowan County. Because of its strategic location on the Great Wagon Road, Salisbury became the principal trading center of the western Piedmont. In an overwhelmingly rural region, Salisbury remained a commercial and cultural mecca until the end of Reconstruction. There the reform movement to bring about internal improvements in the North Carolina backcountry was centered, and in the town blossomed a variety of trades and shops. The antebellum town even had a cotton mill, founded in 1839 when the internal-improvements revolution in North Carolina was gathering steam. This "commendable enterprise," as one civic booster remembered the mill, seldom prospered, however, and it was closed in the wake of the panic of 1857.[6]

The Civil War delayed the recovery of mill and town. Salisbury had been a supply depot for Confederate war efforts, and the old factory was converted into one of the South's principal prisons. Union cavalrymen burned the complex to the ground in 1865. The town soon resumed its previous level of business activity, but the effects of the 1870s depression dampened boosters' hopes for growth. By the 1880s Salisbury was not significantly larger than it had been in 1860. Although it still had a rich elite of bankers, merchants, and wholesalers, the town had not, in the words of a prin-

6. Brawley, *Rowan Story,* 137–75; "The Salisbury Factory: A House with a History" (Unsigned MS in "Cotton Mills" folder, James Brawley Collection, Rowan Public Library, Salisbury, N.C.).

cipal booster, "caught the quick-step of the march of progress" exhibited in neighboring communities. Much of its wholesale trade was going to factors in Statesville. In addition, both the cotton mills in Concord to the south and the tobacco factories in Winston to the north were drawing away farmers who grew the staples those industries needed.[7]

Salisbury's elite would later exaggerate to Broadus Mitchell that the town, by the 1880s, "had done nothing to recover from the war." In truth, the town had two banks in 1887, when few others were nearby, and boasted five tobacco factories at a time when the industry had yet to center in Winston and Durham; it also remained a rail center for the growing trade of the Richmond and Danville line. Still, in the recession of the mid-1880s Salisbury was slow to respond to the problems of a faster-paced, more integrated national market. The town continued to rest upon its longstanding habits and customs. In 1887, for example, the women of the prestigious Presbyterian church called for a new sanctuary to handle the needs of a rising generation. The elders demurred, citing that "in this trying year" the funds could not be raised.[8]

Agitation for a new cotton factory to diversify the local economy periodically cropped up during the 1880s, as Escott and John J. Beck have shown. Potential investors first discussed the matter in 1881, but nothing resulted. A more concerted effort came in 1885, boosted by local newspaper articles that delineated the good effects of mills elsewhere in the South. Again the wealthiest citizens held back, and the scheme never materialized. The third and most sustained attempt came in the spring of 1887. The newly formed Salisbury Improvement Association joined with the jour-

7. John J. Beck, in "Development in the Piedmont South: Rowan County, North Carolina, 1850–1900" (Ph.D. dissertation, University of North Carolina, 1984), 140–53, argued that "the town seemed to stagnate while its rivals moved ahead" and that "town building" climaxed in the 1880s as the result of frustrated efforts to bring Salisbury an additional railroad.

8. Mitchell, *Rise of the Cotton Mills*, 134; Brawley, *Rowan Story*, 220; Session Minutes, June 24, 1887, in the Congregational Archives, First Presbyterian Church, Salisbury, N.C. (hereinafter cited as Session Minutes, First Presbyterian Church).

nalists to spearhead the drive. By April a local editor could report
that "a beginning has been made in this matter." Leaders of the
effort demonstrated "a dogged determination to succeed" and appointed a committee to solicit subscriptions. The "good prospect"
of May, however, turned to the question of August: "How is the
Cotton Mill Scheme?" At that point, the press began to point out
the social necessity for a mill. Not only would a new factory give
"work to the poorer classes of people," but the effort would also
restore some of the racial balance of the town, since what little
growth the local economy had was in tobacco, and blacks filled
most of those jobs. "Race pride, if nothing else, ought to spur us"
in the effort, boosters implored in October, since the factory would
employ exclusively white labor.[9]

Then "it happened" (as Mitchell put it): the religious revival
in November galvanized community sentiment. At the preacher's
urging the wealthier citizens who previously had held back began
to invest in the venture. Within two weeks more than $30,000 was
raised, and within a month incorporation followed. For awhile, enthusiasm ran high enough to allow talk of a second factory, but
eventually only one mill was built. The cornerstone was laid, to
great fanfare, in August of 1888. By early 1889 the factory was operating with 60 looms and 10,000 spindles. Excitement continued
to be so widespread that the factory manager asked the many visitors to be calmer so as not to distract the operatives. By 1895 the
operation had grown to 503 looms and 15,800 spindles, with most
of the 350 operatives producing ginghams. The success of the first
venture led to the construction of two more factories in town by
1900.[10]

9. Escott, *Many Excellent People,* 213–16, and Beck, "Development in the Piedmont South," 171–85, cover these efforts in more detail. See particularly the *North
Carolina Herald* (Salisbury, N.C.), February 24, April 14, May 5, August 17, and October 19, 1887.

10. *North Carolina Herald* (Salisbury, N.C.), November 9, 30, December 21, 24,
1887; March 21, August 8, 1888; January 23, 1889; Board of Directors Minutes, Salisbury Manufacturing Company, January 14, 1895 (Cone Mills Corporate Archives,
Greensboro, N.C.).

With the opening of the mill, most accounts of the crusade end. Although one of the enterprise's founders, Theodore Kluttz, later told Mitchell that "the mill was religion pervaded from the beginning," neither Mitchell nor his critics followed up what happened after operations began.[11] Were the founders actually religious? Was a paternalistic outlook part of their religious belief? Did they pursue religious activities during and after the establishment of the factory? In broader terms, what was Salisbury's religious revival all about? What did it teach its converts about the culture of cotton mills? Finally, what was there in the Salisbury experience that revealed the greater patterns of cultural change engendered by the rise of the mills in the South?

Well into the twentieth century, the events of 1887 remained a benchmark for local residents. Hope Summerall Chamberlain, who had attended the momentous revival, argued that the emotions aroused by the protracted meeting "moved our self-centered, sordid old town as it had never been moved before, and has never been since." Sixty years later, James M. McCorkle, a newspaper columnist, recalled the week as "the greatest revival Salisbury has ever experienced." McCorkle, who also had attended, could "still remember some of the great texts" used in the "soul-stirring" sermons. "It would be impossible," he asserted, "to estimate the good that revival . . . did for Salisbury, both spiritually and industrially."[12]

McCorkle's assertion notwithstanding, it *is* possible to gauge the "good" the revival brought by deconstructing both its content and consequences. Events in Salisbury dramatically exemplified the emergence of an urban, industrial consciousness in most communities of the Carolina Piedmont, as can be seen by studying both the message and the method of the evangelist, the Reverend Robert Gamaliel Pearson. Neither Mitchell nor his critics

11. Mitchell, *Rise of the Cotton Mills*, 135.

12. Hope Summerall Chamberlain, *This Was Home* (Chapel Hill, 1938), 285; James McCorkle, "Salisbury Yesteryears," Salisbury (N.C.) *Post*, November 2, 1947.

studied the minister in any detail; they therefore missed some of the cultural dynamics that were taking place.

Pearson had become a celebrity throughout the Piedmont by the time he came to Salisbury. The Mississippi native was born in 1847 to North Carolinians who had migrated to the Old Southwest. He testified to conversion at the age of six. While a boy, he was known to gather "the children both white and black" on his parent's plantation and "preach to them . . . out in the grove." In 1876 he graduated from the Cumberland Presbyterian Seminary in Lebanon, Tennessee, and by 1880 had done so well during revivals in Nashville that "with no board, assembly, or church behind him, with engagements for only three months of work ahead, he started forth" as an itinerant. For several years Pearson worked the Mississippi Valley, but word of his abilities led to requests to leave the fold of the Cumberland Presbyterians. By the 1890s Pearson had toured many of the southeastern states and ventured as far north as Brooklyn. He capped his whirlwind of preaching by appearing at the Chicago World's Fair with Dwight Moody. Soon afterward, the work telling on his health, Pearson retired to the chair in English Bible at his old seminary.[13]

Pearson took the Carolinas by storm during the late 1880s. Everywhere he preached, thousands came and hundreds professed faith. His impact often puzzled the local churchmen who had called him, for unlike the fiery circuit rider of tradition, Pearson was an unimposing figure. One Concord, North Carolina, observer described him as "exceedingly feminine" in appearance, with a "voice almost like that of a woman." One of the Salisbury enthusiasts recalled him as "a tall, ascetic, corpse-candle of a preacher." Yet, Pearson moved masses. When he first came to North Carolina in February, 1887, at the request of Charlotte's YMCA officials, the result was what one witness called "the first revival of religion in this city in a generation." More than eight

13. Mary Bowen Pearson, "Life Sketch of R. G. Pearson," in "Evangelical Sermons by Rev. R. G. Pearson, D.D." (Pamphlet in the North Carolina Collection, Wilson Library, University of North Carolina, Chapel Hill, N.p., n.d.).

hundred in Charlotte professed faith, and at least three hundred joined local churches. By the time Pearson reached Salisbury, his preaching had become front-page news in Carolina newspapers, and his conversions were tallied with as much enthusiasm as were the baseball scores of the National League.[14]

Who came? Who listened? Who was converted? The Pearson phenomenon was essentially for whites. There is no evidence that black churches participated in the prayer vigils and meetings that Pearson demanded precede his visits. A class analysis, however, is less clear-cut than a racial one. In Salisbury, where the press reported that three hundred were saved and where the Presbyterian session had to hold a special Saturday meeting to examine the penitent, it is clear that most elements of the white community were represented among the converted. Congregational records show that most new members were young and about equally divided between men and women. Most of the converts seem also to have been working class, but then the majority of white Salisbury residents were working class; certainly representatives of professional families came into the churches as well. Among the Presbyterians, for example, were the laborer Jason Hunt, and his wife Martha C. Hunt; the three teenaged daughters of a hardware dealer; the cabinet maker Rowan Horah, and the daughters of I. Henry Foust, Theodore Kluttz, and John M. Knox, all founders of the mill.[15]

14. Descriptions of Pearson are from the *Times* (Concord, N.C.), December 23, 1887, and Chamberlain, *This Was Home*, 285. The initial Charlotte revival is covered in Charlotte *Chronicle*, February 23, 25, March 1, 3, 1887. For Pearson's celebrity, see, for example, Concord (N.C.) *Standard*, April 13, 1888; May 24, September 27, 1889.

15. Among the Presbyterians, forty-five new members joined during the revival, and three more came soon afterward. Six of those were baptized, all on the same Sabbath. Eighteen were teenagers, and eight were over age forty. Sixty-seven came into the local Methodist station, of whom 57 percent were women. Most of the Methodists were teenagers. Only a dozen or so were said to have joined the Lutherans and Baptists, but church records are not extant to verify this. Even fewer became Episcopalians. See Session Minutes, First Presbyterian Church, November 6, 12, 13, 1887, and Church Roster, Salisbury Station, November 6–27, 1887, in Congregational Archives, Methodist Episcopal Church, South, Salisbury, N.C.

Pearson's message, which was the same in Charlotte, Raleigh, Concord, or Salisbury, taught converts to be concerned about more than their individual souls. As a group, southern evangelists tended first to stress the centrality of conversion, and Pearson was no different. Hope Chamberlain remembered him as "a Bible student of the literalist sort." [16] Yet Pearson's true popularity seems to have been rooted in his emphasis on the connection between the sureties of salvation and the rewards for living the sanctified life. "We are free moral agents and may commit any act we choose," he told Charlotteans, "but after we put it to faith, it belongs to God and He makes it an instrument of his Providential administration." [17] Faith was essential, in other words, but once that issue was settled the measure of Christian worth could be deduced from daily pursuits, including the relationships of the market place.

Pearson's rhetoric, Joel Martin has concluded, riveted his listeners by continual references to the metaphors of the developing commercial world around them. At a time when Henry Grady, Richard Hathaway Edmonds, and others were urging southerners to convert their toil to the new industrial system, Pearson was convincing them that as sinners, too, they "had a mortgage on their souls" that if deferred would lead to "spiritual bankruptcy." Christ, Pearson assured believers, was the powerful "locomotive" who could take away the debt of sin. [18]

Pearson's methods could be as materially direct as they were metaphorical. All his revivals followed a standard organization, beginning with prayer meetings, picking up speed with sermons on the hazards of the unconverted life, then proceeding to climax

16. Chamberlain, *This Was Home*, 285.

17. Charlotte *Chronicle*, September 23, 1889.

18. Joel Martin, "The New South Gospel Hour: Salisbury Gets Its Mill" (Paper delivered in George B. Tindall's seminar on the New South, University of North Carolina, Chapel Hill, April 13, 1985, copy in the possession of the author), 34–36. Martin drew his content analysis from Pearson's published sermons in Maxwell Gorman, ed., *The Great Evangelist Sermons of Rev. R. G. Pearson Delivered in the Centenary M. E. Church, Winston, N.C., September 16 to October 4, 1888* (Winston, N.C., 1888). Similar Pearson sermons can be found in the collection *Truth Applied; or, Bible Readings* (Nashville, 1890).

with prescriptions for living within the fold. Pearson particularly played upon the fascination with economic metaphors in delivering "Laying Up Riches" and other sermons in keeping with the gospel of success, the most famous expression of which was Russell Conwell's "Acres of Diamonds."[19]

One sermon, "The Story of Daniel," was preached only to the men of the community at the end of each revival. In this special message Pearson urged the young men to follow the example of Daniel, "the model businessman," who attained material success only after dedicating himself to spiritual obedience. As Martin has noted, Pearson's admonition to males coming of age in the 1880s was to live fully in "the everyday New South world of locomotives, business, credit, and debt and breathe into that world a spiritual dimension."[20] Pearson, whose family suffered financial hardship during Reconstruction, became unusually animated with such themes. At the end of a Charlotte revival he literally shouted to his male listeners: "Let every man, saint and sinner, who wants to be—who feels an impulse to be—a Daniel in his own particular sphere, stand up!"[21]

In Salisbury, the men did more than stand up: they came back to a meeting to discuss the need for a cotton mill. How much Pearson knew about the previous efforts of the Improvement Association is not documented, but someone evidently briefed him. "Mr. Pearson learned there are a great many poor families with children around that need help," the Salisbury correspondent to a Charlotte newspaper reported. Pearson would later "urge that a cotton factory be built to furnish work for these people, that they may help themselves." At the subsequent meeting, the Reverend Francis J. Murdoch, the Episcopal rector, "in strong, eloquent, and

19. The same sequence was followed in Charlotte, Salisbury, and Raleigh during 1887. See Charlotte *Chronicle,* November 8, 1887 (which gave front page coverage to the Salisbury meeting), and Raleigh *News and Observer,* November 12, 16, 18, 19, 23, 1887.

20. Martin, "New South Gospel Hour," 36.

21. Charlotte *Chronicle,* September 23, 1889.

earnest words," echoed Pearson that "it had almost become a necessity to build a cotton mill here, to help the poor whites."[22] The true test of the validity of the revival would come in the founding of the mill by Salisbury's Daniels.

The rhetoric of the organizational meeting provides important clues to an understanding of the Salisbury experience and the general culture of southern industrialization. What Murdoch said was new neither to those present nor to most other industrializers across the Piedmont. More than a month earlier Theodore Bierbaum, one of the local editors, had argued that "the true way to help" the poor was "to enable them to help themselves by giving them a chance to earn their living [in] a cotton factory."[23] The rhetoric of the New South Creed clearly preceded the inspiration of the revival.

Still, the philanthropic impulse was not a false myth, but a cultural theme well rooted in the antebellum Piedmont. Charles S. Fisher, a Salisbury editor, as early as 1828 argued that factories "would build up flourishing villages . . . and improve not only the physical, but the moral and intellectual conditions of our citizens." In large part, the rhetoric of mills as benevolent "institutions" rested upon Whiggish notions of patriarchy, gender, and generation. For decades during which the first cotton mills were being built across the Piedmont, only the most impoverished families, particularly those headed by widows, repaired to the factories. In 1860, for example, somewhere between one third and one half of the workers in most factories were fatherless. Two thirds of the workers were young women, most of them teenaged. Early on, the rationalization that "poor girls who would otherwise be wretched" were benefited by millwork became a part of the managerial ethos in some factories. The general extent to which the earliest factory proprietors—including the ones in Salisbury who remembered "the prattle and song and laughter of the busy factory boys and

22. *Ibid.*, November 11, 1887.
23. *North Carolina Herald* (Salisbury, N.C.), October 19, 1887.

girls"—felt a sense of Christian charity to the orphans they employed is undocumented. Evangelical benevolence, expressed as both attitude and practice, seems to have been evident only in one particular crucible of the southern industrial order.[24] That area, however, produced some of the leaders of the later Salisbury crusade.

Five factories were built along the Deep River in Randolph County, thirty miles to the east of Salisbury, before the Civil War.[25] Many of the Deep River proprietors were Methodists, and the particular social structure of their work forces encouraged them to apply the doctrines of evangelical stewardship to labor relations. According to Holland Thompson, the first historian of North Carolina textiles, the Randolph mill managers "felt themselves to stand in parental relation to the operatives." Thompson, like Mitchell, based much of his research on the oral testimony of manufacturers and was led to believe that Randolph's benevolent paternalism was "somewhat peculiar" for the early phase of textile development.[26] The Deep River proprietors, whom visitors praised for "providentially" providing "opportunity" to "humble and virtuous girls" "reduced by misfortune," taught Sunday school, encouraged thrift by seeking worker loans to the company, and even disciplined recalcitrant workers in a manner similar to congregational trials.[27] Out of the Deep River area were to come three important participants

24. The argument that paternalism was first rationalized in the antebellum period is more fully developed in Gary R. Freeze, "Model Mill Men of the New South: Paternalism and Methodism in the Odell Cotton Mills of North Carolina, 1877–1908" (Ph.D. dissertation, University of North Carolina, Chapel Hill, 1988), 44–56, and is supported by evidence in Richard W. Griffin, "North Carolina: The Origins and Rise of the Textile Industry" (Ph.D. dissertation, Ohio State University, 1954), 3–73. For the quotation about the Salisbury factory, see [Brawley], "Salisbury Factory."

25. The best summary of the industrialization of the Deep River is in L. McKay Whatley, Jr., *The Architectural History of Randolph County, North Carolina* (Raleigh, N.C., 1985), 12–24.

26. Holland M. Thompson, *From the Cotton Field to the Cotton Mill: A Study of the Industrial Transition in North Carolina* (New York, 1906), 62.

27. *Patriot* (Greensboro, N.C.), August 18, 1849.

in the Salisbury crusade, including the first two presidents of the mill.

Most scholars who have looked sympathetically on the religious aspects of the Salisbury crusade have overemphasized the initiating role of Murdoch. Mitchell regarded him as "the chief local instigator of the mill at Salisbury." Actually, that reputation arose from his later work with the factory, which made him "the best textilist ever produced in Rowan." Murdoch was a town booster before the revival, having been a moving force in the Improvement Association. As an Episcopalian, however, he was not at the forefront of the movement to bring Pearson to town—although he quickly capitalized on the emotion of the moment for both the mill and St. Luke's Parish.[28]

More pivotal to the launching of the factory than Murdoch's efforts were those of two other members of the Improvement Association. Both Samuel H. Wiley and I. Henry Foust had spent their younger years in the Deep River valley. Wiley began his teaching career at Middleton Academy on the Deep River in 1851. The academy had been established by George Makepeace and other prominent mill proprietors who mixed paternalism and piety in their relations with workers. Wiley removed to Salisbury in 1859 to teach in an academy housed, ironically, in the defunct cotton factory. After the Civil War, Wiley began to practice law; eventually, he became president of the older of the town's two banks. Foust was the son of a Randolph merchant who had been a partner in some of the factories started by Elliott, Makepeace, and others. In 1862 young Foust was sent to Salisbury to be one of Wiley's pupils. After working in Charlotte during the Reconstruction years, Foust returned to Salisbury and became cashier of the town's other bank.

28. Mitchell, *Rise of the Cotton Mills*, 135–36; Archibald Henderson, "The History of St. Luke's Parish," Greensboro (N.C.) *Daily News*, March 3, 1924; William S. Powell, *St. Luke's Parish, 1753–1953* (Salisbury, N.C., 1953), 37–38. Murdoch, who was the third president of the Salisbury mill, beginning in 1895, was also president of two other cotton mills in the Piedmont, and one of the original incorporators of the Proximity Mill run by the Cone family in Greensboro.

Both Wiley and Foust were Presbyterians and in early 1887 had been elected ruling elders. It is likely that Foust, as secretary of the YMCA, arranged for the Pearson visit, and he may well have been the local official who prompted the sermon on the cotton mill.[29]

Wiley and Foust, more than Murdoch or other members of the local elite, likely kept the spark of the mill-building effort alive during the postrevival lag. In December, 1887, after "fears . . . that the matter is growing cold" were expressed in the press, Wiley induced the eminent cotton manufacturer of the Piedmont, John Milton Odell, to join the venture. Odell was proprietor of the state's fastest-growing cotton mill, at nearby Concord, and had worked with the tobacco magnates of Durham to bring that city its first factory in 1886. Shortly before the Salisbury campaign Odell had become president of the newly founded Cannon Manufacturing Company, also with headquarters in Concord. Odell, too, had spent his formative years in the Deep River valley. Wiley had been his teacher at Middleton Academy. Odell taught school, then became a clerk in the Cedar Falls factory under the tutelage of George Makepeace. With Makepeace's approval and financing, Odell and some associates ventured from Randolph into the cities of the growing Piedmont to become central cogs in the state's postbellum textile growth.[30]

In the 1880s, J. M. Odell was already famous for the paternalistic ethic he brought to mill management, a style he attributed to his Deep River apprenticeship. Around Odell mills throughout the Piedmont, Methodist societies promoted the traditional evan-

29. The background on Wiley is found in a memorial entered into the Session Minutes, First Presbyterian Church, June 28, 1895. Wiley was said to have been a believer in "old fashioned religion" and was praised for having given liberally to the poor and having loaned money to young men to start them in business. For background on both Wiley and Foust, see the *Carolina Watchman* (Salisbury, N.C.), January 15, 1885.

30. Freeze, "Model Mill Men," 77–144. For Wiley's effort to bring in Odell to encourage nervous investors, see the story on Odell in Raleigh *News and Observer*, November 28, 1895.

gelical values of discipline, restraint, and hierarchical control in the new and unsettling environment of the mill village. In Concord, for example, the Odells personally ran the largest Sunday school in North Carolina Methodism, sending their stewards, who were often their overseers, into operatives' homes to drum up support. Thus, not only was Odell, in Wiley's words, "a dividend making and a dividend paying man," as the investors required, but he was presented to the people of Salisbury as a benefactor, the standard bearer, as it were, for a mill-village philanthropy that was to be the legacy of the crusade.[31] With Odell brought in as director, then made president, both pecuniary and philanthropic concerns were woven into one fabric of purpose.

The ideological web of piety and profit, of old and new achievements, which Odell personified, was ritualized during the laying of the factory cornerstone in August, 1888. Theodore Kluttz, the speaker, reiterated the motifs that had become conscious elements of a community ethos. Odell was praised as a "benefactor of his state and people, an educator and employer of skilled labor, a leader in the paths of material prosperity." Kluttz, caught up in his own hyperbole, became carried away by the theme of the factory as asylum, vowing that "throughout North Carolina today, there are hundreds, aye, thousands of white women and children who rise and call blessed the honest name of J. M. Odell." The "good fortune" of Odell's leadership "will begin to diffuse blessings upon our town . . . upon its stockholders, and . . . upon the poor white women and children who are crying out for honest work." Such was the mission of the factory "animated partly by philanthropic motives and partly, of course, by hope of gain."[32]

In addition to building the factory, the three Deep River associates joined with Murdoch and others in perpetuating the evangelical ethos in the mill village. In January, 1889, even before the factory

31. *North Carolina Herald* (Salisbury, N.C.), August 8, 1888.
32. *Ibid.*

opened, the Presbyterian session made plans to open a mission in southern Salisbury. The Reverend Jethro Rumple, who had attended the factory organizational meeting, was to preach there the second Sunday night of each month. By March, with the factory village inhabited, Foust and O. D. Davis, Wiley's fellow banker, began to lead weekly prayer meetings. The efforts toward "chapel, cotton mill, and shop work" were still being pursued in 1897. In 1890, Murdoch helped Methodist mill villagers buy land across the railroad from the factory. More than two hundred communicants joined the Chestnut Hill Methodist Station within two years. Among the Methodist leaders were John L. Odell, who had come from working at his uncle J. M.'s Concord mill, and his wife, Ann Cox Odell. Odell became a foreman in the Salisbury factory as well as a steward in the mission, and his wife was active in all phases of Methodist work. The station built a large brick sanctuary in 1896. Other denominations were active later, the Lutherans founding a Sunday school in 1898, and the Baptists organizing a mission in 1899.[33]

The most active proselytizer during the first decade of the factory was clearly Murdoch, who upon the death of Wiley in 1895 was made president of the company. Murdoch used the original Methodist chapel to hold ecumenical services. One member of St. Luke's Parish recalled that the rector held services twice a month and encouraged a Sunday school "attended by all denominations."

33. Session minutes, First Presbyterian Church, January 25, March 1, 1889, May 28, 1897; "The Story of Coburn United Methodist Church" (Pamphlet in Coburn United Methodist Church Archives); Church Register, 1888–1903, Chestnut Hill Methodist Station, in Coburn United Methodist Church Archives; "Eighty-five Years of Serving the Lord: A Historical Sketch of Haven Evangelical Lutheran Church" (Pamphlet in Haven Evangelical Lutheran Church Archives); Record of Minutes, Chestnut Hill Baptist Church, in Stallings Memorial Baptist Church Archives. (All these archives are in Salisbury, N.C.) J. L. Odell was the only Odell to profess faith late in life, doing so during an 1891 revival at Chestnut Hill. He may have come to Salisbury at the urging of his more pious wife to get him involved in the new mission. See her obituary in the *North Carolina Christian Advocate* (Greensboro), March 20, 1895.

Murdoch "made his sermons so plain for the rural and mill people that they all loved to come and hear him." In 1893 the effort was formed into St. Paul's Chapel, with 10 teachers and 104 students. As president of the factory, Murdoch kept an eye out for aspiring young men whom he trained as protégés, sending the most religiously inclined to seminary and sponsoring others who wanted "to take textile courses."[34]

The web of religiosity imparted to workers outlived the paternalistic founders. Like Pearson's message, the forms of piety demanded in mill-village life drew upon long-standing evangelical traditions that were familiar to workers with agrarian pasts. In 1900, for example, two women were removed from Baptist fellowship for immoral behavior, and in 1902 another was removed for dancing. As late as the 1920s, according to one resident, Chestnut Hill "was a community of churches" where "the Protestant ethic was firmly in control." That is not to say that life there was "another garden of Eden," as another resident of the time remembered. Still, within the limitations that all southern textile workers experienced, Salisbury mill hands had something of a better life. Wages through the 1890s, for example, were higher than the state's average, for both men and women. The founders never set up a company store, instead preferring to encourage local entrepreneurs to set up shop in the mill village. Wages were paid weekly in cash, at a time when scrip and monthly accounts were still prevalent. Murdoch in the mid-1890s became one of the few manufacturers in the state to call for stringently enforced child labor laws to curb the exploitation of younger children whose parents put them to work. On the other hand, little is known about how John M. Knox, who was superintendent of the mill from its inception to 1905, treated any of the workers, young or old. Knox was a Presbyterian, but whether he saw himself in a paternalistic role, like Wiley or Foust, is not known. What is known is that even the enthusiasm of the

---

34. Conference Minutes, December 27, 1893, and Book of Remembrances, 1814–1943, both in Congregational Archives, St. Luke's Parish, Salisbury, N.C.

revival did not remove the stigma of the "public work" of cotton mills from the minds of all Salisbury. The same resident who waxed eloquent about the Eden of the mill village also recalled that the children of "these people" were "not welcome at the Wiley School" across the railroad tracks, but "we had to go anyway."[35]

In sum, it can be argued that the legacy of the 1887 community crusade proved to be a powerful cultural dynamic in the shaping of the Salisbury mill village. As Daniel J. Singal suggested for the whole South, Salisbury was slow to lose the sense of sin and salvation deeply imbedded in Victorian culture. Salisbury's adaptation to the new culture of industrialization had atavistic characteristics grounded in its agrarian heritage. These characteristics were recast in the process of community regeneration. Salisbury's new communal ethos, that the cotton mill could be both benevolent and profitable, was the fruit born of the "institutions and ideas," as Reinhard Bendix has described them, of a New South only partly melded from the Old. The converts of 1887 espoused generally the paternalistic ethos that had been the operative motive of the few who came before them. The paternalistic paradigm that the mill founders then imparted to Mitchell was diffused from a cadre of true believers to the greater community. In turn, through Mitchell, it became part of the lore of southern textiles. The real story of the Salisbury crusade is mythic, as Escott has suggested,

35. Record of Minutes, Chestnut Hill Baptist Church, June 7, 1900, March 31, 1902; Thomas A. Bridges, "Memories of Chestnut Hill," and Francis B. Dedmond, "Remembering Back," both in Salisbury (N.C.) *Post*, August 16, 1987. The obituary of Knox in the *Post*, September 22, 1924, did not mention his approach to labor. The comparison of Salisbury to other mills is drawn from the annual reports of the North Carolina Bureau of Labor Statistics, which began in 1887 and were continued into the early 1900s. No company records have survived to identify who worked in the Salisbury factory. It is impossible, for example, to calculate how many "white women and children," particularly widows, repaired to the mill. By 1895, however, state figures show that all four Rowan mills employed 198 men, 438 women, and 170 children. See North Carolina Bureau of Labor Statistics, *Ninth Annual Report* (Raleigh, N.C., 1895), 55.

but it is the kind of myth, based upon a perceived reality of a genuine past, that George Tindall has found to be essential to the manner in which southerners have made sense of their history and developed plans for their future.[36]

36. Daniel J. Singal, *The War Within: From Victorian to Modernist Thought in the South, 1919–1945* (Chapel Hill, 1982), 1–23; Reinhard Bendix, *Work and Authority in Industry: Ideologies of Management in the Course of Industrialization* (Berkeley, 1974), 444; George B. Tindall, "Mythology: A New Frontier in Southern History," 1–15.

Ignoring the Color Line

Maryville College, 1868–1901

Lester C. Lamon

A lone of all the old colleges of the South, [Maryville] stands connected with the Presbyterian Church (North), *ignores the color line, and educates the rising generation above an intolerant, narrow, sectional spirit."* [1] This bold declaration in 1867 anchored an appeal for funds to support the rebirth of Maryville College (Tennessee) after its closure and financial collapse during the Civil War. This small Presbyterian college had an unusual prewar history, and by announcing publicly their intent to "ignore the color line," its leaders now launched the school into an interracial future that would prove far more controversial and exceptional in the postslavery South than they anticipated in those uncertain early years of Reconstruction.

The college first appeared on the southwestern frontier in 1819, when Isaac Anderson founded the school as Southern and Western Theological Seminary in the small eastern Tennessee town of Maryville. The seminary represented a response to the need for

1. Thomas Jefferson Lamar, "Maryville College, Maryville, East Tennessee" (Broadside in Maryville College Archives, Maryville, Tenn.). Emphasis added.

more Presbyterian ministers among the predominantly Scotch-Irish settlers of the region. A core of preachers had come down the Tennessee River valley as a part of the late eighteenth- and early nineteenth-century wave of evangelical zeal directed at the American frontier. But more Presbyterians were needed if they were to compete for converts with the theologically less demanding Methodists and Baptists.

From the beginning, the seminary at Maryville attracted as students and professors young men who were themselves somewhat flexible in their theology and very sensitive to issues relating to liberty and nationalism. They were strongly influenced, for example, by the teachings of New England's Samuel Hopkins, and most of them demonstrated a commitment to evangelical moral reform.[2] They allied themselves with the more innovative "New School" in 1837 when the Presbyterians split nationally over theological orthodoxy and its entanglement with a variety of social and regional applications. Appeals for temperance and denunciations of slavery punctuated their sermons and revivals in the area. Eastern Tennessee harbored a large number of antislavery organizations and individuals, and Isaac Anderson brought a moderate form of this protest to his school. He refused to sanction slavery among his parishioners, and he brought black students into his home and educated them with the white students at the seminary. It is uncertain that blacks were ever formally admitted to the school before the Civil War, but they were certainly educated there by Anderson and other sympathetic professors.[3] George M. Erskine, for

2. A disciple of Jonathan Edwards, Hopkins refined his mentor's concept of virtue to mean "disinterested benevolence," which Hopkins defined in turn as meaning an attitude that comprises "love to God and our neighbor, including ourselves, and is universal benevolence, or friendly affection to all intelligent beings." Samuel Hopkins, *The Works of Samuel Hopkins* (3 vols.; Boston, 1852), III, 16.

3. A fire in 1856 destroyed Isaac Anderson's home and, with it, most of the college's records, including the catalogs containing the names of students. The strength of Anderson's opposition to the slave trade, however, is well expressed in a quote from one of his sermons: "Any man who will thus chain together his fellow-

example, was purchased and freed by Union Presbytery and then trained at the seminary. Erskine preached to mixed audiences in eastern Tennessee during the 1820s before being formally ordained and sent to Liberia as a missionary by the General Assembly in 1829.[4] Other blacks reportedly attended the school as late as 1848.[5] The college and surrounding community's liberal attitude on race issues drew frequent public attention through stands such as those taken in favor of gradual emancipation in the state constitutional convention in 1834, against the congressional "gag rule" in 1838, and against slavery in general through editorials in several locally published newspapers and in the national columns of the *Emancipator* (New York).[6]

Antislavery sentiment in the South was always vulnerable and often ambiguous, but it never disappeared. On the eve of the Civil War it could be found not only in eastern Tennessee, but also in western Virginia and central Kentucky.[7] Even so, the growing

men and drive them like cattle to market, would sell the Lord of glory for filthy lucre and kidnap the angels of heaven!" "An Appeal for the Loyal College at Maryville, East Tennessee," in Records of the Bureau of Refugees, Freedmen, and Abandoned Lands (hereinafter cited as BRFAL), Record Group 105, Reel M752, National Archives.

4. Samuel Tyndale Wilson, "History of Union Presbytery" (MS in Presbyterian Historical Society, Philadelphia), 6–7; *Calvinistic Magazine*, III (February, 1829), 62–63; Thomas Jefferson Lamar to General Oliver Otis Howard, December 9, 1867, January 23, 1868, in BRFAL, RG 105, M752, NA.

5. Samuel Tyndale Wilson, *A Century of Maryville College and Second Century Beginnings* (Maryville, Tenn., 1935), 48, 195; Lamar to Howard, January 23, 1868, in BRFAL, RG 105, M752, NA.

6. *Millennial Trumpeter* (Maryville, Tenn.), March 7, 1835; Maryville (Tenn.) *Intelligencer*, August 19, 1837, and n.d. (quoted in the *Emancipator*, March 8, 1838); *Emancipator*, March 8, 16, April 19, 1838; Maryville (Tenn.) *Eagle*, November 1, 1856, quoted in Robert E. Corlew, "Some Aspects of Slavery in Dickson County," *Tennessee Historical Quarterly*, X (December, 1951), 326; *Journal of the Convention of the State of Tennessee, 1934* (Nashville), 126.

7. Kenneth M. Stampp, "The Fate of the Southern Antislavery Movement," *Journal of Negro History*, XXVIII (1943), 17–22.

pressures of economic expansion, power politics, and emotional sectionalism made effective antislavery activity nearly impossible. Most dedicated abolitionists moved from the region in the 1830s. Left were the men of Maryville College and a few others like them—men who courageously spoke their feelings, edited their small papers, and preached their sermons, but who made little organized, direct effort to free many slaves.

The evangelical messages of Isaac Anderson and his colleagues did not call for outright abolition or direct emancipation, but they carried the conviction that slavery conflicted with Christian teachings of love and liberty—and the warning that if it was not rejected on the basis of love, God would find other means to destroy it. In the short run, slaves should receive better treatment and be given opportunities such as education. Slave owners must recognize, however, that in the long run the institution had to be dissolved. By the 1850s this antislavery message had lost some of its vigor and leadership to the inevitable toll of age, an emphasis upon "balance and restraint" by a new generation of evangelical ministers, and the vehemence of proslavery forces in the South.[8]

The foremost and continuous mission of Maryville College (as it officially was called after 1842) was to provide the educational and spiritual training necessary to meet the challenges of Christian leadership in the Old Southwest. Isaac Anderson and his followers believed all men to be brothers in Christ; man's institutions, therefore, should serve the benefit of all comers—blacks included. Coupled with this devotion to Christian education and an attendant rejection of slavery, however, was a firm commitment to national union. Anderson had spoken out sharply in defense of the Union at the time of the nullification controversy in 1832, and he

8. *Calvinistic Magazine*, 2d series, V (June, 1850), 184–85; *Presbyterian Witness* (Knoxville), June 11, 1852; James W. Patton, "The Progress of Emancipation in Tennessee, 1796–1860," *Journal of Negro History*, XVII (January, 1932), 92; Carter G. Woodson, "Freedom and Slavery in Appalachian America," *Journal of Negro History*, I (April, 1916), 145; David T. Bailey, *Shadow on the Church: Southwestern Evangelical Religion and the Issues of Slavery, 1783–1860* (Ithaca, N.Y., 1985), 101, 247.

also chastised the most vociferous abolitionists in the North for the divisiveness caused by the immediacy of their demands. This restrained and moderate approach characterized the college's general stand on the eve of the Civil War. When war forced Anderson's successors to cast their lots in 1861, at least half of the faculty and students rejected the call of the Confederacy and supported the Union.[9]

War ravaged a divided people. Materially poor before the Civil War, eastern Tennessee suffered even more at its conclusion. Maryville College had been stripped of its physical assets by neglect and war appropriation, and its students and staff were scattered from Indiana to Georgia. The school might easily have vanished into the pages of frontier history, taking with it its heritage and tradition of theological and racial liberalism. Its days as a seminary were indeed over, but its life as a struggling Presbyterian college with a ministerial focus and a tradition of unorthodox racial attitudes would be revived.

In effect, Maryville College required complete refunding after the Civil War. Only a fraction of its endowment could be reclaimed, and a contemporary described its physical plant as "a huge old building without a decent room in it, and without a pane of glass in its windows." Union soldiers had used window sills and door frames as firewood when they occupied the structure as a stable during the war.[10] The person who almost single-handedly raised the institution back to life was Thomas Jefferson Lamar. Born in eastern Tennessee and graduated from Maryville in 1848 and Union Seminary in New York in 1852, Lamar had been professor of languages at Maryville from 1857 until its closure in 1861. During

9. Ralph Waldo Lloyd, *Maryville College: A History of 150 Years, 1819–1969* (Maryville, Tenn., 1969), 11, 202; Gideon Stebbins White Crawford, *The History of Maryville College* (Maryville, Tenn., 1876), 11; Wilson, *A Century of Maryville College*, 112.

10. Crawford, *History of Maryville College*, 9; Maryville (Tenn.) *Weekly Index*, March 5, 1880.

the war he remained in the town of Maryville, preaching at several small Presbyterian churches and maintaining a firm loyalty to the Union.[11] By his own admission, his "first impression was that Maryville College was dead to live no more," but when in 1865 the newly reconstituted Synod of Tennessee appointed Lamar to solicit funds for the institution's reopening, he undertook a task that consumed almost all of his energies until his death in 1887.[12]

Encouraged by the temporary return to Maryville (from Indiana) of his old antislavery professor John Sawyers Craig, Lamar tackled the formidable problem of financing the reopening.[13] Local economic conditions were not promising, and in December, 1865, he made his first trip north in search of assistance. Although he returned empty-handed in April, 1866, he proceeded to reopen the school in the fall. Lamar had the strong support of prominent eastern Tennessee Unionists, and he now had a sense of the interests of potential Presbyterian lay contributors.[14] He was no longer naive to the political considerations of the Reconstruction era.

Lamar pursued several routes to obtain federal Reconstruc-

11. John Edminston Alexander, *A Brief History of the Synod of Tennessee, from 1817 to 1887* (Philadelphia, 1890), 106–107; Edwin J. Best, "New Providence Presbyterian Church: The First Hundred Years," *Publications* [East Tennessee Historical Society], XXX (1958), 89.

12. Thomas Jefferson Lamar to Professor Herrick Johnson, July 16, 1883, in Correspondence of the College Board, Presbyterian Church in the United States of America (PCUSA), Presbyterian Historical Society; Crawford, *History of Maryville College*, 9.

13. Craig's return and work with Lamar is noted in the Minutes of the Presbytery of Union, April 23, 1866, Maryville College Archives, and Best, "New Providence Presbyterian Church," 90.

14. Particularly prominent in their support of the college's reopening were Horace Maynard and Seth J. W. Luckey. Both were eastern Tennessee Presbyterians. Maynard had been a Whig Congressman, state attorney general under the military government, and would serve briefly as postmaster general under President Hayes. Luckey was a former antislavery figure and judge from Jonesboro. Minutes of the Board of Trustees of Maryville College, September 27, 1867, Maryville College Archives, Maryville (Tenn.) *Times*, November 24, 1900.

tion funds for the college, but not until he approached General O. O. Howard of the Freedmen's Bureau did he receive any encouragement.[15] Howard's interest corresponded with conclusions Lamar had reached from his first fund-raising trip: Maryville had a "marketable" past. Many educational institutions now "stood in a row, as at a post office" competing for the same funds, but no southern school could match Maryville College's record of political loyalty and opposition (albeit somewhat hesitant) to slavery.[16] At first Lamar had appealed for funds solely on the basis of the college's ability to provide much-needed education in the South. When this approach drew little tangible interest, he did not hesitate to stress those contributions currently attractive in the North— loyalty to the Union and education for the freedmen.

When the board of trustees met in September, 1867, preparatory to the beginning of the college's second fall term since reopening, Lamar made his fund-raising report. He proposed the question, "Shall persons be excluded from the benefits of Maryville College because of race or color?" Clearly at stake was aid from the Freedmen's Bureau and most probably from certain northern philanthropists as well. The trustees responded with a strongly worded resolution, saying that "if there was no exclusion during the proscriptive reign of slavery, by reason of race or color, there can be no adequate reason for such exclusion now."[17] On this authority Lamar and other agents constructed their appeals so as to give primary emphasis to the characteristics that made Maryville

15. Early efforts to obtain federal aid are noted in "History, Maryville College: Extracts from the Records of the Synod of Tennessee" (Typescript in Maryville College Archives); Lamar to Howard, December 9, 1867, BRFAL, RG 105, M752, NA.

16. "Memorial to Mr. William Thaw," in "The Bible in College and Theistic Realism: Address at the Inauguration of Rev. Samuel Ward Boardman, D.D. as the Fourth President of Maryville College, September 5, 1889" (MS in Maryville College Archives); Maryville (Tenn.) *Times,* November 24, 1900, quoting a letter from the Maryville College Faculty to Mr. William Thaw, March 4, 1880.

17. Minutes of the Board of Trustees of Maryville College, September 28, 1867, Maryville College Archives.

unusual in the South: its connection with the "Northern" Presbyterian Church, its stand on color, and its goal of instilling an education that transcended narrow sectionalism.[18]

In opening the school's doors to black students as well as white, the directors committed Maryville College to what would become an almost unique path in southern higher education. To Lamar and the new faculty, directors, and students, however, the decision to admit blacks was neither a statement of racial egalitarianism nor a deliberate effort to challenge prevailing racial beliefs and practices in the South. The officers reached a very practical decision, consistent with the school's pre–Civil War history of racial and theological liberalism.

In a very real sense, these Presbyterian educators and students simply offered a restatement of their commitment. In addition, by looking for support in the northern states, they were reconnecting with prewar theological and denominational ties. Although these ties had represented minority strains in the ideological and institutional makeup of the Old South, they had remained strong and vital until forcibly severed by the debate over slavery and the subsequent military conflict. And yet these southerners also saw the opportunity to cause change in the leadership and practices of their state and region—change that their loyalty to the Union already had defined as highly desirable. The idea of "reconstruction" could have tangible meaning; a war and its associated ideological arguments had been lost, and it should be no surprise that adjustments could and would be made in the wake of this defeat.

Racial reform was far from the primary motivation of the founding participants in the rebirth of Maryville College, but these men saw creative potential in the postwar chaos and accepted fundamental alterations in race relations as legitimate corollaries to

18. See Lamar, "Maryville College" and other appeals distributed by Lamar, J. W. Healy, Samuel Sawyer, and Elias Boing, all in Maryville College Archives. See also Josiah Copley, "Maryville College, Tennessee," *Presbyterian Banner* (Pittsburgh, Pa.), November 2, 1881.

emancipation. Their views did not go uncontested, even within the ranks of eastern Tennessee Unionists and New School Presbyterians (the Synod of Tennessee ratified the action of the board of trustees by a majority of only one vote), but the men at Maryville prevailed within the church and community. They gained support from the North, but Thomas Jefferson Lamar remained the key figure in the school, and he was a southerner, as were the students, trustees, and community supporters. College officials allied themselves politically with the brief period of Republican Radicalism in eastern Tennessee and thus strengthened their credentials as pragmatic educators and socially flexible southerners.[19] Maryville College would struggle, but it would survive—with its formal policy of admitting black students uncompromised.

Once Maryville's decision not to exclude blacks became official policy and was made public, Lamar's fund-raising efforts began to pay significant dividends. In October, 1867, William Thaw of Pittsburgh contributed $1,000, and in February, 1868, General Howard sent $3,000 from the Freedmen's Bureau. Thaw made another gift of $3,000, and he, Preserved Smith of Dayton, Ohio, William E. Dodge of New York City, and John C. Baldwin of New Jersey began a practice of annual donations that literally financed the college's current account. In February, 1869, General Howard approved an additional $10,000 grant to Maryville to finance a new main building, and in January, 1870, he authorized $3,000 more from his agency's by-then rapidly diminishing funds.[20]

19. "Extracts from Minutes of Union League Council, Maryville, Tennessee," January 2, 1867–January 14, 1869, prepared by Edwin J. Best for the author. Original minutes in McClung Collection, Lawson McGhee Library, Knoxville.

20. Mary C. Thaw to Rev. E. P. Cowan, September 4, 1901, Mary C. Thaw to Mrs. Nettie F. McCormick, July 10, 1902, Mary C. Thaw to Dr. Samuel T. Boardman, April 20, 1904, Mary C. Thaw to Dr. J. Stuart Dickson, January 3, 1906, all in Thaw Correspondence, Maryville College Archives; T. J. Lamar to Dr. James G. Craighead, February 18, 1876, in James Geddes Craighead Papers, Presbyterian Historical

The northern philanthropists Lamar solicited so successfully generally had two characteristics in common: they were loyal New School Presbyterians, and they had solid antislavery (not necessarily abolitionist) backgrounds. Consequently, college representatives stressed not only their Unionism, but also the school's importance to the uncertain survival in the South of New School Presbyterianism and its brave record of opposition to slavery. Thaw, Dodge, Smith, Baldwin, and the later donors had no formal connection with each other, but represented a particular approach to racial philanthropy. They channeled their gifts so as to encourage the gradual "uplift" of blacks through education and sound religious instruction. The training of black ministers and teachers under white Presbyterian leadership fit their view of controlled and practical elevation for the freedmen. Each of these men gave money to other institutions that served only blacks, and some gave to white-only schools, as well; coeducation of the races was not critical for their support, but it *was* a crucial factor in their support for Maryville College.

Aid from the Freedmen's Bureau, of course, *required* the admission of blacks. Lamar sent letter after letter to General Howard and his staff, assuring them of Maryville's long history of educating blacks and opposing slavery, and of its firm commitment to equal educational opportunities for black students in the future. President Andrew Johnson had sought to keep the Freedmen's Bureau out of his native eastern Tennessee, but with the decline of his influence and the narrowing focus of the bureau upon the work of educating the masses of knowledge-hungry blacks, the possibili-

---

Society; Lamar to Johnson, July 16, 1883, in Correspondence of the College Board, PCUSA; Lamar to C. E. Compton, July 28, 1869, Compton to Lamar, January 7, 1870, Henry M. Whittlesey to Compton, January 12, 1870, Lamar and P. M. Bartlett to General O. O. Howard, January 24, 1870, Compton to Bartlett, March 11, 1870, and C. E. Compton, *Semi-Annual Report of the Condition of Freedmen's Schools in Tennessee for the ½ Year Ending, December 31, 1869*, all in BRFAL, RG 105, M1000, NA.

ties of such a program as that at Maryville gained a favorable hear-ing.[21] In Tennessee as elsewhere, the real need in black education was for qualified teachers, preferably black teachers. Thus, normal training was a primary criterion for bureau support at Maryville, as it also was at other, better-known schools for educating blacks, such as Fisk University in Nashville.[22] Methodists in eastern Tennessee also sought to win federal support for the founding of a new college in Athens, some fifty miles southwest of Maryville. Playing upon the interest in training teachers, they promised to educate blacks in a normal department of what came to be called East Tennessee Wesleyan College, but after receiving $3,000 from the bureau, never delivered upon the promises.[23] The New School Presbyterians at Maryville, however, unlike the Methodists, had made a deal that was consistent with their tradition and their willingness to adapt to or encourage a moderately reconstructed set of race relations in the South. In the end, they would not educate even a fraction of the number of blacks as would a school such as Fisk, but their sincere biracial promise eventually earned $16,000 in support from the Freedmen's Bureau, a dollar-per-black-student ratio far exceeding what the $25,000 contributed to Fisk provided.[24]

Without the open-door racial policy, it is highly unlikely that Maryville would have received even a small fraction of this government and private largesse. Even with such aid, the college struggled constantly to survive; without the aid it most certainly would have failed. Denominational subscriptions offered the only other source of outside income, and despite regular appeals these

21. William S. McFeeley, *Yankee Stepfather: General O. O. Howard and the Freedmen* (New Haven, 1968), 115.

22. John Cimprich, *Slavery's End in Tennessee, 1861–1865* (University, Ala., 1985), 129.

23. H. M. Whittlesey to C. E. Compton, June 11, 1870, Compton to Board of Trustees of East Tennessee Wesleyan University, June 14, 1870, J. Richmond to Compton, June 17, 1870, all in BRFAL, RG 105, M1000, NA.

24. Joe M. Richardson, *A History of Fisk University, 1865–1946* (University, Ala., 1980), 23–24.

never reached a significant level. Key factors in this regard were the small number of "Northern" Presbyterians in the South and the overall poverty of the region encompassed by the Synod of Tennessee.

Lamar's detractors and opponents would later charge that he had sold out to northern radicals—agreeing to conduct an experiment in social equality in return for financial support. Such a view ignored both the history and context that gave meaning to the college's choice in 1867. The decision to educate blacks and whites together was not as extraordinary as it appeared. Slavery had prevented neither Maryville College from educating black students nor the Presbyterian church in Maryville from admitting blacks to membership. Furthermore, black ministers often addressed mixed audiences in the area. With the hurdle of slavery removed, church leaders who made up both the local Union Presbytery and the board of trustees of the college were in a position to fulfill their long-standing commitment to the spiritual and educational elevation of blacks. They organized Sabbath schools and churches for the freedmen of eastern Tennessee; where necessitated by small numbers or where desired by those involved, schools and churches were "mixed" in membership.[25] Schools and churches required trained teachers and ministers just as they had in the frontier days of the Southern and Western Seminary. There were, as yet, no colleges in the area for blacks, and to have divided meager resources between a new school for freedmen and the struggling effort at Maryville College would have doomed both to failure. The need and desire for financial support from the North now required a formal and publicly recorded position, but the decision to allow blacks to matriculate openly at the reopened school was consistent with a genuinely felt, deep-rooted, evangelical Christian responsibility to the former slaves. The college's leaders and the early white

25. Best, "New Providence Presbyterian Church," 84–85; Minutes of the Presbytery of Union, April 23, 1866; Vera Wilson Gilmore, ed., *Union Presbytery, 1797–1976* (Knoxville, 1976), 41.

students were not necessarily egalitarian social crusaders, nor were they selling out to such folk from the North. They had a long-standing commitment, they adapted it to new circumstances, and they intended to keep it.

Opening the doors to all qualified students did not bring a rush of black applicants. The relatively small local black population, the virtual absence or only recent creation of elementary and secondary schooling for freedmen, and undoubtedly, a hesitancy on the part of qualified blacks to risk the potentially hostile and uncertain atmosphere of a predominantly white institution, restricted the pool of candidates. In 1866 the black members of the large and traditionally biracial congregation of New Providence Presbyterian Church had underscored the reluctance of blacks to enter or perpetuate a relationship dominated by whites (even "sympathetic" whites) when they formally and amicably withdrew to form Maryville Second Presbyterian Church.[26] But opportunities for advanced educational training for blacks were scarce. Three black students enrolled in 1868, and a total of thirty had matriculated when Maryville College awarded a bachelor's degree to a black student for the first time, in 1880.[27]

During these early years most black students were local residents, and there were occasional complaints that they were set apart in some college activities. Nevertheless, these first blacks did interact freely with fellow white students and faculty in the politically powerful Union League chapter in Maryville.[28] By the 1870s, moreover, at least some black students lived in college dormitories and, if they chose, participated in sporting and literary societies. William Henderson Franklin, for example, entered Maryville in

26. Edwin J. Best to the author, February 9, 1987, in possession of author.

27. "Roster of Students of Maryville College to 1903" (Maryville College Archives); Dr. P. M. Bartlett to C. E. Compton, May 6, 1870, in BRFAL, RG 105, M1000, NA.

28. "Extracts from Minutes of Union League Council, Maryville, Tennessee."

1872 and established a thirty-year pattern of active participation in a wide range of college activities. Not only was he the first black graduate, but during his student days he became an integral part of the Reckless Baseball Club, the Athenian Literary Society, and the YMCA. After graduation, Franklin worked actively in the Society of Alumni and served on the college's board of trustees from 1893 to 1901.[29] His long association with Maryville College was an exception, however, among black alumni. In spite of the efforts of a committed faculty—especially Lamar, Oberlin-educated Alexander Bartlett, and former Maryville student G. S. W. Crawford—the nonacademic environment of black students deteriorated after 1880.[30]

Maryville's decision to admit students irrespective of race brought some opposition almost immediately. As noted earlier, the Synod of Tennessee in September, 1868, had given its support to the plan by a majority of only one vote; an unsuccessful petition to rescind this action was presented to Union Presbytery the following year.[31] College faculty and officers found themselves regularly criticized and their efforts to gain local financial support greatly hindered by racial antagonisms. "We are the target," Lamar noted on one occasion, "at which is aimed all that malignant hate of that class who continually fight against the just rights and elevation of the colored race." To this group, educating blacks "in any way," Lamar continued, "is bad enough, but to educate them with the

29. Dr. P. M. Bartlett to Mary C. Thaw, September 12, 1901, in Thaw Correspondence; Minutes of the Proceedings of the Reckless Baseball Club, 1876–1877; *College Days*, 1894; *College Days*, 1895; "Records of the Society of Alumni of Maryville College"; and Minutes of the Board of Trustees of Maryville College, 1893–1901; all in Maryville College Archives.

30. Lamar to Howard, December 28, 1869, in BRFAL, RG 105, M1000, NA; Alexander Bartlett to James H. Fairchild, November 4, 1878, in Fairchild Papers, Oberlin College Library, Oberlin, Ohio; Author's interview with Dr. S. E. Crawford, August 9, 1976.

31. Bartlett to Mary C. Thaw, September 12, 1901, in Thaw Correspondence; Minutes of the Presbytery of Union, April 16, 1869.

whites is an unpardonable sin."[32] The local press was divided in its general support of the college, depending upon the views of editors and newspapers that came and went in the years from 1868 to 1880, but opposition appeared frequently. In addition, national Reconstruction policies, particularly the oft-debated Civil Rights Bill of 1874, periodically caused hostility toward Maryville's racial liberalism to boil to the surface. College officials had spoken out in favor of the highly controversial integrated-schools provision of Charles Sumner's civil rights proposal, earning denunciation from newspapers across the state. And locally, "clods and missiles" were hurled at participants in a predominantly black political rally in Maryville at the time of the 1874 fall elections.[33]

Maryville escaped the Reconstruction-era violence so common elsewhere in the state and in the South, but the creative uncertainty of the postwar years hardened considerably during the 1870s, even in eastern Tennessee, and by the early 1880s constant pressure threatened to undermine the college's commitment to racial integration. Other religious denominations and philanthropic groups were addressing the need for higher education among the small black population of the area. Quakers had founded the Freedmen's Normal School in Maryville; the United Presbyterian Church in North America had opened Knoxville College for Negroes in Knoxville, fifteen miles away; only a bit more distant, in Morristown, the Methodists were preparing to launch Morristown College in 1881. This local competition made it difficult for Maryville College—already handicapped by the small pool of black

32. T. J. Lamar to General O. O. Howard, December 28, 1869, Dr. P. M. Bartlett to Howard, December 18, 1869, Bartlett and Lamar to Howard, January 24, 1870, C. E. Compton to Howard, January 8, 1870, all in BRFAL, M1000; Alexander Bartlett to Fairchild, November 4, 1878, in Fairchild Papers; Maryville (Tenn.) *Republican*, May 30, 1874.

33. Maryville (Tenn.) *Republican*, May 30, 1874; Nashville *Union and American*, May 28, 1874; Verton M. Queener, "A Decade of East Tennessee Republicanism, 1867–1876," *Publications* [East Tennessee Historical Society], XIV (1942), 82–83; Stafford Allen Warner, *Yardley Warner: The Freedman's Friend* (Abingdon, Va., 1957), 280–81.

Presbyterians in the South, by the hostile rivalry of the southern branch of the denomination, and by a general decline of interest in work among the freedmen within the college's own parental church organization—to increase its small black enrollment. Furthermore, the segregated approach taken by this competition found support among the sizable number of eastern Tennesseans who, while favoring education for blacks, adamantly opposed coeducation of the races.[34]

Beginning in 1869, Peter Mason Bartlett held the title of president of Maryville College. He was an able campus administrator, freeing Lamar for most of the fund-raising efforts. Bartlett, however, was an outsider from the North, and he possessed an argumentative and abrasive manner; consequently, he became the focus for much of the criticism of the college's policy. By his own later admission, Bartlett had never really believed in the coeducation of the races, but for many years he dutifully carried out the commitments made to the original financial benefactors. By 1878, however, the slow growth of the college, the difficulty in attracting black students, and the carping criticism of whites had convinced him that the interracial effort should be abandoned in the best interests of the school.[35] From this point until he was removed from office in 1887, he was a divisive force on the faculty. As early as 1880, William Thaw had sensed a wavering of spirit and let it be known that if Maryville became indifferent "as to the outworking of obligation to colored students," he would "feel absolved from any further [special] interest in the institution."[36] A substantial

34. Blount County *Democrat* (Maryville, Tenn.), April 14, 21, 1880; *Independent*, XXXV (March 1, 1883), 261; Charles F. Bryan and JoVita Wells, "Morristown College: Education for Blacks in the Southern Highlands," [East Tennessee Historical Society] *Publications* (1980–81), 64.

35. Maryville (Tenn.) *Republican*, May 30, 1874; Blount County *Democrat* (Maryville, Tenn.), April 14, 21, 1880; Alexander Bartlett to Fairchild, November 26, 1878, in Fairchild Papers; Dr. P. M. Bartlett to Mary C. Thaw, September 12, 1901, in Thaw Correspondence.

36. William Thaw to the Faculty of Maryville College, February 14, 1880, quoted in "Injunction by the Trustees of Maryville College" (Maryville College Archives).

white student rebellion during the course of 1881 and 1882 under-scored Thaw's general concern.

In August, 1881, the faculty faced the refusal of one of the college's two social and literary societies to admit black students to membership. The Animi Cultus Society, the offending party, was formally directed to amend its constitution immediately in order to make clear that no student would be denied membership "on account of race or color." The society reluctantly agreed to this demand, but six months later the faculty faced a major crisis. In February, 1882, the Animi Cultus Society not only rejected a black student and expelled the members who had solicited his membership, but the society also sent a letter (signed by twenty-seven students) to the faculty denying the faculty's right to exercise any authority in the matter. In response the faculty suspended the students involved and permanently dissolved the society.[37]

At issue, however, was the basic question of integration. The Animi Cultus Society had taken its case to supporters outside the college, and the institution found it necessary to answer friend as well as foe. Periodicals representing both Northern and Southern Presbyterianism joined the debate, and William Thaw again suggested that his "interest and cooperation" might have to be "terminated."[38] The board of trustees responded to criticism from both sides with a strongly worded resolution stating:

> Whereas the impression has become, to a degree prevalent in the public mind that the co-education of the races in

37. Faculty Meeting Minutes, 1881–82, in Maryville College Archives; "Correspondence and Letters Relating to Discipline in 1882" and "Action of Faculty" folders, Maryville College Archives.

38. *Presbyterian Banner* (Pittsburgh, Pa.), March 8, 15, 1882; *Christian Observer* (Louisville), February 22, March 8, 22, 1882; William Thaw to the Board of Trustees of Maryville College, February 20, 1882, quoted in "Injunction by the Trustees." Opposition from the Presbyterian Church in the United States (Southern) was nothing new. Its representatives regularly attacked the policy of "race mixing" and had attempted to gain legal control over the college in a series of legal actions between 1872 and 1880. For a discussion of the legal dispute, see Lloyd, *Maryville College*, 63–66.

Maryville College is still a debatable topic, or its expediency questioned, or at least there is such a difference of opinion among the authorities of the College that the success of the policy is likely to be hindered, if not wholly thwarted . . . we do, hereby, reaffirm our adoption of this policy, and declare it to be our sincere purpose to execute it impartially and honestly, and strictly enjoin upon the Faculty and Teachers of the College to do nothing by word or deed, directly or indirectly, seeming evasion or equivocation to produce the impression that the co-education of the races in Maryville College is any longer a debatable question.[39]

These Presbyterians had made a commitment to co-education during more optimistic and flexible times, and they remained resolved to keep it. During the 1880s and 1890s, however, pressure upon them grew rather than diminished. At first during these years, blacks in Tennessee had found themselves in a position of some political influence as whites divided sharply over local issues and such state-wide concerns as the public debt. In eastern Tennessee, two black former students at Maryville College, both Presbyterian ministers, took especially outspoken stands in favor of expanded black equality. William Henderson Franklin, by now the founder and principal of Swift Memorial Institute in Rogersville, commented regularly in the national black press regarding the need to end separation and discrimination in public education and the importance of black political participation and service on juries. He urged blacks to "know their rights" and to have "the courage to demand and to defend them."[40] In Knoxville, meanwhile, Job Lawrence, minister at Shiloh Presbyterian Church, became visibly and personally involved in local politics. He applied pressure and won appointment to the Knoxville Board of Education, was

39. Minutes of the Board of Trustees of Maryville College, August 23, 1882.

40. Joseph H. Cartwright, *The Triumph of Jim Crow: Tennessee Race Relations in the 1880s* (Knoxville, 1976) is a superb account of black political activity in the state during this period of "revival." Cartwright notes Franklin's communications in the New York *Freeman, Globe,* and *Age.* See pp. 89, 175, 177, 183, 251–52.

the target of "an immediate public explosion," and eventually lost his seat after a much-publicized lawsuit. Before deciding to leave the area, Lawrence lambasted Republicans for ignoring blacks except at election time, and concluded that "we are no more free than in the days of bondage."[41]

White reaction to black political assertiveness in Tennessee took two forms, both of which implied new pressures upon the college's racial policies. First, white Republican friendship toward blacks started to decline below even the "election time" interest deplored by Job Lawrence. After receiving considerable criticism for their support of the Lodge Force Bill and experiencing a number of defeats in the elections of 1890 and 1892, white Republican leaders in eastern Tennessee began to view black political support as a liability. A steady incline toward Lily-Whitism within the party began. Second, the legislature passed a series of laws designed to disfranchise most black voters. By bringing about what the historian Joel Williamson has implied to be an "echo redemption" in the state, white Tennesseans strongly rejected both black activism and whites who associated themselves with blacks and their causes.[42]

Furthermore, in addition to the political context, there was clear evidence that the Presbyterian Church in the United States of America (PCUSA—the "northern" branch) held a declining interest in statements of racial equality and in work among blacks in general. Discussions regarding reunion with the southern church and with the Cumberland Presbyterian Church (predominantly southern) during the 1880s and 1890s, for example, led to regular proposals for segregated presbyteries, proposals finally adopted by the General Assembly in 1904 and 1906. Corresponding with this reduced commitment to blacks was a growing emphasis by

41. Michael J. McDonald and William B. Wheeler, *Knoxville, Tennessee: Continuity and Change in an Appalachian City* (Knoxville, 1983), 31.

42. Gordon B. McKinney, "Southern Mountain Republicans and the Negro, 1865–1900," *Journal of Southern History*, XLI (November, 1975), 507–509; Joel Williamson, *A Rage for Order: Black-White Relations in the American South Since Emancipation* (New York, 1986), 155–57.

Presbyterian and other denominations upon bringing education and Christian education to mountain whites. Mission schools sprang up in Kentucky, western North Carolina, and eastern Tennessee, and pressure came to bear upon schools such as Maryville and Berea College in Kentucky to do more for the sons and daughters of white mountaineers. Adapting to this pressure would require coming to grips with the growing southern antipathy toward flexible or liberal racial ideas and practices.[43]

Given these general and specific conditions, representatives of Maryville College could not avoid ostracism and public denunciation, and no matter how strongly or how often the faculty and trustees declared their commitment to coeducation to be beyond debate, in practice changes occurred. The folk at Maryville had never been driven strongly by an interracial vision (as compared with their counterparts at Berea, for example); they simply had strong sympathies for blacks and were genuinely committed to blacks' inclusion in a reconstructed South. And as pragmatists in their commitment rather than visionaries, they were more vulnerable to outside pressure.

Ironically, President Bartlett, the northerner, yielded first—his divisiveness and "equivocation" led to his removal in 1887—while the southern faculty and trustees remained publicly firm. But the college also had lost its two most effective defenders of its racial policy—Alexander Bartlett died in 1883 and Thomas Jefferson Lamar in 1887. Blatant student confrontations such as that of the Animi Cultus Society would not be repeated for almost twenty years, but black students became less and less a part of the general college community as the decade of the 1890s began.

43. James M. McPherson, *The Abolitionist Legacy: From Reconstruction to the NAACP* (Princeton, N.J., 1975), 238–39; Elizabeth R. Hooker, *Religion in the Highlands* (New York, 1933), 199; James C. Klotter, "The Black South and White Appalachia," *Journal of American History*, LXVI (March, 1980), 832–49. Social pressure similar to that applied in Maryville was found by the whites associated with Morristown College. See Bryan and Wells, "Morristown College," 64. For relevant situations elsewhere, see McPherson, *Abolitionist Legacy*, 181–82.

For the most part, separation became a matter of custom rather than formal policy. The few black students sat in the back of the classroom, kept as a group to themselves in chapel, and no longer lived on the campus. Although the Animi Cultus Society was dissolved for its flagrant racism, no black students in fact joined the social and literary societies after that dispute ended in 1882. The faculty denied that any changes had occurred and maintained that any withdrawal was voluntary on the part of the blacks. Nevertheless, some formal compromises did take place. In 1895, for example, Paris A. Wallace, an outstanding black graduate, won the prize for the best commencement oration. In the words of a fellow student, his award "caused quite a stir." The faculty met and declared that henceforth the medals were to be given in private ceremonies and the "speeches which are made in public at the presentation of Diplomas . . . must be limited to 250 words each."[44]

Although Maryville's coeducation policy contained less and less "integration," the college's strong liberal arts curriculum continued to attract a small number of black students.[45] Furthermore, William Thaw and the other major northern Presbyterian benefactors had expressed their renewed confidence by contributing heavily to a successful drive to expand the endowment in 1883. A new president, Vermont-born Samuel W. Boardman, took office in 1889, pledged to uphold the commitments to educate blacks. Also, in 1892 and again in 1895 the Synod of Tennessee rejected proposals to rescind the support it had given to the coeducation policy in 1868.

Opposition persisted, however. Former president P. M. Bartlett, following rejection by the board of trustees in a bid for

44. Dr. P. M. Bartlett to Mary C. Thaw, September 24, 1901, in Thaw Correspondence; Author's interview with Mr. and Mrs. J. H. Daves, July 2, 1970; Author's interview with Dr. S. E. Crawford, August 9, 1976; Wilson, *A Century of Maryville College,* 134; Maryville (Tenn.) *Times,* December 15, 1900; John C. Crawford, "Ramblings and Reminiscences" (MS in Maryville College Archives); Faculty Meeting Minutes, 1891–1913.

45. Eight of the nine black students who graduated with B.A. degrees from Maryville College between 1868 and 1901 did so in the ten-year span 1889–1898.

reinstatement, stayed in Maryville and became a regular critic—arguing that blacks would receive better treatment in their own separate schools and that Maryville's educational mission would be better served because, without blacks, it would attract many more needy white students from the region. Several prominent alumni and students also helped to keep this issue alive.[46]

Shortly after the fall term began in 1900, the Synod of Tennessee, meeting in Maryville on October 4, received a petition signed by 153 students (almost 50 percent of the total enrollment and not including any of the 5 black students). The petition requested "that the negros [sic] be either excluded from the College or be given free and equal rights with white students, rights which they are not enjoying at the present time." The students (among whom was the son of former president Bartlett) had no expectations of gaining the full equality side of their request; given past compromises and prevailing attitudes and customs, this would have been practically impossible. Encouraged by the public sermons and counsel of George D. McCulloch, the new pastor of the influential local Presbyterian church, the students actually were seeking to force a repeal of the thirty-three-year-old policy of integration.[47]

The synod referred the petition to the Maryville College board of trustees, which was not scheduled to meet again until January, 1901. The issue persisted, however, among the trustees, within the churches of the area, and in the local and state press. P. M. Bartlett became a public figure, repeating his long-standing arguments for all who would listen. McCulloch contended that "we [the whites] had to learn the impossibility of carrying out such

46. Rev. Donald McDonald to Will A. McTeer, [?], 1887, in Will A. McTeer Papers, McClung Collection, Lawson McGhee Library; Samuel T. Wilson to Mary C. Thaw, October 29, 1900, Dr. P. M. Bartlett to Mary C. Thaw, September 12, 1901, both in Thaw Correspondence; Lloyd, *Maryville College*, 210.

47. Student petition, Maryville College Archives; Samuel T. Wilson to Mary C. Thaw, October 29, 1900, in Thaw Correspondence; Rev. George D. McCulloch to Will A. McTeer, October 24, 1900, in McTeer Papers; Maryville (Tenn.) *Times*, October 13, 1900.

a plan" and that "God's providence must be recognized" in the issue of segregation. When the board of trustees met on January 16, however, a new and potentially more serious form of attack was under way. The college had received private warnings that unless it took action on its own, "a settlement will be forced in the courts and state legislature by those who are indifferent to the honor of the college or the welfare of the colored race."[48] Sensing correctly that the college intended to resist student and public pressure, a prominent local white graduate had drafted legislation that would require total segregation of students in private schools (segregation long since had been mandated—by the Tennessee Constitution of 1870—for public-supported schools). The legislation subsequently was introduced by a state senator from Knoxville and became known as the Murphy Bill. As a result of this pending threat, the board of trustees referred action on the student petition to a special committee, which was to make a detailed report in May. By that time, the Murphy Bill had become law through an overwhelming vote of both houses of the legislature.[49]

When the special Committee on Coeducation of the Races reported to the trustees on May 28, it made four recommendations, which the board then adopted as formal policy: (1) that no attempt be made to test the constitutionality of the law; (2) that since the Murphy Law required schools to teach either blacks or whites, but not both, Maryville henceforth admit "only white students"; (3) that the trustees "equitably divide the interest accruing from such portion of the endowment as was given on the specific conditions of co-education"; and (4) that $25,000 of the endowment (approximately one tenth) be set aside so that the interest could be "applied

48. "Minutes of the Eighty-fourth Annual Session of the Synod of Tennessee, October, 1900" (Maryville College Archives), 45; Knoxville *Journal and Tribune,* October 5, 1900; Maryville (Tenn.) *Times,* October 13, December 15, 1900; McCulloch to McTeer, October 24, 1900, in McTeer Papers.

49. Lloyd, *Maryville College,* 210; Minutes of the Board of Trustees, January 16, 1901; *Maryville College Monthly,* III (February, 1901), 86–87; Lester C. Lamon, *Black Tennesseans, 1900–1930* (Knoxville, 1977), 61n.

to the education of the colored people in Swift Memorial Institute at Rogersville, Tennessee so long as it shall remain a Presbyterian Institution." [50] In reaching these decisions, members of the committee rejected suggestions that a fight be made in the legislature, consulted with legal counsel (which advised against testing the constitutionality of the state legislation), considered the unsolicited proposals of a group of black alumni, and sought the advice of persons representing the interests of the Reconstruction-era donors. [51] Officials clearly intended to honor the spirit of earlier financial commitments even though the school's operating budget had run a deficit in each of the past two years. [52]

And yet the decisions appear to have been made rather quickly and without debate—almost perfunctorily. There were no special meetings of trustees, presbytery, or synod, and not even a public threat of court action that might have been interpreted as "showing the flag." In short, the reversal of a thirty-three-year practice—a practice for which many sacrifices had been made and abuses withstood—took place with remarkably little public protest or notice. The manner in which the college dealt with this manifestation of the now-pervasive southern demand for complete black exclusion from the white world remained consistent, however, with the school's historical practice and approach in racial issues. Maryville College had never intended to be a symbol of diehard

50. Report of Committee on Coeducation of the Races" (MS) and Minutes of the Board of Trustees, May 28, 1901, both in Maryville College Archives.

51. *Ibid*; W. H. Piper to Will A. McTeer, January 14, 22, 26, 1901, John P. Smith to McTeer, January 21, 1901, Calvin A. Duncan to McTeer, January 23, 31, 1901, E. A. Elmore to McTeer, January 29, February 15, 1901, William A. Cate to McTeer, April 8, 1901, Mary C. Thaw to Frank Semple, January 29, 1901, Semple to McTeer, February 2, 1901, all in McTeer Papers; Seven black alumni to the Board of Trustees, May 7, 1901, in Maryville College Archives; Mary C. Thaw to Samuel W. Boardman, July 10, 1902, April 20, 1904, Mary C. Thaw to President Samuel Tyndale Wilson, September 5, 14, 16, 1901, and Mary C. Thaw to Rev. E. P. Cowan, September 4, 1901, all in Thaw Correspondence.

52. Samuel Tyndale Wilson, "Report to the Directors," May 27, 1902 (Typescript in Maryville College Archives).

resistance or fundamental challenge to the place blacks were expected to occupy in southern society. Even before the Civil War, when the school's stand against slavery clearly set it apart from the mainstream of southern thinking, Maryville's minority view of race was only a small part of its mission to bring its own brand of evangelical Christianity to the people of the region. The stand against slavery emanated from broadly applied principles of liberty and Christian duty, not from an overt commitment to racial equality.

Similarly, when T. J. Lamar and the Synod of Tennessee decided to rebuild and reopen the college during the uncertain years following the Civil War, they had given race little consideration one way or the other. But when they were reminded that Christians had a duty to educate the freedmen, that no higher educational institutions for blacks existed, and that money was available if Maryville admitted black students, they readily adopted a policy of integration or coeducation. They took this position, not as part of a social experiment or even as a self-conscious challenge to traditional southern race relations, but out of a willingness to adapt their mission and duty to changed circumstances. During the Reconstruction decade it had seemed entirely possible to the Unionists in eastern Tennessee that meaningful changes should and would occur in southern society, and Lamar and the faculty, trustees, and students were willing (perhaps some were even eager) to put some of these changes into practice at Maryville.

The experience of black students during the late nineteenth century illustrated the nature of the commitment of Maryville's white leadership. William Franklin, as one of the early students, participated freely with whites on almost every level because he and most of his mentors and colleagues honestly expected freedom to mean more than an end to slavery, perhaps even equality. When these expectations were shown to be too optimistic and solid opposition to a more equitable place for blacks began to assert itself, Maryville's interracial practices remained firmly grounded in duty but less influenced by racial ideals. Challenges from unofficial bodies such as the Animi Cultus Society threatened the college's sense of honor and responsibility to its benefactors, and were dealt with severely. But to insist that blacks actually join student organizations or to allow black scholars such as Paris Wallace to be on prominent public display at commencement would constitute unnecessary idealistic challenges to the increasingly rigid racial views of the overwhelming southern majority. Even the more visionary experiment at Berea was also making subtle adaptations to such white racial demands.[53]

Action by the duly elected General Assembly of the State of Tennessee absolved the school of its continuing formal obligation to the federal government, William Thaw, and others, if not of its Christian duty. There were regrets and stirrings of conscience among officials at Maryville College in the spring of 1901. Awarding Franklin an honorary doctorate at the last commencement before the Murphy Law took effect perhaps symbolized a desire to atone for what one professor described as "an unfavorable beginning for the twentieth century's interpretation of the brotherhood of man."[54] Such symbolic action aside, however, the most difficult decision, in the view of a former student, professor, and soon-to-be president Samuel Tyndale Wilson, involved "giving away $25,000 of our little endowment; but it was the right thing to do."[55] Maryville College had been founded and led by southern men dedicated to doing the "right thing." They were sensitive, pragmatic, Christian educators who willingly took blacks into their mission alongside whites, but they were not out to force racial reform on the South. The message remained the same from 1819 until 1901, but the context changed several times. And as the context changed, so did the practice. Maryville's remarkable witness had opened a small door to a few black southerners; with the beginning of the new century, even that meager access had disappeared.

53. Elizabeth S. Peck and Emily Ann Smith, *Berea's First 125 Years: 1855–1980* (Lexington, Ky., 1982), 47–57.

54. Elmer B. Waller, Editorial in *Maryville College Monthly*, III (February, 1901), 87.

55. Tyndale quoted in Lloyd, *Maryville College*, 214.

New Negroes for a New Century

Adaptability on Display

Walter B. Weare

The question of an "adaptable South" would have held a rather different meaning for New South blacks than for New South whites. As southerners and Americans, the former slaves lived with an extra measure of uncertainty in a larger society that seemed always poised on the edge of a "southern" past and an "American" future, its own uncertain identity bound up in classifying one third of its population as neither slaves nor citizens. Whites looked to a mythic past as they faced the future, adapting to change as they wished for continuity. Blacks looked to a dreamlit future as they endured the past, adapting to continuity as they wished for change. The equation was never balanced, however, because the problem became ever more complex on the black side, and because the power weighed ever more heavily on the white side. Blacks seldom had an unmediated relationship with the material forces determining history; they relied more directly on the cultural and the spiritual—on their own devices and the authority of a distinctive other world—to act as mediators and to deflect the crushing weight of this world. In the penetrating view of W. E. B. Du Bois, Afro-Americans lived behind a veil, performing a shadow act as a reflection of white power.

At the most complex level of accommodation, black leaders adapted to those who were themselves adapting, charting their marginal course carefully along the rift that made up the "divided mind of the New South," seeking to modernize their people while paying obeisance to the old order. But as the nineteenth century came to a close, white leaders—even as they differed in their own adaptation to the opposing forces of modernization and tradition, forming independent partisan allegiances or competitive camps of planters and industrialists—also increasingly formed overlapping alliances or advocated *Herrenvolk* unity. Their common resolve to manage the social relations of a developing country whose great promise, they now agreed, lay in industry as well as in agriculture, led them to embrace a political economy designed to keep things as they were while changing them—to maintain a familiar system of caste and class while moving toward modernization, to divide black and white workers racially while compressing them economically as subordinate strata of low-cost labor. In this restructuring, most of the southern economy traveled a route somewhere between the "Prussian Road" and Wall Street, and black leaders learned to adapt to white leaders who simultaneously espoused the Lost Cause and the New South Creed.[1]

1. The debate over the nature of the New South political economy has generated a voluminous literature, which in oversimplified terms can be characterized as derivative of the class analyses of C. Vann Woodward (a rising dominant bourgeoisie) and Eugene Genovese (a lingering hegemonic aristocracy), or of the market analysis of Robert Fogel and Stanley Engerman (neoclassical economics explains everything). Jonathan Wiener, *The Social Origins of the New South: Alabama, 1860–1885* (Baton Rouge, 1978), extended Genovese's approach in suggesting that the New South followed a "Prussian Road" of industrial development under the hegemony of planters persisting from the old regime, not unlike the Junkers of nineteenth-century Germany. An early but excellent discussion of the overall debate is Harold D. Woodman's "Sequel to Slavery: The New History Views the Postbellum South," *Journal of Southern History*, XLIII (1977), 523–54. For an exchange among Wiener, Woodman, and Robert Higgs, see "*AHR* Forum: Class Structure and Economic Development in the American South, 1865–1955," *American Historical Review*, LXXXIV (1979), 970–1001. See also the comprehensive historiographical pieces by Numan V. Bartley, "In Search of the New South," and Gavin Wright, "The Strange Career of the New

But the white synthesis was not merely structural or benign; from the black point of view it carried an ominous immediacy growing out of what Joel Williamson has classified as Radicalism— the vicious hardening of race relations between 1889 and 1915, with the image of the "black beast rapist" overtaking that of the "old-time Negro," and with the specter of genocide, either at the hands of white men "defending white womanhood" or at the hands of God and Darwin extinguishing an "unfit race," supplanting a moderate vision of faithful labor and peaceful coexistence. This hateful turn of the dialectic produced a black synthesis, a broad albeit uneven agreement on adaptability that cut across political persuasion and formed the centerpiece of Afro-American thought during the age of Booker T. Washington.[2]

As Du Bois so clearly saw it, Washington "grasped the spirit of the age—triumphant commercialism." In Washington's version of historical materialism, the "souls of black folk" amounted to an embarrassing superstructure of a feudal past whose dying hand would surrender a dependent, spiritual people to a New South whose material forces would transform them into economic men— "New Negroes for a New Century," as Washington called them— who could solve the race problem. In response to the charge that the freedmen and their children had lapsed into a state of moral and material decay and could not survive outside of slavery, the southern black leadership, with Washington as high priest (and Du Bois not always as dissenter) launched an accommodative counter-attack, preaching a gospel of progress, proselytizing the premodern black masses, and seizing every opportunity to testify before skeptical whites. Adaptability, quite literally, became the issue; and

Southern Economic History," both in *Reviews in American History,* X (1982), 150–80. Within this theoretical framework little has been done on the internal social history of black southerners; a good exception is Crandall Shifflett, *Patronage and Poverty in the Tobacco South: Louisa County, Virginia, 1860–1900* (Knoxville, 1982).

2. See Joel R. Williamson, *The Crucible of Race: Black-White Relations in the American South Since Emancipation* (New York, 1984).

this essay would like to suggest that as black defenders rallied around the Darwinian challenge, accepting the burden of proof for black compatibility with a modern industrial state and placing the proof of "race progress" on elaborate display in an effusion of expositions, they produced a significant social and intellectual movement in Afro-American history.[3]

It came as no accident that this black New South creed, with its emphasis on progress, modernization, materialism, racial solidarity, business enterprise, scientific agriculture, self-help, and public relations, coincided with the climax of the career of Jim Crow, the vogue of scientific racism, and the heyday of industrial capitalism. As the southern economy expanded and racism intensified, as disfranchisement obliterated the base of black politicians who found themselves isolated token figures dependent on a decreasing number of powerless patronage appointments, and as traditional relationships between an old servant elite and a white aristocracy faded into the past, a black bourgeoisie of professionals and businessmen based in the segregated black community appeared on the scene as the adaptive, self-styled, self-conscious, last best hope for the race. Indeed, in the popular lexicon of bourgeois black society they became known as "race men." As products of both Western civilization and racial oppression, they pitted one profoundly American ideology (progress) against another (racism), seeing little choice except to believe passionately that the race, like Washington himself, was going to go up from slavery, that history was on their side, that the invisible hand of Darwin would favor the man farthest down, whose greater struggle rendered him the fittest.[4]

Thoroughly modern in outlook and expectations, but de-

3. W. E. B. Du Bois, *The Souls of Black Folk: Essays and Sketches* (London, 1903), 43; Booker T. Washington, N. B. Wood, and Fannie Barrier Williams, *A New Negro for a New Century* (Chicago, 1900), *passim*.

4. August Meier, *Negro Thought in America, 1880–1915* (Ann Arbor, 1963), 151–55. See also August Meier and David Lewis, "History of the Negro Upper Class in Atlanta, Georgia, 1890–1958," *Journal of Negro Education*, XXVIII (1959), 128–39.

prived of status, they chafed under racial proscription only to turn their dissonance toward, rather than against, the core values of the society that rejected them. Forbearance and optimism became their trademarks. The alternatives—turning against the regime to retaliate or turning away from the regime to emigrate—seemed suicidal or alien to those whom E. Franklin Frazier distinguished as the "old black middle class." So they gritted their teeth and redoubled their efforts to bolster a battered image and lay claim to a bountiful future as free persons in the Western world.[5]

It is impossible to attach time and place precisely to the origins of the Afro-American exposition movement and its symbolic universe—what one writer has summarized matter-of-factly as "show and tell race relations."[6] According to August Meier, "This larger complex of ideas that included racial solidarity and self help . . . had been especially popular in the discouraging decade before the Civil War. It was based on the assumption that by the acquisition of wealth and morality—attained largely by their own efforts—Negroes would gain the respect of white men and thus be accorded their rights as citizens."[7] These antebellum underpinnings probably extend back to the eighteenth-century free African societies and their offspring of religious institutions, moral reform and literary societies, and especially the Negro Convention Movement. In 1853, at the important convention in Rochester, New York, concerned free black leaders founded the National Council of Colored People, which decried racial persecution and resolved that given the unparalleled progress "in the midst of . . . disparagement," black Americans could "take courage, having placed ourselves where we may fairly challenge comparison with more highly favored men." This message—success against the odds—became the stock-in-trade presentation of the old middle class as they re-

5. Edward Franklin Frazier, "Durham: Capital of the Black Middle Class," in *The New Negro*, ed. Alain Locke (New York, 1925), 333–40.

6. John H. Haley, *Charles N. Hunter and Race Relations in North Carolina* (Chapel Hill, 1987), 180.

7. Meier, *Negro Thought*, 42.

hearsed for Reconstruction and a New South, when race men would transform statistical reporting into jubilees.[8]

The institutionalized celebration of emancipation and progress in the black South began even before emancipation itself, most notably in the Sea Islands of South Carolina and in those parts of Tennessee where Confederate control gave way to Union occupation by 1862. By January, 1865, Tennessee had abolished slavery and was willing to hear John Mercer Langston, Virginia's future black congressman, deliver the emancipation address in the state capitol at Nashville. A local white newspaper described the event as a solemn occasion "attended by several white persons . . . besides a very large number of civil, well dressed and orderly colored people." Later that year another celebration in Nashville more typically combined the formal and festive. According to the pioneer black historian Alrutheus Ambush Taylor, "This celebration consisted of a procession, a barbecue, speaking and music. The procession included three colored associations in regalia. . . . General [Clinton B.] Fisk spoke on 'the gospel of work, the gospel of economy, and the gospel of virtue.'"[9]

Despite the efforts of the black bourgeoisie to shape them, these events increasingly blossomed into less somber folk festivals, a healthy reminder that Afro-American culture is not merely mimetic and seldom just a response to white oppression. The emancipation jubilees, some held on January 1, others on September 22, a few on the Fourth of July or the anniversary of the ratification of the Thirteenth Amendment, and still others on the anniversary of the announcement of emancipation in a specific region (in Texas, for example, June 19, 1865, or "Juneteenth Day"), took on a life of their own as they spread throughout the South. As social history they are akin to the proliferation of "colored fairs," whose origins

8. Quoted in John Hope Franklin, *From Slavery to Freedom* (3d ed.; New York, 1967), 237.

9. Willie Lee Rose, *Rehearsal for Reconstruction: The Port Royal Experiment* (New York, 1964), 167–68, 195–97; Alrutheus Ambush Taylor, *The Negro in Tennessee, 1865–1880* (Washington, D.C., 1941), 230–31.

lay somewhere between the carefully staged expositions as public-relations events and the more spontaneous emancipation celebrations as social events. There may in fact be a linear history of these institutions, beginning with emancipation or Fourth of July celebrations, proceeding to local and state fairs, and giving rise ultimately to international expositions. In practice, however, there was considerable blurring of the lines among these events, and any notion of a hierarchical relationship resided more in the minds of the black elite than in the minds of the freedmen.[10]

By the 1880s many of the southern states had established colored state fairs, complete with state-chartered fair development companies and separate grounds and buildings. Again, Tennessee seems to have taken the lead. In 1870, the Davidson County and Middle Tennessee Colored Agricultural and Mechanical Association established a site for what became the annual state fair on the outskirts of Nashville. The association built an amphitheater and a full set of exhibition buildings; horse racing, music, baseball, speeches, and contests enlivened the four-day event, and railroad excursions from Memphis and other cities brought thousands of visitors. In 1873, Frederick Douglass gave the annual address, prompting the Nashville newspaper to predict that "this fair promises to be the best ever held by the Association. . . . The colored hotels and boarding houses will be overrun for a few days and an appeal will be made for all colored citizens to open their doors for the accommodation of strangers."[11]

As black fairs and festivals proliferated throughout the southern states, whites occasionally recoiled, especially during Re-

10. William H. Wiggins, Jr., *O Freedom! Afro-American Emancipation Celebrations* (Knoxville, 1987), xvii–48. A mine of original documentation on this subject exists in the Hampton Institute Clipping Files, Hampton Institute Library, Hampton, Va. (hereinafter cited as HC).

11. Taylor, *The Negro in Tennessee*, 240–41. Other state studies dealing with fairs include Vernon Lane Wharton, *The Negro in Mississippi, 1865–1900* (Chapel Hill, 1947), 270; Lawrence D. Rice, *The Negro in Texas, 1874–1900* (Baton Rouge, 1971), 180–81, 197; John Dittmer, *Black Georgia in the Progressive Era, 1900–1920* (Urbana, Ill., 1977), 169, 183; and Tindall, *South Carolina Negroes*, 119–20.

construction, at the energy and enthusiasm of the celebrants, not to mention their sheer numbers. In some cities, the black citizens rolled celebrations of the Fourth of July and their own freedom all into one, causing whites to concede the Fourth as a black holiday. With every intention of irony, the Petersburg (Va.) *Dispatch* registered its impression of July 4, 1873: "Nearly all the attention extended yesterday to the 'glorious fourth' was accorded it by the truly loyal representatives of the colored race. The white people generally went fishing; but the Senegambians were out in full glory, and crowded the pavements from dawn to dewy eve. A special train from Richmond and another from Gaston brought over large delegations from those points. . . . One of the features of the day was the parade of the colored company, the Petersburg Guard, under Captain Hill. The march was followed by a multitude that darkened the face of the earth." [12]

The end of Reconstruction also brought an end to much of the white anxiety, especially in regard to black troops—but there was no end to the black anxiety heightened by doomsayers who predicted racial extinction for an uncivilized people deteriorating as dead weight on the progress of a New South. [13] This intolerable assumption became the bane of existence for the men and women of the old black middle class, who believed, in theory, that they would be judged by their individual achievements, but knew that in practice they would be judged by their racial identity. They nonetheless maintained faith in the formula that as more and more black individuals became a credit to their race—as measured by white, middle-class standards—they would convince more and more of the world that they belonged to a creditable race. This was the essence and the burden of being a race man.

It was more than coincidental that the Western world at this time proposed the exposition-as-forum for all those who would

12. Quoted in Alrutheus Ambush Taylor, *The Negro in the Reconstruction of Virginia* (Washington, D.C., 1926), 63–64.

13. Williamson, *Crucible of Race,* offers a grand synthesis and a creative interpretation of the deterioration of southern race relations and the resurgence of white anxieties by the turn of the century.

make any claim to civilization—and thus to racial progress—and in retrospect it appears that the black bourgeoisie were drawn ineluctably into the Darwinian game of invidious display. From this larger perspective, they were once again adapting to those who were adapting. The Old World—in this case, England—had set the standard with its 1851 Crystal Palace Exhibition in London. Although it would take nearly the remainder of the century, the United States would show that it had come of age at the 1893 World's Columbian Exposition in Chicago. In the meantime, the American South felt obliged to prove through a succession of expositions that it was not a backward subnation. At the bottom of the three-tiered model, black southerners had no choice, in the eyes of their leaders, except to demonstrate their capacity to compete in a rising New South in a demanding new age.

In an insightful analysis of this compulsive age of the exposition, Robert Rydell has explained that America's world's fairs from 1876 to 1916 represented more than competition among Western nations. Agreeing with Robert Wiebe that the United States during this period was bent on a "search for order," Rydell argues that the directors of the expositions "offered millions of fairgoers an opportunity . . . to reaffirm their collective national identity in an updated synthesis of progress and white supremacy." Race and progress formed a mutually inclusive "idea complex" that lay at the heart of the exposition. "The idea of technological and national progress became laced with scientific racism" in the late nineteenth century as "the epistemological frame of reference was shifting from religion to science." This shift, with its "emphasis on classification . . . diversity of racial 'types' and an evolutionary hierarchy . . . tended to blur class distinctions among whites while it invited them to appraise the relative capabilities of different groups of nonwhites for emulating the American model of progress."[14]

The black devotees of racial progress believed that they

14. Robert W. Rydell, *All the World's a Fair: Visions of Empire at American International Expositions, 1876–1916* (Chicago, 1984), 4–5.

could beat the scientific racists at their own game, but they were up against more than abstractions. The Smithsonian Institution, with congressional funding, virtually emptied its ethnographic collections and brought them to expositions as degrading displays of exotic peoples of the non-Western world. Visitors at the Columbian Exposition came away from the Smithsonian exhibits "nearly unanimous . . . about which people belonged at the respective extremes of the racial spectrum." Witnessing the line-up of races, one journalist sounded an ominous warning to his readers: "The negro types at the fair represented very fairly the barbarous or half-civilized state of a people who are a numerous and rapidly increasing class of American citizens." *Frank Leslie's Popular Monthly* similarly suggested that "in these wild people we easily detect many characteristics of the American negro." And a woman from Boston, sorting out the Smithsonian's darker races of the world, concluded that she now thought the American Indian was "a thing of beauty and joy forever." [15]

If these world's fairs did not create racial thought, they certainly gave it the stamp of authority and provided the most powerful and popular medium for its expression before the advent of the motion picture. Rydell believes an examination of the fairs helps to explain "how scientific ideas about evolution, race, and culture were disseminated from academic circles to the level of popular consumption . . . a partial but crucial explanation for the interpenetration and popularization of evolutionary ideas about race and progress." [16]

There is enormous irony in the black leadership's choosing as a means to redeem the reputation of the race the very vehicle that drove it deeper into disrepute. But if they were to meet the argument on its own terms—race and progress—there was, of course, no better means of presentation. To transcend the terms of the debate, to move beyond the "received culture," was asking too

15. *Ibid.*, 55, 65–66.
16. *Ibid.*, 5.

much of middle-class moderns who in many cases shared with their adversaries not only a faith in science and progress, but also a condescending view of the premodern peoples with whom they were identified. Not until the 1920s with Garveyism and the Harlem Renaissance, or until the 1930s with a new intelligentsia embracing class over race, would Afro-American thought move much beyond the orbit of the nineteenth-century race man. Du Bois was always brilliantly ahead of his time in synthesizing the issues of race, class, and culture, but he never pretended that he could outdistance Western space and time.[17]

The imperative that cut across Afro-American class and culture was a creative capacity for survival—in a word, adaptability. It would be folly to try to distinguish the cultural from the tactical, but black Americans regardless of class have had no peers in making the best out of a bad situation, "drawing sweet juice from bitter fruit, " as the folk prescribed, or "taking advantage of the disadvantages," as Booker T. Washington and his cohort advised. The best evidence for this ability was the existence of a black professional class in the first place, who carefully carved a refuge of proud institutions out of a hostile world that intended little beyond slavery. Thus it should come as no surprise, given the implications for survival in the great forums on race and progress, that black

17. In addition to standard works such as Meier's *Negro Thought,* Louis R. Harlan's *Booker T. Washington: The Making of a Black Leader* (New York, 1972) and *Booker T. Washington: The Wizard of Tuskegee* (New York, 1983), and Elliott Rudwick's *W. E. B. Du Bois: A Study in Minority Group Leadership* (Philadelphia, 1960), other useful secondary works dealing with the black intelligentsia of the time, especially with Du Bois, include Samuel P. Fullenwider, *The Mind and Mood of Black America* (Homewood, Ill., 1969); Harold Cruse, *The Crisis of the Negro Intellectual* (New York, 1967); Arnold Rampersad, *The Art and Imagination of W. E. B. Du Bois* (Cambridge, Mass., 1976); William Toll, *The Resurgence of Race: Black Social Theory from Reconstruction to the Pan African Conferences* (Philadelphia, 1979); William J. Moses, *The Golden Age of Black Nationalism, 1850–1925* (Hamden, Conn., 1978); and Alfred A. Moss, Jr., *The American Negro Academy: Voice of the Talented Tenth* (Baton Rouge, 1981). For a broad view of the decline of the "race man" by the 1930s, see James O. Young, *Black Writers of the Thirties* (Baton Rouge, 1973).

leaders would seek a way to adapt the exposition movement to their needs.

Their first major effort (beyond the emancipation celebrations) took place in the North rather than in the South, at the 1876 Centennial Exhibition in Philadelphia. Despite high expectations of being invited to exhibit the contributions of Afro-Americans to the progress of the Republic, the black delegation met with denial and condescension. With the exception of two books by black authors and a statue of a freedman, the centennial permitted no black presence save for waiters and janitors. Frederick Douglass, possibly the nation's finest orator, was not invited to speak and was further humiliated when police denied him seating at the opening ceremonies. Prominent black women, who had answered their white sisters' call to assist with fund raising for the exposition, received additional evidence that they would have to establish their identity within the framework of race when they discovered their exclusion from the Woman's Building. Throughout the exposition movement, white women conspicuously called attention to their contributions; hence, it may have occurred to both black women and black men that a building identified by race, like one identified by sex, would offer some recognition and reward. But in this instance, instead of gaining any representation of their own, black Americans were insulted at the centennial by a demeaning concession entitled The South—actually a restaurant put together by a white Atlanta businessman who proposed to greet visitors with a "band of old-time plantation darkies who will sing their quaint melodies and strum the banjo."[18]

From this moment forward, leadership in the national black exposition movement would shift to the South in a pattern of separation in lieu of exclusion, a pattern not unlike that which Howard Rabinowitz has described for southern race relations in general. In many ways such an arrangement played into the hands of those preaching black progress. Separate displays, ultimately to be ex-

18. Rydell, *All the World's a Fair*, 27–29.

hibited in impressive separate buildings, placed the progress message in high relief and a respectable distance from the minstrel shows on the midway and the Smithsonian's Wild Men of Borneo. In this shift from moral suasion to material suasion, Alexander Crummell, the leading black intellectual of the nineteenth century, signaled the new departure (the arrest of the old idealism) when he counseled a strategic retreat from civil rights and political protest to self-help, racial solidarity, and separate institutions, which, he declared, together would "settle all the problems of caste . . . though you were ten times blacker than midnight."[19]

With the exception of Booker T. Washington and a handful of notables, the black southerners who planned and organized the separate expositions are generally forgotten figures in Afro-American history. Charles Norfleet Hunter, arguably the founder of the black exposition movement, is a pertinent example. A former slave from North Carolina, Hunter represented the middle-level leaders of the distinctive generation that knew both slavery and freedom, an invisible, marginal elite, profoundly self-conscious about their pivotal place in history and desperately, sometimes angrily, in search of status and recognition commensurate with their achievements—accommodationist activists who often had multiple careers within a variety of black institutions. If they came of age during Reconstruction, they were almost without exception active in politics; and although most took Crummell's counsel after Reconstruction, a few were able to extend their political lives for a season in the South or, like Hunter's brother Osborne, followed a white-collar exodus to Washington, D.C., in search of federal appointments. For those who remained in the South, adaptability became a way of life as they read the winds of social and political change and sought economic security within the increasingly complex institutional apartheid that provided jobs in teaching, business, and service professions. Hunter has an

---

19. Howard N. Rabinowitz, *Race Relations in the Urban South, 1865–1900* (New York, 1978). Crummell quoted in Meier, *Negro Thought,* 43–44.

added historiographical importance because he left papers and therefore preserved a window to the little-known world of those who searched for a new life during the medieval period of Afro-American history, a long night of fitful struggle between the first and second Reconstructions.[20]

If Hunter struggled in common with other educated freedmen in the postwar South, there was much about him that was uncommon. He was born in 1851 to urban-artisan slave parents in Raleigh, North Carolina. His father, Osborne Hunter, Sr., belonged to the genteel William Dallas Haywood family, who permitted the senior Hunter to maintain his own residence in the city and apparently allowed him the opportunity to earn enough income as a carpenter-wheelwright to hire permanently the time of his wife, who belonged to another family. Charles scarcely knew his mother; she died when he was four years old, and he was sent to the big house to be reared by the Haywoods.[21]

If there was a divided black mind in the New South, it belonged to Hunter. Amphibianlike he moved between ancestral waters of white paternalism and the distant islands of racial democracy. On occasion he could give adaptability a bad name. He once invited Charles Sumner and the author of North Carolina's Black Codes to appear on the same platform; and he arranged master-slave reunions for twentieth-century expositions at the same time he joined the NAACP and supported Booker T. Washington.[22]

But Hunter's zeal for personal success—and hence racial success—along with his quest for white approval, embodied much of what the exposition movement was about. He symbolized the

---

20. Charles N. Hunter Papers, Perkins Library, Duke University; Haley, *Charles N. Hunter*, chaps. 1–3.

21. Hunter Papers; Haley, *Charles N. Hunter*, chaps. 1–3.

22. Hunter's papers reveal amazing twists and turns as he sought to serve himself as he served his people. Haley, *Charles N. Hunter*, captures this well; see esp. 24–25, 33–35, 45–49, 69–71, 78, 84–85, 117, 126–27, 146–49, 154–57, 174–77, 185–86, 195–96, 208–209, 244–46, 284–86.

broad umbrella of black stratagems during the stormy age of disfranchisement and Jim Crow. Under the aegis of the exposition, he would find himself in the company of everyone from Frederick Douglass and W. E. B. Du Bois to Booker T. Washington and Bishop Henry M. Turner. For Hunter, the exposition would lend at least some institutional shape to his life, from his passionate creation in 1879 of the North Carolina Industrial Association (NCIA) and its public relations organ, the *Journal of Industry,* to his pathetic efforts to reenlist white support for the NCIA and the North Carolina Colored State Fair just before his death in 1931.[23]

By the time Hunter, at age twenty-eight, launched the NCIA and the *Journal of Industry,* he had passed through a lifetime of careers in state and local politics, the Freedmen's Savings Bank, two fraternal orders, and the emerging black school system. As a precocious teenager and valedictorian at the Johnson Normal School (Kittrell College), he had attended North Carolina's constitutional convention in 1868, and a year later he took control over Raleigh's Fourth of July and Emancipation Day celebrations.[24]

The NCIA was another matter—all business. Its purpose, declared Hunter in the state charter, was to "encourage and promote the development of the industrial and educational resources of the colored people of North Carolina, to gather statistics respecting their progress . . . peculiar to civilized and enlightened Nations, [and] to hold annually an exhibition of the progress of their industry and education."[25] He reserved the message of the black New South creed, however, for the pages of the *Journal of Industry,* a professionally printed newspaper that continued to promote his ideas well into the twentieth century. In 1879, a year before Henry Grady ushered in the New South Creed with his Atlanta *Constitution* editorial calling for "fewer stump speakers and more stump

23. *Journal of Industry,* April, 1879, p. 1, in Hunter Papers; Haley, *Charles N. Hunter,* 46–49, 55–56, 71, 280–82.

24. Hunter Papers; Haley, *Charles N. Hunter,* chaps. 1–2.

25. NCIA Charter, North Carolina Laws, chap. 120-1879 (Copy in Hunter Papers).

pullers," Hunter was exhorting "our young men [to] take hold of this industrial movement." The "solution of the great Negro problem," he continued, "may . . . not be reached at the ballot box. It is to be performed in the field, in the work shop, in the school room, at the counter, in the various professions." With self-help advice that echoed Crummell and anticipated Washington, Hunter trained his bourgeois black nationalism on the twin themes of the exposition movement, prejudice and pride: "Let us all, young and old of both sexes go to work and . . . refute the oft repeated assertion that the Negro race has no inherent element of progress." Above all, Hunter counseled an "exhibit of everything and anything that will reflect credit upon the race. Every colored man having the slightest vestige of race pride will interest himself and his neighbors in this movement."[26]

In Hunter's mind the NCIA was the opening stroke in a national black exposition movement. He worked toward this end for the 1893 World's Columbian Exposition, but as he and others discovered, the plan better suited the South, where in tandem with the advance of Jim Crow and the influence of Booker T. Washington the movement would come to fruition in four major expositions: the Cotton States and International Exposition at Atlanta in 1895, the Tennessee Centennial Exposition at Nashville in 1897, the South Carolina Interstate and West Indian Exposition at Charleston in 1902, and the Jamestown Tercentennial Exposition in 1907.[27]

These expositions were not, of course, Afro-American in origin; rather, they embodied the spirit of Henry Grady and the New South Creed. Before Grady's death in 1889, his message of a dynamic, industrial New South had already become the *raison d'être* of several southern expositions, most notably the International Cotton Exposition at Atlanta (1881), the Southern Exposition at

26. *Journal of Industry,* April, 1879, p. 1, in Hunter Papers. Grady quoted in Paul M. Gaston, *The New South Creed: A Study in Southern Mythmaking* (New York, 1970), 42.

27. Haley, *Charles N. Hunter,* 85–86; Rydell, *All the World's a Fair,* 52.

Louisville (1883), the World's Industrial and Cotton Centennial Exposition at New Orleans (1885), and the Piedmont Exposition at Atlanta (1887). These "solemn circuses," as C. Vann Woodward characterized them, offered the best evidence that "the South had come to believe—with at least a part of its divided mind—in Progress." Indeed, millions of white southerners and their Yankee guests flocked to the huge "temples of plaster and iron erected to the alien gods of Mass and Speed . . . to invoke the spirit of Progress and worship the machine." On a less exalted level, according to Woodward, southern expositions were what expositions were everywhere: "modern engines of propaganda, advertising, and salesmanship geared to . . . attracting capital and selling the goods."[28]

But southern expositions had an additional theme—perhaps a central theme for those after 1895: they proposed a solution to the "Negro problem." What distinguished these later expositions from those of the 1880s (aside from the presence of the South's most popular figure, Booker T. Washington), was an institutionalized black participation, conspicuously housed in separate "Negro Buildings," whose proportions and design by all accounts—many of them photographic—were grand and beautiful. Even in their most prosaic form, expositions were exercises in symbolism, outward signs of underlying values; and perhaps nothing was more revealing in this regard than the anomaly of structures representing race and gender—the Negro Building and the Woman's Building—rising elegantly among exhibition halls devoted to agriculture, industry, and science.

The attention paid to Booker T. Washington's famous 1895 address has obscured the history of the larger format, the exposition movement, from which the speech arose. Ten years earlier at the World's Industrial and Cotton Centennial in New Orleans, thousands of black exhibits were displayed in the United States Government Building. The usually sardonic Henry M. Turner pro-

---

28. C. Vann Woodward, *Origins of the New South, 1877–1913* (Baton Rouge, 1951), 124–25; Gaston, *New South Creed,* 74–75.

claimed that this bold inclusion, especially the portraits of black and white abolitionists and a life-sized silk embroidery of Toussaint L'Ouverture, stood as a rebuke to the Supreme Court for its 1883 decision in the Civil Rights Cases. It was "so unexpected, so marvelous," rejoiced Turner, but he would soon understand that this was an exceptional moment in the history of race relations (as was the brief postwar integration of the public schools in New Orleans); for the trend was toward separation, toward the Atlanta Compromise and *Plessy* v. *Ferguson*. In fact, the separate and unequal railway cars bringing black visitors to the New Orleans fair stirred Booker T. Washington to protest that these cars be made equal with the white ones. Rehearsing a cryptic phrase that would become more accommodative a decade later, he declared, "We can be as separate as the fingers, yet one as the hand for maintaining the right." [29]

Nowhere were the imaginary possibilities for separate and equal expressed with greater zeal than in the symbolic setting of the exposition. By early 1894, black leaders in Atlanta had convinced the directors of the Cotton States Exposition to establish a separate Negro Department. Later that year, Booker T. Washington joined a delegation of black and white leaders from Atlanta on a journey to Washington, D.C., where—"one as the hand"—they lobbied Congress for federal funding. The black testimony, especially Washington's, was so effective that Congress voted the exposition a sum of $200,000 on the condition that part of the money be spent to construct a Negro Building. The step that insured the Atlanta Compromise, however, took place when the directors agreed, under black insistence, that it would not be "purely social" for Washington to sit with the white dignitaries and make an address at the opening ceremonies—as Frederick Douglass had not been permitted to do at Philadelphia in 1876. [30]

29. Herbert S. Fairall, *The World's Industrial and Cotton Centennial Exposition, New Orleans, 1884–1885* (Iowa City, 1885), 12, 19, 161, 163–65, 273, 379–80; Rydell, *All the World's a Fair*, 80–83.

30. William Ziegler Schenck, "Negro Participation in Three Southern Expositions" (M.A. thesis, University of North Carolina, 1970), 14–15; Rydell, *All the World's*

Throughout the fall of 1895, thousands of blacks and whites visited the Negro Building, a tasteful structure with slate-colored clapboard siding and white trim, its rambling thirty thousand square feet punctuated by porticos and a profusion of lace-curtained windows. Built by two black contractors from Georgia using only black labor, the spacious pavilion was given over mostly to southern black institutions: colleges, hospitals, orphanages, fraternal societies, churches, banks, and businesses—representatives of a growing, separate world-within-a-world, which stood in relation to white society as the Negro Building stood to the surrounding exposition.[31]

That the building appeared as a powerful symbol was a point lost on no one at the time. Vice-President Adlai Stevenson toured the building and declared it "a credit to the colored race," whose "industrial progress . . . and the manner in which it is permitted to be displayed" convinced him that "it may be safely left for the southern people and the negroes to settle their own problems without outside interference." Atlanta's white leaders congratulated themselves for having "ushered in a veritable era of good feeling between white and black," and the Atlanta *Constitution* concluded that on the entire exposition grounds, "large as they are," there was nothing "more significant or more hopeful than the negro building and its contents."[32]

For a moment, Washington must have wondered if it was not all too easy—a well-honed metaphor, coupled with the best black people on display, had transformed the best white people

---

a Fair, 79–80, 83–84; Harlan, *Making of a Black Leader,* 209; Ruth M. Winton, "Negro Participation in Southern Expositions, 1881–1915," *Journal of Negro Education,* XVI (1947), 34–43.

31. *Official Catalogue: Cotton States and International Exposition, Atlanta, Georgia, U.S.A., September 18 to December 31, 1895, Illustrated* (Atlanta, 1895); Schenck, "Negro Participation," 38–41.

32. Atlanta *Constitution,* October 19, 24, 1895, quoted in Schenck, "Negro Participation," 43.

into an admiration society. But Washington had predicted as much; Du Bois, too, at this time believed that the elite served as agents of social change; and the son of Frederick Douglass, Charles Remond Douglass, made no departure from the ideology of his father in declaring, "Our people [the black aristocracy of Washington, D.C.] made no mistake in going to Atlanta—a large gathering of well-dressed, intelligent and well-behaved colored people cannot but make a favorable impression among those who know us as menials in rags and ignorance." The only thing at Atlanta more important than the Negro exhibit, quipped Alice Bacon from Hampton Institute, "was the exhibit of the Negro."[33]

In his theory of trickle-down race relations, Booker T. Washington became obsessed with cultivating the art of display—an all-consuming burden of the old black middle class, whose individual lives and institutions became everyday expositions. Tuskegee Institute, for example, functioned above all else as an ongoing exposition, quite literally on parade before all manner of inspectors passing powerful judgment. The world was watching: as went Tuskegee, so went the race. It is no exaggeration to characterize Tuskegee as a boot camp for the bourgeoisie. Wilson Moses has summed up Washington's approach as a "military-industrial model," and according to Louis Harlan, Washington ran Tuskegee as a dictatorship sustained by a sense of "high duty to make of Tuskegee a black utopia, a proof that Negroes were capable of the petit bourgeois life." The intensity of this burden has been captured best by Ralph Ellison (himself a student at Tuskegee) in his opening chapters of *Invisible Man*, where the protagonist commits the unforgivable sin of allowing a white philanthropist to venture off campus into the seamy netherworld of the black underclass—an antiexposition.[34]

In his effort to convince whites that the Negro was the solu-

33. Alice Bacon, *The Negro and the Atlanta Exposition* (Baltimore, 1896), 23, 11.

34. Moses, *Golden Age*, 75; Louis R. Harlan, "Booker T. Washington in Biographical Perspective," *American Historical Review*, LXXV (1970), 1582; Ralph Ellison, *Invisible Man* (New York, 1947), chaps. 2–6.

tion rather than the problem in building a New South, Washington told whites what they wanted to hear and showed them what they needed to see. Perhaps he was too successful. In their most wistful moments, heightened by the siren song of the exposition, white devotees of the New South Creed not only acknowledged "Negro Progress," but also took credit for it as they embraced a self-congratulatory vision of a kind of utopian apartheid—an orderly, productive world governed by a gentle Darwinism that shaped an adaptable black population into sweet-tempered servants of both a vibrant economy and a tranquil social order.

The black response to the Atlanta exposition was more complex, more urgent, than the white response, and in many ways a microcosm of Afro-American thought under the onslaught of Jim Crow. Those who followed Washington in the great leap forward saw themselves as sober, secular realists tapping into the science of material progress. But their capitalist realism rested on faith, faith in the Protestant ethic and the American dream. The severe testing of this faith, in a secular world of denial and danger, produced a psychic need to translate the worst of times into the best of times, a kind of middle-class millenarianism. The antidote to extinction was to drink an extra measure from the adversary's cup. In part this response came out of a traditional Afro-American mechanism of defense, the psychocultural necessity of finding the good in the bad—and so it was with the black middle-class Darwinians who put a higher gloss on the meaning of struggle and progress. In the words of a disciple from Virginia, "This history of this race of ours in America in the intense and direct competition with the most powerful forces that the world has ever known has been the very thing we needed to insure our development." A kindred source suggested that "God worked in mysterious ways" in presenting the challenge of discrimination "to stimulate the Negro to accumulate wealth . . . while the poor white man in the South will sink lower in the scale of human existence." Another Bookerite predicted that "money power will raise the Negro as it has the Jew, who was once as persecuted as the Negro is now. The almighty

dollar is the magic wand that knocks the bottom out of race prejudice."[35]

Washington, like Charles Hunter before him, believed that
the display of progress would work wonders on black pride as well
as on white prejudice. Doubtless he would have felt vindicated had
he met the ninety-year-old black woman who traveled sixty miles
to see the Atlanta fair, and "when at last she stood in the Negro
Building and saw all the work of her own people whom she had
known only as slaves or peons, the sight was too much for her, and
she just stood and cried for joy." Just as dramatic, however, were
the negative black responses: for all those who testified to their bol-
stered pride, there were just as many who refused to attend the
fair, lest they swallow their pride. Supporters of the exposition dis-
counted this opposition as emanating from northern blacks who
"could not believe that a Negro exhibition at a fair in the heart of
Georgia, devised by Southern whites, could be . . . anything but a
by-word and a laughing stock." The most cutting criticism, however, came from Atlanta itself, from the anti-Bookerite *People's Advocate*, whose editor blasted the fair as a "big fake" where "the
white man holds sway" and "Negroes have not even a dog's show
inside the Exposition gates, unless it is in the Negro Building."
Otherwise, the editor complained, there were very few jobs for
blacks, and "several buildings on the grounds the Negro dare not
enter . . . especially if he has a lady, for he might be told 'no niggers
allowed.'"[36]

The divided and sometimes heated opinion on separate
black expositions in the South would continue to trouble their or-

35. *Colored Virginian*, November 4, 1915, New York *Age*, February 8, 1901, both in
"Negroes in Business," Vol. I, HC; National Negro Business League, *First Proceedings*
(Boston, 1900); Washington *Post*, August 15, 1900, New York *Age*, March 14, 1901,
both in HC, "Negroes in Business," I.

36. Bacon, *The Negro and the Atlanta Exposition*, 24, 19; *Official Catalogue Cotton
States and International Exposition; People's Advocate* quoted in "The Negro at the Atlanta Exposition," *Literary Digest*, XII (November 2, 1895), 6; Schenck, "Negro Participation," 22, 54–61.

ganizers at Nashville in 1897, at Charleston in 1902, and especially at Jamestown in 1907. Most of the black critics were not opposed on principle to separate expositions or to preaching the gospel of progress or even to appealing for white approval; rather, they opposed the surrounding moat of discrimination, the "danger of being grossly insulted" while crossing the white man's territory to attend one's own exposition. To be sure, this little debate had the effect of calling attention to the larger debate over accommodation versus protest in regard to civil rights. But on the question of black expositions, pure and simple, there was less controversy, as would be revealed after 1907 when the era of the New South expositions came to an end, while the separate black fairs and expositions, in black rather than white settings, continued with great vigor. As George Tindall demonstrated long ago, there was nothing unusual about black leaders supporting self-help, racial solidarity, and autonomous institutions while at the same time protesting for civil and political rights.[37]

Neither the Tennessee Centennial nor the South Carolina Interstate and West Indian Exposition generated as much publicity, positive or negative, as did the Atlanta exposition. The much-heralded Atlanta Compromise probably explains the disparity, for surely the black exposition at Nashville was a grander affair than was its counterpart at Atlanta, and Booker T. Washington, even with nothing new to announce, was nonetheless much more in view at Charleston than he was at Atlanta.

The Nashville exposition, moreover, created a lasting, if anomalous, monument to the New South: the stupendous replica of the Parthenon that, according to a contemporary observer, stood as "the symbol of a great recovery in American life, a reinstatement of Art as the Crown of Commerce." This odd fit between the architecture and the announced purpose of the exposition extended to

37. Tindall, *South Carolina Negroes,* has many such examples, most notably that of Congressman Thomas Ezekiel Miller, 56, 121. Meier, *Negro Thought,* is full of original insight on this theme.

the white-designed Negro Building, a Spanish Renaissance pavilion of white stucco and Mediterranean tile, more exotic than industrial, even slightly Moorish with its domes and towers.[38]

Without an appreciation for what Paul Gaston has called the "vital nexus" between the mythology of the Old South and the creed of the New South, one could be only puzzled at the romance and redolent symbolism from the past that suffused these celebrations of the future. What were the New South qualifications of the white-appointed director of the Tennessee Centennial's Negro Department, Richard Hill, known among Nashville whites as the "son of 'Uncle Jim Hill,' long a favorite fiddler and prompter at balls and parties given by the best families of Tennessee." Richard Hill functioned as pure symbol, a comforting transition that would preserve southern leisure and civility in the throes of change. "The aristocratic negro of the future," continued the official historian of the centennial, "will be the descendants of men like 'Uncle Jim Hill,' 'Uncle Bob' of Belle Meade, and 'Uncle Alfred' of the Hermitage." Or one could ask why John W. Thomas, president of the Tennessee exposition, would extol to the point of tears the virtues of his "black mammy" and the loyalty of his slaves in an address dedicated to an industrial New South; or why, indeed, the "Old Plantation" would become one of the favorite concessions on the exposition midway.[39]

This fractured *mentalité* of the New South bears testimony to the original insights of C. Vann Woodward, to irony and tragedy, to the distinctiveness in the original shape and in the emotional weight of the burden of history that white southerners carried into the future—things the exposition allowed them to express in tan-

38. Herman Justi, ed., *Official History of the Tennessee Centennial Exposition* (Nashville, 1898), 473–74, 196–98; Rydell, *All the World's a Fair*, 103–104.

39. Gaston, *New South Creed*, chap. 5. For an interpretation that sees the Lost Cause as less obsessive, see Gaines M. Foster, *Ghosts of the Confederacy: Defeat, the Lost Cause, and the Emergence of the New South* (Baton Rouge, 1988); Justi, *Official History*, 194; Rydell, *All the World's a Fair*, 87.

gible form. The point here, however, is that black southerners, in addition to bearing their own burden, had to measure and adapt to the burden of others, to be always a step ahead, behind the veil.

Thus, when Booker T. Washington and his cohort put themselves and the race on public display—even when they sang spirituals for their supper—they did so with a deadly serious sense of the realpolitik. Studies of the New South political economy that cite the persistence of a plantation base have a point, but they miss the mark completely when they characterize Washington as a one-dimensional plantation type, a predictable piece of the superstructure. Washington knew perfectly how to wear the old-time mask, but his eyes were always turned toward the future. His values lay in New England, not in Alabama. He was Yankee to the bone, profoundly imbued with the Protestant ethic and Victorian morality. His heroes were white, northern businessmen, and his education at Hampton Institute had reinforced their every axiom: order, industry, thrift, persistence, optimism, pragmatism, and efficiency. Hampton, and hence Tuskegee, were to teach the freedmen self-sufficiency, mold them into efficient producers and consumers, into modern workers prepared for the realignment of the South and the North as a unified industrial nation. This was the program that appealed to Andrew Carnegie and other northern patrons of Tuskegee who sensed, along with Washington, that the South was a developing country and that together they could launch a campaign making the old slave states safe for long-range investment, if not for immediate democracy.[40]

This was the larger message of the exposition at Nashville, no less than at Atlanta; and although most black leaders acceded to Washington's underlying dialectic, some dissented once again to

40. See n. 1 above. See also Dwight B. Billings, Jr., *Planters and the Making of a "New South": Class, Politics, and Development in North Carolina, 1865–1900* (Chapel Hill, 1979) and esp. Jay R. Mandle, *The Roots of Black Poverty: The Southern Plantation Economy After the Civil War* (Durham, N.C., 1978). Williamson, *Crucible of Race,* argues that Washington reigned lordlike over a "black feudatory," but I would argue that he did so in a Stalin-like quest to modernize.

the sacrifice of immediate rights and liberties, especially to the Negro Building's being "Jim Crowed" in its placement across the lake
from the classical White City and uncomfortably close to the midway and the minstrel shows. In any case, perhaps owing to the
long history of black fairs in Tennessee, the exhibits and attendance at Nashville outdid those at Atlanta and evoked considerable
pride. A five-mile parade preceded the official opening of the Negro Building on "Negro Day," July 5, 1897, which attracted thirty
thousand visitors. Charles W. Anderson, the "Booker T. Washington of the North," gave the main address, reminding his people
that their every act was "unconsciously pleading the cause of the
race before the great tribunal of the civilized world." He further
counseled "the vigorous young men" to remember that "martyr-
dom butters no parsnips," and sounding a note of ambiguity reminiscent of the great wizard from Tuskegee in addressing mixed
crowds, Anderson declared that "all things come to him who
waits, if he hustles while he waits." The wizard himself came to the
exposition on Emancipation Day, September 22, and delivered a
version of his Atlanta address; in the meantime a host of white notables had spoken at the Negro Building, including President William McKinley and William Jennings Bryan. Tennessee officials
lauded the black participants for their "remarkable showing"—further proof that, without altering "the natural order of things,"
blacks and whites could "work together in building up the South
in wealth, power, and influence." Self-satisfied and secure, southern whites savored the moment as they looked out across Lake Wa-
tauga from the Parthenon to the "delightful Negro Building" and
indulged themselves in the make-believe world of exposition race
relations—separate and serene.[41]

Serenity could have been the central theme of the South Carolina Interstate and West Indian Exposition, held near Charleston
during the winter and spring of 1901–1902. The white directors of
the fair entertained grand notions of hemispheric economic devel-

41. Justi, *Official History of the Tennessee Centennial Exposition*, 196–204; *Guide to the
Tennessee Centennial Exposition* (Nashville, 1897), 18–19.

opment, the motive being to link the South, especially Charleston as entrepôt, with the Caribbean. This transnational New South regionalism would thus elevate southern commercial centers into the role of the metropolis profiting from an uneven relationship with less developed partners—not unlike the existing relationship between the North and the South. In yet another nod to the great White City of the Chicago World's Fair, the directors of the Charleston exposition produced the "Ivory City," a collection of Spanish Renaissance buildings coated in cream-colored plaster and topped with red tile. The setting evoked a lost world of antebellum grandeur beneath a veneer of twentieth-century boosterism—a mixed vision reflected in the site of the fair, which stood an hour's buggy ride from downtown Charleston on the old Lowndes estate, nestled between the Ashley and Cooper rivers amidst live oaks and perfumed gardens. One reporter thought the tone betrayed an Old South or Latin casualness that would not yield to the New South Creed, producing instead a languid "scene of quiet restful experiences" without "the spurring of weary feet" or the press of "industrial missionaries."[42]

As for the Negro Department, "now a settled and well-established feature of every exposition held in the South," the vision remained fixed. Booker T. Washington, nominal head of the department, described the Charleston exposition as another "large opportunity to exhibit our progress [and] to solve what is called the race problem." Thomas Ezekiel Miller, a long-time black leader from South Carolina, challenged visitors to Charleston to "read our history through our products and thereby know us as we are."[43]

But not many came, black or white. The anomalous location may have been telling, for certainly the Charleston exposition

42. Letterbook, South Carolina and West Indian [SCWI] Exposition, in Record Group 43, Records of the U.S. Department of State, National Archives; George Kennan, "The Charleston Exposition," *Outlook*, LXX (March 22, 1902), 714.

43. Washington *Times*, December 1, 1901, in "Expositions," HC; Charleston *News and Courier*, August 15, September 13, 1901, quoted in Schenck, "Negro Participation," 25.

lacked the energy of Atlanta and Nashville. Purported to be the first "purely southern" exposition, it attracted little attention outside the section, and the Caribbean connection scarcely materialized. The black presence, especially that of Booker T. Washington and the Tuskegee-dominated Negro Building, accounted for much of the excitement generated by the fair. Also, the word went out that Du Bois would accompany his prize-winning display on Negro progress from the 1900 Paris Exposition; but in the end he and other black visitors may have been kept away by what Washington's local lieutenant, William D. Crum, acknowledged were "poor railway accommodations" along with "other incidents that made them feel they were not as welcome as their money."[44]

Five years later, at the 1907 Jamestown Tercentennial Exposition, these complaints would multiply many times over, but nobody could characterize that event as casual or parochial. The celebration of the "English settlement of America" had been done twice before, in 1807 and 1857; hence, the Tercentennial kept pace with an evolving nationalism to make it the most elaborate of the southern expositions. With its emphasis not only on industrialism, but also on militarism, it provided a grand stage for President Theodore Roosevelt to strut the status of America as a world power and to parade the Great White Fleet at Hampton Roads in favorable comparison with the fleets of twenty-one other invited nations. Commensurately, black leaders saw the exposition as the ultimate forum, something of a showdown on racial progress and the integrity of American Negro history. As one black editor put it, "The gauntlet is thrown down to us in a manner so unmistakably strong that we are compelled to take it up in self-defense. We are building up a distinct civilization, parallel with that of our white neighbors and equal at many points with theirs, notwithstanding the caucasian's superior advantages and centuries of bodily freedom." Speaking to the critics of segregated exhibitions, the editor argued

44. Schenck, "Negro Participation," 45, 62–65; William D. Crum, "The Negro at the Charleston Exposition," *Voice of the Negro*, I (1904), 331, as quoted *ibid.*, 65; Letterbook, SCWI Exposition, RG 43, NA.

that the Negro Building at Jamestown should not be seen as a retreat, but as an opportunity for "open competition with the whites." Since the black citizen "is forced to label his triumphs with the Negro tag in order to get the credit that is justly due him . . . the wisest colored men and women of the country are justifying the separate exhibition idea of Jamestown. Decry it as we may, the Negro's capacity for civilization is on trial for its life."[45]

Jamestown uncovered the hidden anger in the accommodationist's task of perennially proving oneself before whites; even that most malleable soul, Charles Hunter, bristled at the assertion that the essence of the Jamestown exposition was "to properly celebrate the three-hundredth anniversary of the birth of Anglo-Saxon influence in America." Hunter, the inveterate impresario who resurfaced with a vengeance at Jamestown, launched a campaign to prepare a tercentennial textbook in Negro history that would set the record straight on black contributions to America since 1619. "To do otherwise," affirmed his editorial supporter, "would be to rob the nation of vital portions of its history and to deny the Negro his heritage that is his richest possession."[46]

The more strident and possibly more desperate tone at Jamestown reflected not only a maddening frustration with white insensibilities but also a deepening division among black leaders over tactics and strategies, especially those geared to the Tuskegee machine. Much had happened between the Charleston and Jamestown expositions that added to the ferment: the "Boston Riot" in 1903; the publication of *Souls of Black Folk*, also in 1903; the founding of the Niagara Movement in 1905; and the Atlanta and Brownsville race riots of 1906. These and other events invited the leader-

45. "Plan of the Jamestown Exposition," in RG 43, Box 2412, NA; *The Official Blue Book of the Jamestown Ter-Centennial Exposition* (Norfolk, Va., 1907), 1–2; John T. Maginnis, *The Jamestown Exposition* (N.p., 1907), 5, 7, 11, 13, 19, 21, 59; Unidentified clipping in "Expositions," HC.

46. Haley, *Charles N. Hunter*, 162–63; Schenck, "Negro Participation," 31, 33; Unidentified clipping in "Expositions," HC; Charles N. Hunter to Senator Joseph Foraker, January 12, 1907, Hunter to Senator J. W. Graham, January 31, 1907, both in Hunter Papers.

ship to look into the widening gulf between the Bookerites and anti-Bookerites, with the Jamestown exposition serving as something of a referendum on the Atlanta Compromise. Jamestown sounded the last hurrah for the high symbolism of separate spheres and mutual progress. The impressive Negro Building stood as a striking emblem of material suasion at the same time it acted as a clearing house for dissent.[47]

On the one hand, in the words of a Bookerite booster, the building "bespoke grandeur in all things . . . the premier exhibit of the entire exposition." Designed by Booker T. Washington's son-in-law, William Sidney Pittman, a black architect from Washington, D.C., and constructed entirely by black contractors, including a black electrician (as the black modernists hastened to point out), the building occupied nearly sixty thousand square feet and housed more than nine thousand exhibits, two thousand of them provided by Charles Hunter's North Carolina Negro Development Company. Science, technology, and business constituted the theme of the exhibition, with an emphasis on black mastery of the modern age. One exhibit listed five hundred patents held by black Americans; Fisk University ran continuous demonstrations in chemistry, physics, astronomy, biology, and mathematics; and a Howard University professor gave hourly lectures on "the progress of the race." Information abounded on black business, including a display on black-owned oil wells in Kansas and Oklahoma; the True Reformers Bank from Richmond set up an operating branch in the Negro Building. But the *pièces de résistance,* in the estimation of Fred R. Moore, editor of the New York *Age* and Booker T. Washington's voice in the North, were the "historic tableaux of Negro progress . . . fourteen clay tablets by the black sculptress Meta

---

47. Other than the Hampton Institute clippings, the best original source on black participation at Jamestown is Giles B. Jackson and David Webster Davis, *The Industrial History of the Negro Race of the U.S.* (Richmond, Va., 1908), a four-hundred-page document written as a vindication for the separate exposition and those who supported it. Jackson, a Richmond attorney and former slave of General Fitzhugh Lee, was director general of the Negro Development and Exposition Company, and the driving force behind the Jamestown fair.

Vaux Warrick," tracing Afro-American history "from the low estate of 1619 to the thrifty, industrious and progressive people we find in 1907." Moore sounded the familiar themes of the larger ideology: "The Exposition has inspired a new faith in ourselves and our possibilities. It has disarmed the enemy, who have made wholesale accusations that the Negro is incapable of achievements that require intelligent initiative, scientific skill, and business acumen. It is a 'star witness' in support of the Negro's claim to full fledged American citizenship."[48]

On the other hand, in the words of Dr. Nathan F. Mossell, founder of the Frederick Douglass Hospital in Philadelphia and passionate anti-Bookerite, "the fact that the usual Southern methods will be practiced . . . is to my mind sufficient grounds for self-respecting persons of color to avoid contact or patronage with the whole miserable affair." Noting that he had been in Norfolk recently and "was driven out of a public park like a dog," and that at the very moment when black citizens were making their way to Jamestown, the Virginia state legislature had passed a Jim Crow railway bill, Mossell thought the fair was a cause for censure: "It is sad to feel that our manhood as a people has been so nearly crushed out that we supinely submit to such outrages without general protest." A spokesman for the Negro Development and Exposition Company, a black corporation chartered especially for organizing and administering the exhibition at Jamestown, responded that Mossell and other detractors represented "a little camp of irreconcilable idealists, who live up in the clouds and breathe an artificial atmosphere," and that for them to refer to the exposition as a "Jim Crow affair was no less appropriate than to refer to Tuskegee Institute as a Jim Crow school."[49]

48. *Official Blue Book,* 675; Unidentified clipping in "Expositions," HC; *Jamestown Magazine,* I (1906), 27; Savannah *Tribune,* November 16, 1907, *Afro-American Presbyterian,* March 7, 1907, New York *Age,* December 5, 1907, all in "Expositions," HC; Jackson and Davis, *Industrial History,* 138–280.

49. New York *Age,* December 5, 1907, Unidentified clipping, both in "Expositions," HC.

The defender had a point; Dr. Mossell could ill afford to undercut black institutions. Yet for Mossell, Du Bois, and a growing body of restive critics, the problem was more complex, its solution more akin to ethnic pluralism. Ideally, one ought to be able to express one's "twoness," as Du Bois suggested, in a positive fashion, both as a friend of black institutions and as an enemy of racial discrimination. The controversial airing at Jamestown of Afro-American thought, the least intended yet most revealing exhibit of the black exposition, placed another milestone down the road from the Atlanta Compromise. This last of the great southern expositions forced harder thinking about the costs and benefits of casting the pearls of black progress before an audience ever more committed to white supremacy. It was one thing to acknowledge Jim Crow in theory as a backdrop for separate development, but it was another thing to suffer in practice its daily insults as the ironic price of staging a production to improve race relations. Du Bois, for example, had been in "hearty sympathy with the exposition idea," but the indiscriminate assaults on conservative black businessmen during the 1906 Atlanta race riot, along with the disheartening news of outrageous discrimination at Jamestown, led him to boycott the fair, as did Atlanta University and the Niagara Movement.[50]

The idea died hard, however, because its roots lay twisted deep in a peculiar American soil that nourished both slavery and freedom; there could be no better American story than *Up from Slavery*. Given the imperative of teleology in Afro-American culture, tales of material deliverance could never afford to be prosaic or merely secular. Witnessing Booker T. Washington's christening in 1912 of a $100,000 black-owned cottonseed-oil mill in the all-black town of Mound Bayou, Mississippi, a black journalist reported that "strong men wept and women cried for joy. A glimpse of the millennium seemed to have [been] vouchsafed them." Stand-

50. Newport News *Star*, March 23, 1907, in "Expositions," HC; Schenck, "Negro Participation," 66–70.

ing on the boundaries of American life, being able to see in while being shut out (as the veil suggested), the black millenarians caught a vision of what they took to be a higher law. By adapting themselves—religiously so—to the modern forces of material progress, they challenged the intolerable assumption that blacks might go down rather than up from slavery. Against this assumption they searched for social justice when there was none, and thus overrated the engine of uplift—the deus ex machina—they had fashioned to take its place.[51]

After Jamestown, a train of events (the Springfield, Illinois, race riot in 1908; the founding of the NAACP in 1909; Washington's death in 1915; World War I; and the Great Migration of blacks to the North) would carry Afro-American thought along lines of greater independence—an obverse corollary of black adaptability that would shift from accommodative efforts to gain white recognition and approval to more direct efforts to achieve political power and cultural autonomy. As Langston Hughes asserted in 1926, "We younger Negro artists" had overcome the "racial mountain" of whiteness, and were now "free within ourselves . . . to express our individual dark-skinned selves without fear or shame. If white people are pleased we are glad. If they are not, it doesn't matter." The New Negro movement, along with Garveyism and the rise in the 1930s of a Marxian black intelligentsia, would dominate the first generation of these post-Washington efforts.[52]

Subsequent generations would come to suspect *progress* as a counterrevolutionary code word used by whites to signal blacks that they should be grateful and go slowly. The civil rights revolution of the 1950s and 1960s presumed that material liberation would grow out of political liberation, only to witness economic Thermidor and a neo-Darwinian disarray that in the 1980s seemed to carry the modern movement in a confounding full circle, albeit

51. *Star of Zion*, December 19, 1912, in "Negro Towns," HC.

52. Langston Hughes, "The Negro Artist and the Racial Mountain," *Nation*, CXXII (June 23, 1926), 692–94.

to a postmodern destination without the certitude of race men or the solidarity of their institutions.

One would like to think that if W. E. B. Du Bois were alive, he could supply the larger perspective for understanding and action. Nowhere does the American penchant to measure history by the moment serve us more poorly than in the case of the Afro-American experience, which surely qualifies as the *longue durée* of our national past—with Reconstruction as the continuing revolution. Du Bois suggested this ahead of his time, and his own long life suggests that in demanding immediate victory one should prepare for a lifetime of struggle. Among the constants in this struggle, deep in the souls of black folk, have been hope and endurance, wrath and resolve, the forces that sustained the black middle-class moderns of the exposition era no less than the folk.

In talking with his graduate students about such a world of eternal hope and relentless travail, George Tindall often turned from history to literature, from the American South to South Africa and the sobering, strengthening last lines of Alan Paton's *Cry the Beloved Country:* "Yes it is the dawn that has come . . . as it has come for a thousand centuries, never failing. But when that dawn will come, of our emancipation, from the fear of bondage and the bondage of fear, why, that is a secret."[53]

53. Alan Paton, *Cry the Beloved Country: A Story of Comfort in Desolation* (New York, 1948), 273.

New Woman, Old Family

Passion, Gender, and Place in the Virginia Fiction of Amélie Rives

Wayne Mixon

In the South, the years after Reconstruction witnessed the ascendancy of what W. J. Cash called the "savage ideal" of intolerance, which made it extremely difficult for southerners to criticize their region.[1] Because fiction is not "fact," however, imaginative literature can permit writers to do things they might be reluctant to do in expository writing. And because of the internal dynamics involved in the working out of a novel or story, imaginative literature may contain meanings of which the author himself is not fully conscious. Close readings of many novels and stories by

The author is grateful to Michael Plunkett of the University of Virginia for permission to quote from manuscript materials housed there; to Dan Carter, Carlos Flick, Elizabeth Jacoway, Lester Lamon, Robert McMath, and Eric Sundquist for critical readings of the essay; and to Bessie Killebrew for typing numerous drafts. Some of this material was originally published in " 'A Great, Pure Fire': Sexual Passion in the Virginia Fiction of Amélie Rives," in *Looking South: Chapters in the Story of an American Region*, ed. W. B. Moore, Jr., and J. F. Tripp (Greenwood Press, Westport, Conn., 1989). Copyright © 1989 by Winfred B. Moore, Jr., and Joseph F. Tripp. Used with permission.

1. W. J. Cash, *The Mind of the South* (1941; rpr. New York, n.d.), 137–45.

writers born in the South between 1850 and 1880 and raised there—writers belonging to generations either too young to have participated in the Civil War or unborn when it occurred—unearth much strikingly unconventional treatment of things southern: a deromanticizing of the gentry; a concern to portray life among the poor and the middle class; and criticism of racism, sexism, romantic agrarianism, the abuses of industrialism, and the general inability or unwillingness of the South to engage in honest self-examination. At the same time, however, these writers were self-consciously and proudly southern. They cherished the region's folk culture, its sense of honor, its identification as pastoral alternative to materialistic America. They did not want to annihilate the South, but rather, as they saw it, to create a better South.[2]

One writer whose work supplies ample evidence of many of these traits was Amélie Rives. Not only her writing, but also her life supports George B. Tindall's contention that "few parts of the modern world have bred so great a variety of styles or so diverse a cast of character types as the American South."[3] At first glance, Rives would seem to be an unlikely candidate for iconoclast. Without question she was to the manner born. Her ancestors were early settlers of piedmont Virginia. One grandfather, a United States senator and twice ambassador to France, was a significant figure in antebellum America. Her godfather was General Robert E. Lee, on whose staff her father was serving when Amélie was born in 1863. Her namesake was a French queen. Her home, Castle Hill, near Charlottesville, dated back to pre-Revolutionary times. There the beautiful, nature-loving Amélie roamed the picturesque foothills of the Blue Ridge. There, even during the dark days after the Civil War, she enjoyed a life of culture and refinement. There, by her

2. For a fuller discussion of these points, see Wayne Mixon, "Humor, Romance, and Realism at the Turn of the Century," in *The History of Southern Literature,* ed. Louis D. Rubin, Jr., *et al.* (Baton Rouge, 1985), 246–51.

3. George B. Tindall, "The Resurgence of Southern Identity," in *The American South: Portrait of a Culture,* ed. Louis D. Rubin, Jr. (Baton Rouge, 1980), 161.

own account, she was brought up in "a wise and systematic manner." Between sojourns north and abroad, she would spend most of her long life at Castle Hill. Her surviving correspondence demonstrates a deep love and a fierce loyalty toward home and family.[4]

An early interest in writing developed into a lifelong career. From the publication of her first story in the *Atlantic Monthly* in 1886, when she was only twenty-two, to the appearance of her final work in 1930, Rives wrote twenty-four books, including plays, novels, two volumes of poetry, and a collection of short stories set outside the South. She also wrote a number of plays that were performed but not published.[5] Roughly half of the published work consists of novels laid wholly or partly in Virginia. Some of the Virginia novels are of little interest to the historian—for example, a horse story with a twist and two tales of the occult—but others merit study not only because the stories are well told, but also because they treat certain themes in a manner rare for the times.

Although Rives embodied the Virginia gentry's attachment

4. Amélie Rives Chanler to Mildred Nelson Page, February 25, 1889, Clipping from London *Nation,* September 20, 1913, Amélie Rives Troubetzkoy to Frances V. Beverly, May 17, 1932, all in Amélie Rives Troubetzkoy Papers (Nos. 2495, 6287-g, 6754), Manuscripts Division, Special Collections Department, University of Virginia Library (hereinafter cited as ART Papers, U. Va.); Amélie Rives Troubetzkoy to Harlie Cooper, August 12, 1940, in Amélie Rives Troubetzkoy Papers, Duke University; J. D. Hurrell, "Some Days with Amélie Rives," *Lippincott's Monthly Magazine,* XLI (April, 1888), 531–36; Welford Dunaway Taylor, *Amélie Rives (Princess Troubetzkoy)* (New York, 1973), 20–22, *passim.* Scholarship on Rives is scant. In addition to Taylor's book—a competent study circumscribed by the format of the Twayne Authors series—the most significant work is Helen Lojek, "The Southern Lady Gets a Divorce: 'Saner Feminism' in the Novels of Amélie Rives," *Southern Literary Journal,* XII (Fall, 1979), 47–69, which argues that Rives's feminism was limited by her perspective as a southern aristocrat. Generally reliable but tending to understate the importance of Rives's Virginia background to much of her fiction is the biographical sketch by Lloyd C. Taylor in *Notable American Women, 1607–1950: A Biographical Dictionary,* ed. Edward T. James, Janet Wilson James, and Paul S. Boyer (3 vols.; Cambridge, Mass., 1971), III, 169–71.

5. Taylor, *Rives, passim.*

to home and kin, she did not settle into the niche reserved for the southern lady of the late nineteenth century. As a person of exceptional breadth, one whose family had encouraged her intellectual development and whose experience was expanded by association with northern socialites and European aristocrats, she struggled against the strictures imposed by popular opinion. Married at twenty-four to a great-grandson of John Jacob Astor after having thrice rejected his proposals, she secured a divorce in 1895, a difficult undertaking in Victorian America.[6] The next year she married Pierre Troubetzkoy, a Russian prince and painter, royal but not rich, whom she had met two years earlier when she and her husband attended a London party given by Oscar Wilde. Disdaining propriety in other matters as well, she was smoking cigarettes openly when such behavior could get a woman arrested even in a cosmopolitan place such as New York City. "I cannot," she told a newspaper interviewer in 1914, "tolerate prudishness. I take a little slap at it whenever I can."[7]

That remark was very much an understatement, for in her fiction Rives often landed crippling blows against prudery with an acknowledgment of women's sexuality and a portrayal of sexual passion that are astonishingly forthright for the times. In an early novel, *The Quick or the Dead?*, the heroine, a young widow, is nearly driven mad by mixed guilt and desire because her lover, her late husband's cousin, so closely resembles the dead man. The protagonist, Barbara Pomfret, reflects the author's sentiments when she tells her lover, "Let us give each other our red-hot thoughts, not wait for them to cool to cinders in the breath of conventionality and

6. *Ibid.*, 14–15; Welford Dunaway Taylor, "A Real Lily: The Story of Amélie Rives Troubetzkoy" (Graduate paper, University of Richmond, 1961), 14–17 (Copy in ART Papers, U. Va.). To effect the divorce, Rives briefly lived in South Dakota, where divorce laws were more liberal than in most other states. Taylor, "A Real Lily," 17.

7. Taylor, *Rives*, 14; Taylor, "A Real Lily," 16; New York *Times*, April 19, 1914, Sec. 6, p. 4.

commonplace."[8] Rives subsequently portrays the lovers' relationship in a number of "red-hot" scenes. On a walk in the woods, Barbara encounters her suitor, Jock Dering. Although she resists, he embraces her, "his lips against her ear. His breath streamed down her cheeks in among the black furs at her throat, thrilling her to the quick, and she began to pant frantically." Later, on a coach ride, Dering, to fool the driver, pretends to arrange something on the carriage floor. "In truth," Rives writes, "he was pressing his lips rapidly, first against Barbara's gown, and then against the curve of her instep." Later still, after Barbara has told Jock that she wants him, he "pressed his lips, now on one foot, now on the other; then, kneeling up, he kissed her dress, her knees, her waist, her arms, while she bent over him, panting, intoxicated."[9] If these scenes appear to the reader of today to lie somewhere between D. H. Lawrence and a Harlequin Romance, to verge on powerful eroticism and yet to be anchored in what by now seem clichés, such duality underscores both the difficulty of treating sex candidly a century ago and the noteworthiness of Rives's effort.

By confessing her desire for Jock, Barbara openly initiates the love-making in the last-mentioned scene, boldly defying conventional standards of ladylike behavior. The passage that some readers found most objectionable, however, is one in which she repeatedly asserts her desire with even greater force. Interrupting a trip to return to Barbara, who mistakenly thinks he's been hurt in an accident, Jock urges her to love him, not pity him. Throughout his entreaty, Barbara responds, "Kiss me."[10] That a Virginia lady fairly recently widowed would behave in such a manner was more than many readers could stand. Preachers damned the novel, and vitriolic letters flooded the publisher's office.[11]

Despite the novel's impressive sales—300,000 copies in the

8. Amélie Rives, *The Quick or the Dead? A Study* (1888; rpr. Philadelphia, 1904), 52.

9. *Ibid.*, 108, 132, 233.

10. *Ibid.*, 222–23.

11. Taylor, *Rives*, 39–40.

first three years after publication—Rives was stung by the intemperate criticism and retreated, although only slightly.[12] *Barbara Dering,* the sequel to *The Quick or the Dead?* published in 1892, four years after its precursor, contains fewer descriptive scenes of sexual passion, but Rives did not shy from using the book to criticize masculine perceptions of women. In conversation with a close friend, Barbara says:

> We [women] are not the bloodless creatures we are generally thought to be. Did you notice how, when a woman is considered very ardent, she is thought to be an exception to the general rule? Men are fond of saying that we cannot keep a secret; and yet, when I think of how well we have hidden that fact for ages, until even scientists speak of us as lacking in fire, I cannot help smiling at the popular belief! We are trained to regard all healthy, natural, vivid impulses as unrefined, unfeminine, immodest. A girl likes even her lover to fancy that she yields unwillingly to his kisses. Oh, if I had a daughter, I would teach her that passion . . . is a great, pure fire created by God, and not to be scorned by man![13]

To Rives's way of thinking, the fire of passion might be felt as keenly and as sensitively by poor white women as by a Virginia lady. *Virginia of Virginia,* a novella published the same year as *The Quick or the Dead?* and praised by no less a figure than Thomas Hardy, contains a number of poignant scenes that convey the sensuality of the heroine, Virginia Herrick, an overseer's daughter who is the victim of unrequited love.[14] Riding horseback up a mountain with the man she loves, Virginia silently admires the muscles in his back. Watching him sleep, she cuts off a lock of his

12. Taylor, "A Real Lily," 9. In the preface to the 1904 reprint of the novel, Rives said that she had not intended for the protagonist to be viewed sympathetically. Rives, *Quick or Dead?*, iv. Barbara's characterization belies that statement.

13. Amélie Rives, *Barbara Dering: A Sequel to "The Quick or the Dead?"* (1892; rpr. Philadelphia, 1893), 106.

14. Taylor, *Rives,* 49.

hair. Noticing his shirt hanging near her deathbed, she says to a servant: "It's sorter got his shape now, ain't it? Hand it here, mammy. Don' it smell good?—kinda briery an' soapy, mammy?"[15] Such recognition of that kind of feminine feeling was rare in southern fiction of the time.

Five years after the publication of *Virginia of Virginia*, Rives completed another novel with a similar protagonist, setting, and theme. Like Virginia Herrick, Tanis Gribble, the central character in *Tanis, the Sang-Digger*, is young, poor, and sensual. Finding work as housekeeper for a transplanted New England couple in a valley town near the mountains where she once dug ginseng roots for a living, Tanis yearns for a settled, respectable life with a decent, sensitive husband. Having grown up among the ginseng diggers, a rough lot, and being aware of her own attractiveness, she is no sheltered innocent. When the husband of her employer offers her a gift, denying that he expects something in return, Tanis calls him a fool. "They been't a feller," she says, "wi' any gumption under his hat, t'wix hyuh an' the Blue Ridge, ez ud lemme go onct he got a holt o'me."[16]

Passionate and self-respecting, Tanis faces a dilemma. The man she loves, Sam Rose, a handsome, conceited, domineering mountaineer, has "ruined" three other mountain girls. Determined that Sam will not use her so, Tanis nonetheless candidly acknowledges her desire for him as she thinks to herself that if only Sam were a good man, "I'd kiss [his blue eyes] twel they shut. . . . I cud make him trimble . . . though he do be suh strong an' tall."[17] Unable to understand the paradox of physical attraction and spiritual repulsion that characterizes her feelings for Sam, Tanis seeks guidance from her employer, asking her to define love. This proper New England lady emphasizes love's lofty, ennobling aspects. Tanis wonders about the fire, the passion, which the New Englander dismisses as infatuation. The agony that Tanis suffers as a

15. Amélie Rives, *Virginia of Virginia* (New York, 1888), 61, 116–17, 213.
16. Amélie Rives, *Tanis, the Sang-Digger* (New York, 1893), 20.
17. *Ibid.*, 109.

result of her conflicting emotions is the product of something far deeper than infatuation. It is her misfortune to love a man who is unworthy of her, and the story ends tragically. Like *Virginia of Virginia*, it is a tale of hopes unfulfilled and of dreams shattered, of a big-hearted woman unappreciated by a small-minded man.

Such, too, is the fate initially suffered by the protagonist of Rives's finest novel, *World's-End*, published in 1914. Issued more than twenty years after *Tanis*, *World's-End* appeared at a time when opposition to the explicit fictional treatment of passion had abated considerably. Nonetheless, as reviewers remarked, the novel is noteworthy in terms of Rives's portrayal of passion because of the nature of the heroine and the trouble she faces.[18] Phoebe Nelson Bruce, twenty, single, and of impeccable Virginia pedigree, gets pregnant by Richard Bryce, a young New York sophisticate, who refuses to marry her. Despairing, Phoebe attempts suicide but is stopped by her lover's uncle, Owen Randolph, who, suspecting her plight, marries her himself. Highborn, well-bred, and compassionate, Owen would "far rather take a generous, impulsive, warm-blooded free-lance to wife than an immaculate but mean-natured virgin."[19]

Prudes could find much to condemn in *World's-End*—not only the situation of a proper Virginia girl's getting pregnant out of wedlock, but also the rendition of certain scenes. While the Randolphs are in England on their wedding trip, Phoebe, having drunk too much champagne at a fashionable party, exaggerates the attention Owen pays to a woman who has just finished a seductive dance. Phoebe thinks, "I am far prettier . . . my breasts are like white flowers . . . are like little . . . pears." Then, dancing, she says to Owen: "I can do it too. . . . Don't I do it as well as she does?" She continues to tempt until "desire shook him." Later, at a dinner party at World's-End, Owen's Virginia estate, Richard surrepti-

18. Frank Luther Mott, *Golden Multitudes: The Story of Best Sellers in the United States* (New York, 1947), 249; Editorial comment, *Book Review Digest*, X (1914), 541; *New York Times Book Review*, April 26, 1914, p. 206.

19. Amélie Rives (Princess Troubetzkoy), *World's-End* (New York, 1914), 366.

tiously gazes at Phoebe. "He saw that red mouth which had melted and quivered under his own that May night after the storm . . . the shining hair, with which he had laced her to him . . . the lovely throat,—the little breasts that had beat against his."[20]

If Phoebe's passion for Richard at the outset of the story generates her misery, the fault lies with the object of the feeling, not with the feeling itself. And it is the desire that Phoebe and Owen come to have for each other that helps bring about Phoebe's reclamation. "Passion," Rives once told a friend, "is its own excuse and raison d'etre."[21] Establishment values around the turn of the century, however, condemned the expression of passion, especially by women, as morally wrong and socially dangerous. When Rives began publishing her fiction, Comstockery was in its heyday. In 1887, the year before her first novels came out, the Women's Christian Temperance Union established its Department of Pure Literature, the purpose of which was to suppress "impure" writing. By the mid-1890s, the esteemed physician John H. Kellogg was stating as a matter of fact that "exorbitant demands of the sexual appetite encountered among civilized people are not the result of a normal instinct, but are due . . . [in part] to the seduction of prurient literature." Many other people agreed with Dr. Kellogg and the WCTU that romantic novels were among the worst offenders against good health and right morals; reading such books purportedly caused everything from uterine disease to violent crime. As part of a vocal minority of writers who, in the words of Peter Gay, were "averse to moral uplift, at least of the conventional brand, and uneasy with the evasive treatment of erotic themes," Rives rebelled against the moralizers and the Genteel Tradition, which reigned supreme in American literature and, in her view, threatened to ruin it.[22]

Fiction like Rives's early novels faced a formidable opponent

20. *Ibid.*, 224–25, 328.

21. Emily Clark, *Innocence Abroad* (New York, 1931), 78–79.

22. David J. Pivar, *Purity Crusade: Sexual Morality and Social Control, 1868–1900* (Westport, Conn., 1973), 117, 151, 182; John S. Haller and Robin M. Haller, *The Physician and Sexuality in Victorian America* (Urbana, Ill., 1974), 103; Peter Gay, *The Tender*

in the increasingly influential Social Purity Movement, which advanced "a new ideology of sexual behavior" against an older view that had "recognized and encouraged women's sexuality." The crusaders for purity argued that women should not want or need sex, and that its function should be exclusively procreative. Popular sex-in-life manuals, some written by physicians, advanced the cause of sexual purity. Young men were moved to make public profession of their own abstinence from illicit sex by joining the White Cross Society, which by 1887 boasted branches in every state and territory. Women themselves often enlisted under the purity standard because, as Carl N. Degler writes, "by asserting their own lack of sexual passion, [they] gained a certain moral superiority over men," whose frequent need of sexual expression relegated them "to the status of lesser beings." Only loose women, usually poor and ill-informed, were supposed to enjoy sex. As one sex-in-life manual of 1876 put it, "The higher a woman rises in moral and intellectual culture, the more is the sensual refined away from her nature."[23]

Rives, as her novels show, thought otherwise. To be sure, Virginia Herrick and Tanis Gribble are poor and passionate, but they are also decent and upright. Phoebe Bruce is wellborn, and Barbara Dering is the quintessential Virginia aristocrat. They, too, are passionate and yet morally sound. Unlike those real-life Victorian women who, according to John and Robin Haller, "sought to achieve a sort of sexual freedom by denying [their] sexuality . . . in an effort to keep from being . . . treated as . . . sex object[s]," Rives's protagonists demonstrate their full humanity by insisting

---

Passion (New York, 1986), 165, 168, Vol. II of Gay, *The Bourgeois Experience: Victoria to Freud*, 2 vols. In a writers' symposium published in the New York *Sun*, Rives singled out the late Anthony Comstock for special condemnation. New York *Sun*, April 15, 1916 (Clipping in Henry Sydnor Harrison Papers, Duke University).

23. Carl N. Degler, *At Odds: Women and the Family in America from the Revolution to the Present* (New York, 1980), 253, 258; Pivar, *Purity Crusade*, 114, 172; Haller and Haller, *Physician and Sexuality*, 100.

upon their right to equal participation in affairs of passion.[24] Rives saw and described what the sexual purists wanted to wish away: namely, that respectable and self-respecting women might enjoy carnal pleasures as much as low women, or any men, did.

Rives paid a high price, in terms of critical reception, for her challenge to convention. Reviewers in prestigious journals, the arbiters of high culture, often either panned her work or else could not bring themselves to take it seriously. After all, Rives was only a woman, and a pampered southern one at that, writing "love" stories.[25] Reviews of her earliest novels illustrate the failure of many critics to appreciate Rives's attempt to deal seriously and sensitively with relations between the sexes. Of *Virginia of Virginia*, the *Nation* said, "The incidents of the story are cheaply sensational [and] Virginia's character is hysterical and an offence against taste and common sense." A short time later, the New York *Times* denounced the "essential vulgarity" of *The Quick or the Dead?* and called the book "ridiculous trash." The review of *Barbara Dering* in the *Critic* referred to Rives's "bold handling of delicate subjects" and opined that "there are many people who will not like this story, finding it outspoken to the verge of coarseness."[26]

It was not without cause, then, that Rives believed that her treatment of passion hurt the acceptance of her work. The damage perhaps was greater in the South than elsewhere. Although Anne Goodwyn Jones asserts that "the South has always welcomed and praised its women writers," she points out that this reception re-

24. Haller and Haller, *Physician and Sexuality*, xii.

25. Rives deeply resented the patronizing treatment she received from critics because of her sex. "Poet Turns on Her Critic," New York *Sun*, December 31, 1910 (Clipping in ART Papers, U. Va.).

26. *Nation*, XLVII (October 4, 1888), 274; Taylor, *Rives*, 40; *Critic*, n.s., XIX (March 11, 1893), 140. See also *Catholic World*, LVI (January, 1893), 579; *Godey's Magazine*, CXXVI (January, 1893), 104; *Atlantic Monthly*, LXXII (July, 1893), 125. As late as 1915, a major literary journal ran a review of Rives's somber story *Shadows of Flames* under the heading "Light-Hearted Novels." *Bookman*, XLII (November, 1915), 324–28.

sulted in part from southerners' refusal to take literature seriously.[27] And one should add that the welcome and the praise were contingent upon what these women wrote. Local-color sketches and historical romances often received warm endorsement. Discussion of the taboo subject of sex was almost sure to bring censure. Certainly, the conventional southern view of the southern lady left precious little room to accommodate Rives's attitude toward sexual passion.[28] Even so, Rives wrote out of the conviction that sex was far too important an element of human life to be treated with anything other than all the candor she could muster. More than ten years before Kate Chopin published *The Awakening*, Rives had depicted passion much more explicitly in *The Quick or the Dead?* Stretching the boundaries of Victorian fiction to the limit, Rives's writings helped to make readers aware of the significance of women's sexuality.

But Rives went further. Throughout her Virginia fiction her portrayal of women protagonists mounts an unrelenting attack upon gender discrimination. Gender is the underlying factor, the great determinant of developments, in virtually all of her Virginia novels. Clearly, Rives was among the vanguard of southern women who, in the words of Jean E. Friedman, began "to perceive themselves as a discrete class and recognize the limitations imposed upon them by the southern male-dominated community."[29] In Rives's work the sisterhood of women transcends race (an issue to which Rives, like many other southern women writers of the time,

27. New York *Times*, April 19, 1914, Sec. 6, p. 4; Anne Goodwyn Jones, *Tomorrow Is Another Day: The Woman Writer in the South, 1859–1936* (Baton Rouge, 1981), 39, 41–42.

28. R. T. W. Duke, Jr., "Amélie Rives (Princess Troubetzkoy)," *Library of Southern Literature* (Atlanta, 1909), X, 4455; Jones, *Tomorrow Is Another Day*, 32; Anne Firor Scott, *The Southern Lady: From Pedestal to Politics* (Chicago, 1970), 217. Even in reputedly cosmopolitan New Orleans, a reviewer bridled at Rives's portrayal of relations between the sexes in *Barbara Dering*. New Orleans *Picayune*, November 27, 1892.

29. Jean E. Friedman, *The Enclosed Garden: Women and Community in the Evangelical South, 1830–1900* (Chapel Hill, 1985), xiii.

devoted relatively little attention).[30] It also transcends social class, a matter that deeply interested her.

Here and there in Rives's fiction poor whites are depicted with the patronizing humor that had figured heavily in some southern writing since the days of her fellow Virginian William Byrd of Westover.[31] By and large, however, Rives presents such characters, particularly women, with a sensitivity and sympathy that are all the more remarkable in light of her own social station. So interested was she in the matter of class that it serves as a major theme in two of her works, *Virginia of Virginia* and *Tanis*.

The very writing of two novels centering upon poor whites was rare in late nineteenth-century southern literature. Concerned to present the South in a favorable light, local colorists, who dominated fiction writing in the postbellum era, generally believed that the lives of the poor "were unpleasant and brought no honor to the area," and therefore relegated them to minor roles.[32] Virginia Herrick and Tanis Gribble, however, occupy center stage. That their lives are unpleasant and their fates tragic demonstrates that Rives in telling their stories was not concerned to bring honor to the South but to show how aristocratic insensitivity (*Virginia of Virginia*) and a brutalizing environment (*Tanis*) could make it virtually impossible for poor white women to fashion satisfying lives.

Tanis' attempt to secure social respectability by reforming Sam fails to overcome his belief that women exist only to serve men, especially to satisfy their carnal appetites. Her independence infuriates him; he refuses to grant that she has a mind of her own.

30. Blacks in Rives's novels always appear in minor roles, and she sometimes employed conventional "darky humor" in portraying them. Her view of blacks generally reflected the paternalism often associated with her class. For evidence that she considered gender a more fundamental concern than race, see *Barbara Dering*, 246–47.

31. See *Quick or Dead?*, 126–44, and *Barbara Dering*, 29. A standard work on poor whites in southern literature is still Shields McIlwaine, *The Southern Poor-White: From Lubberland to Tobacco Road* (Norman, Okla., 1939). It fails to mention Rives.

32. Merrill Maguire Skaggs, *The Folk of Southern Fiction* (Athens, Ga., 1972), 21.

The forceful Virginia persistently acts in ways that defy polite notions of femininity. She hunts; she rides, excellently and stride-saddle; she dresses mannishly; and what is most significant, she takes charge in emergencies. When Jack Roden, the man she loves, is thrown during a horse race, she, not the dumbstruck men nearby, saves him. During a fire in the stables, it is Virginia rather than the men "running frantically about—omnipresent—useless" who rescues Roden's prize horse.[33] But Roden, conventional English gentry, prefers the proper lady on the neighboring estate and rejects Virginia's love.

Although insurmountable barriers cause both Virginia and Tanis to fall short of their goals, these women stand in sharp contrast to the mountain girls depicted by local colorists. Neither fits the popular stereotype of the sexually promiscuous character that, according to Merrill Maguire Skaggs, "flits alluringly in and out of southern local color fiction," although never fully portrayed. Both are earthy and passionate, but they are not promiscuous; both are poor and white, but they are not trash. Nor do they resemble the innocents created by Mary Noailles Murfree, the period's best known chronicler of southern mountain folk, who regularly "languish . . . away for love" that is not returned by men from the outside world.[34] While Virginia's death is indirectly the result of her love for an outsider, neither she nor Tanis waits passively for fate to take its course. Intelligent, ambitious, and assertive, both challenge convention—and lose. Yet given the period's constraints upon people who were both poor and female, their struggle elicits admiration.

Rives's most powerful critique of gender discrimination comes in her examination of its effects upon the kind of woman she knew best, the southern lady. The limitations imposed upon upper-class southern women often resulted from what men perceived to be noble efforts on their—men's—part to preserve and

33. Rives, *Virginia of Virginia*, 107, 202, *passim*.
34. Skaggs, *Folk of Southern Fiction*, 151, 153.

protect their ideal of femininity. At the very time Rives began writing, another Virginian gave loving expression to the masculine ideal of the southern belle. In *The Old Virginia Gentleman*, published in 1885, George W. Bagby described the belle and her world thus "More grace, more elegance, more refinement, more guileless purity, were never found in the whole world over, in any age; . . . a complete, immaculate world of womanly virtue and home piety was [hers], the like of which . . . was . . . never excelled, since the Almighty made man in his own image. . . . Young gentleman, hold off. . . . Lay not so much as a finger-tip lightly upon her, for she is sacred."[35] As Rives's fiction shows, she believed that such sentiments resulted from wishful thinking rather than from a clear-eyed view of reality.

Of all Rives's protagonists, the aristocratic Barbara Dering is the most forceful advocate of feminism. Her very appearance belies the popular stereotype of the petite, demure heroine. Attractive but not beautiful, Barbara is tall and large-framed. Like Virginia Herrick an excellent rider, she is much more at ease in the outdoors than in the drawing room. She, too, takes charge in adversity, her actions confounding the man whom she saves from serious injury. Because she has wealth and social position, Barbara, unlike Virginia and Tanis, has acquired education to complement her native intelligence. Brighter and far more sensitive than her husband Jock, she is angered by the masculine tendency to generalize, usually disparagingly, about women and to dominate them. The institution of marriage would be much improved, she believes, were the words "serve and obey" to be struck from the wedding ceremony.[36] She insists that married women be considered individuals in their own right, rather than merely creatures of their husbands. Barbara sees little hope, however, of transforming masculine views of women; so she resolves to devote her energies to promoting the sisterhood of women. As she tells a close friend and neighbor, "Let

35. Quoted in Kathryn Lee Seidel, *The Southern Belle in the American Novel* (Tampa, 1985), xi.

36. Rives, *Barbara Dering*, 92.

us live for [other women]. Let us teach . . . [our daughters] to live for them, too! Oh, if I could only write great poems and books to help them! But, at least, I can live my life, so that those who come in contact with it will be helped and comforted."[37] Ironically, sensitivity to the plight of women steels her to bear the burdens of a married woman in a patriarchal world. At the end of the story, when Jock returns after a long absence following a bitter fight, they begin again, wiser and sadder. One suspects that the road ahead will be a rocky one.

Thirty years before many other American women novelists began, as a hostile critic in the 1920s put it, to "disregard the tradition that this is primarily a man's world and . . . [to describe] boldly their own primary interests, among themselves, for themselves," Rives was doing so in her unconventional portrayal of passion.[38] Like many of the women writers of domestic fiction that had enjoyed wide popularity in the nineteenth century, Rives declared war on male-oriented society. But she waged that battle without resorting to the bathos that often characterized that genre. Plot resolutions in her Virginia novels of the late eighties and early nineties foreshadow the work of later women writers like Willa Cather and Edith Wharton who, according to an admiring critic in the twenties, faced life "with scant truckling to any public thirsting for spurious joy and the conventional happy ending."[39] In her portrayal of women, Rives prefigured the novels of such tough-minded writers

37. *Ibid.*, 139.

38. Quoted in Paul Lauter, "Race and Gender in the Shaping of the American Literary Canon: A Case Study from the Twenties," *Feminist Studies,* IX (Fall, 1983), 448.

39. Quoted *ibid.* On the domestic novel, see Russel Nye, *The Unembarrassed Muse: The Popular Arts in America* (New York, 1970), 26–27. Cather herself dismissed Rives's fiction as "irretrievably silly." Lojek, "Southern Lady Gets a Divorce," 55. Cather also denounced Kate Chopin's *The Awakening* for its "trite and sordid" theme. Margaret Culley, ed., *Kate Chopin: "The Awakening"* (New York, 1976), 153. It has been suggested that Cather's lesbian tendencies contributed to her belief that "women artists . . . wrote only insipid stories of love and marriage." *New York Times Book Review,* December 14, 1986, p. 3.

of the Southern Renaissance as Ellen Glasgow, Frances Newman, and Margaret Mitchell. Anticipating the psychoanalyst Karen Horney's insights into the "patriarchal ideal of womanhood," which caused women to see themselves as "infantile and emotional creatures," Rives sought to counter that ideal by creating women protagonists who were at once independent, strong-willed, and passionate, and as a result were disappointed and hurt by the world around them.[40]

Essentially, in *Barbara Dering* and in other novels of the eighties and nineties Rives was arguing, first, for an appreciation of the feminine sensibility, which like the sociologist Lester Frank Ward and the reformer Jane Addams she believed was distinct from and superior to the masculine; second, for what in an interview twenty years later she called "sex cooperation."[41] Like the early southern suffragists and the women in the Southern Farmers' Alliance, Rives believed that the most effective way to advance the cause of women entailed cultivating the support of men of good will, rather than considering all men enemies.[42] For the condition of women, particularly that of married women, to be improved, there must be mutual respect in the man-woman relationship. Such mutual respect was predicated upon self-respect, which for women could best be achieved through intellectual independence. Women should not identify themselves in terms of men; a married woman should resist, as strenuously as she could, becoming the

40. Karen Horney, *Feminine Psychology*, ed. Harold Kelman (New York, 1967), 146, 182. On Glasgow, Newman, and Mitchell, see Jones, *Tomorrow Is Another Day*, 225–350.

41. New York *Times*, April 19, 1914, Sec. 6, p. 4. On Ward and Addams, see Jill Conway, "Women Reformers and American Culture, 1870–1930," in *Our American Sisters: Women in American Life and Thought*, ed. Jean E. Friedman *et al.* (4th ed.; Lexington, Mass., 1987), 405–406. Unlike Addams and other women reformers, Rives did question Victorian sexual stereotypes.

42. On the suffragists, see Scott, *Southern Lady*, 176–84, and on the Alliance women, see Julie Roy Jeffrey, "Women in the Southern Farmers' Alliance: A Reconsideration of the Role and Status of Women in the Late Nineteenth-Century South," in *Our American Sisters*, ed. Friedman *et al.*, 273–96.

property of her husband. A woman should strive to develop culturally worthy interests that brought individual fulfillment; thereby, she might acquire the intellectual independence essential to self-respect. Even so, given the dominance of men in American society, it was crucial to enlighten those of them who were potentially friendly to the cause of women so that their help could be enlisted.

Such men were distinguished by what Rives called, in lamenting its absence from Jock Dering, "a certain feminine quality without which the character of no man is wholly lovable, and the possession of which does not signify weakness but strength."[43] That quality consists of tenderness, gentleness, selflessness, an ability to empathize, a willingness to value another's well-being more than one's own. Rives had been writing for twenty-five years before she was able to invest a leading man with those traits. In her concern to counter the stereotype of the weak, passive woman, she had created one-dimensional men who were callous, ineffectual, or downright villainous. They exist primarily to highlight the superiority of the heroines.

In Owen Randolph of *World's-End*, however, Rives finally fashioned a major male character who elicits the reader's admiration. The lowborn Sam Rose had been overly sensuous, the highborn Jack Roden and Jock Dering myopic and insensitive. The women who loved them suffered for that love. Owen, however, is worthy of the heroine Phoebe's love, and it is her association with him that makes her a better woman, that teaches her the self-forgiveness that leads to self-respect. The relationship between Owen and Phoebe is one of equals, largely because he, although twenty-seven years her senior, encourages that equality. He can be an advocate of what Rives described elsewhere as "saner feminism"—by her definition synonymous with sex cooperation—and lose none of his masculinity.[44]

Owen is such a man because he does not have to prove any-

43. Rives, *Barbara Dering*, 84.
44. New York *Times*, April 19, 1914, Sec. 6, p. 4.

thing. Sam Rose's baseness is insured by his environment; Jack Roden and Jock Dering are outsiders (Dering, although born in the South, has lived most of his life elsewhere). But Owen is a Virginia gentleman so secure in his sense of self that he can weep in Phoebe's presence. Because of his own emotional security, he can treat women with unpatronizing sensitivity and with fairness.

In *World's-End*, for one of the few times in her Virginia fiction, Rives uses a man to voice her views. Moreover, the behavior of that man, Owen Randolph, often mirrors her own. She gave much of the money she earned from *The Quick or the Dead?* to help poor blacks around Charlottesville, and she tried frequently to improve labor conditions. At the age of seventy-seven, she rose from her sickbed during winter and, as she wrote to a friend, "went out over the fields [at Castle Hill] to see a new baby that had come to one of the nice families on the estate."[45] Sharing his creator's sense of noblesse oblige, Owen uses his money to provide opportunity for the poor—male and female, black and white—over the opposition of certain kinsmen who object to the "socialistic enormities" of his willingness to share "all profits equally with the workers [in his factories], exclude child-labour, and reduce the [daily] working-hours to eight." At the same time he does everything in his power to conserve what he considers worthy in tradition: buy a virginal forest to save it from a sawmill; prohibit automobiles from World's-End; and insure that his nephew Richard, "with his decadent, Montmartre-ish ideas" and lack of feeling for the "negroes and white country folk whose problems [Owen] had spent so many years trying to solve," will not become master of the Randolph estate.[46]

Owen's attachment to World's-End is second only to his love for Phoebe, just as Rives's love for Castle Hill was exceeded only by

45. Taylor, *Rives*, 23; Amélie Rives Troubetzkoy to Luther Greene, January 31, 1941, in ART Papers, U. Va.

46. Rives, *World's-End*, 12, 21, 47, 162. As Owen prohibited automobiles from World's-End, so Rives forbade them at Castle Hill. Troubetzkoy to Beverly, May 17, 1932, in ART Papers, U. Va.

her love for Pierre, to whom she was happily married for forty years. For all of her iconoclastic treatment of the themes of passion and gender, Rives was traditional to the core in her love of place. The Virginia that she knew is the great constant in her fiction. Her descriptions of settings, which in virtually all of her Virginia novels are based upon Castle Hill, call forth her most lyrical writing. Her characterizations of Virginians high and low, and her portrayal of their interactions constitute some of her best work. Among her impulses to write was one shared by many other southern writers for as long as a regional consciousness has existed. As Eudora Welty once remarked: "I am . . . touched off by place. The place where I am and the place I know . . . are what set me to writing. . . . Place opens a door in the mind . . . [and bestows] the blessing of being located—contained." [47]

Nowhere else does Rives express her gratitude for such a blessing with greater force and poignancy than in *World's-End*. Like Rives herself, Owen enjoys an "Anchises-like sense of regeneration from contact with the soil of his old home." His sojourns in New York, a microcosm of the urban North, are spiritually debilitating, and Rives uses those trips to highlight the superiority of the rural South. New York is a place of stark contrasts, of the affluent avant-garde that promote unintelligible art and the abjectly poor callously disregarded by the fortunate. One winter morning, Owen, who has traveled to New York to help the poor, is struck by two *Times* headlines "printed side by side with no thought of dramatic contrast": EIGHT DEAD OF COLD—CITY'S POOR SUFFER; and $200,000 FOR A PAINTING. Rives continues her savage indictment by portraying Owen "staring up at the ugly, brown church from which a stone had fallen that autumn and crushed a workingman as though to remind him that his class were outsiders and must not venture too near sacred edifices where millionaires handed round the plate." Owen's longing for home is so apparent that even casual

47. Quoted in C. Vann Woodward, *The Burden of Southern History* (Rev. ed.; Baton Rouge, 1970), 23–24.

observers note it. In conversation with him at a performance, an Englishwoman says: "It's so very nice and so odd, too, to see an American so fond of a place. But I suppose you call yourself a Virginian—eh?" He responds: "A Virginian first, perhaps. . . . It's in the blood, you know."[48]

The love of Virginia is also in the blood of Sophy Taliaferro, the heroine of Rives's last significant Virginia work, *Shadows of Flames*, published the year after *World's-End*. Although only one sixth of this six-hundred-page novel is set in Virginia, the idea of home as refuge is a dominant theme. It is to Virginia that Sophy returns after each of two disastrous marriages, the first to an English lord addicted to morphine, the second to a northern socialite addicted to drink and other women. Not only her husbands individually, but also English aristocrats and northern plutocrats collectively, fare poorly at Rives's hands. As in *World's-End*, the most sympathetically drawn characters are the unpretentious, honorable, home-loving Virginia gentry, the most conspicuous of whom is Sophy herself. Loyal to husbands who hardly merit her allegiance— to the first until his death, to the second until his philandering— trapped in places and among people who cause her only misery, Sophy longs "for the foothills of the Blue Ridge as Pilgrim yearned for the Delectable Mountains."[49]

Rives expressed her love of place not only in her fiction but also in her life. Old, widowed, reduced to a condition a friend described as "near indigence," with even her newspaper subscription a Christmas present, she resolutely refused offers to purchase Castle Hill even though selling the place would have enabled her to live in affluence somewhere else. "I should never be able to breathe away from Castle Hill," she said. "It is the only life I have left."[50] All of Rives's life and most of her fiction provide further evidence to support the contention that a strong sense of place is a

48. Rives, *World's-End*, 7, 28.

49. Amélie Rives (Princess Troubetzkoy), *Shadows of Flames* (New York, 1915), 64.

50. Louis Auchincloss, *A Writer's Capital* (Minneapolis, 1974), 138. Castle Hill was recently sold and closed to the public.

prime determinant of southernness. As John Shelton Reed has argued, this high regard for place goes beyond mere parochialism to include "a sensitivity to the things that make one's community unique and, in particular, the existence of a web of friendship and, often, kinship that would be impossible to reproduce elsewhere."[51]

Yet within the masterpiece of nature that was piedmont Virginia, and within its protective web of friendship and kinship that Rives deeply appreciated, she perceived that all was not well. No apologist for the status quo despite her social station, she was deeply interested in educational reform, and she gave strong support to Virginia's Equal Suffrage League.[52] Fundamental to achieving social progress, as she saw the matter, was the need to change the South's conventional view of the status and role of women, high and low. Flaws of form in her work, resulting in part from hasty composition and scant revision, should not be allowed to obscure the importance of what she was about—the liberation of the "caged bird" that was woman.[53] The emancipation of women was far too urgent a matter to be dealt with through local color and historical romance, popular genres ill suited to critical realism. It is no accident that virtually all of her Virginia novels are set not in the past, but in the present. Significantly, she hoped that a more sympathetic understanding of woman's plight could be achieved in the South. Given the admirable qualities that Rives ascribed to certain Virginia gentry, male and female, why should they not lead the way to an enlightened resolution of a fundamental problem?

While seeking to conserve what she considered worthy in southern tradition, Rives brought into the open concerns that had

51. John Shelton Reed, *One South: An Ethnic Approach to Regional Culture* (Baton Rouge, 1982), 136.

52. Sidney R. Bland, "Comments: Session on Southern Letters—Case Studies in Controversy" (Fifth Citadel Conference on the South, Charleston, S.C., 1987), copy of typescript in possession of author.

53. New York *Times*, April 19, 1914, Sec. 6, p. 4. Rives was occasionally derelict in ascribing adequate motivation for a character's actions, was sometimes careless of plot detail, and was often guilty of resorting to overwrought language.

long been hidden, and she did so in a way that should still command attention. Like a very few other Virginia authors of her time—James Branch Cabell, Ellen Glasgow, Mary Johnston—Rives must be numbered among the vanguard of southern writers who, in the words of Edgar E. MacDonald, broke with "the aesthetics, social attitudes, and community assumptions of the older, late-Victorian South."[54]

A neglected writer from a forgotten time in southern literature, Rives candidly and courageously brought a new, fresh perspective to regional writing. The neglect that she and other southern writers of her time have suffered is the result in part of a dramatic change in critical criteria that occurred after the First World War.[55] For the cultural historian, if not for the literary critic, southern writing from 1890 to 1920—the "forgotten decades" of regional literature—is a fertile, unplowed field rather than the arid waste that H. L. Mencken and others after him descried and then abandoned.[56] There were oases in the "Sahara of the Bozart"; Rives's work created one of them. And there was thematic continuity between pre-1920s writing and that of the Southern Renaissance, which could not have flowered so luxuriantly without roots.

54. Edgar E. MacDonald, "The Ambivalent Heart: Literary Revival in Richmond," in *History of Southern Literature,* ed. Rubin *et al.,* 264.

55. The onslaught of modernism relegated much that was premodernist to the ash heap. Writing that was pre-Freud, pre-Eliot, and pre-Joyce seemed no longer to appeal to many critics. A new critical emphasis upon form at the expense of cultural context, along with a severely judgmental attitude, had the effect of extolling a few writers and pushing the rest into insignificance. Although the best contemporary critics of southern literature emphasize its historical dimension, they are rightfully impressed by the brilliance of the Southern Renaissance and tend to focus their work upon regional writing since 1920. See Morris Dickstein, "Popular Fiction and Critical Values: The Novel as a Challenge to Literary History," in *Reconstructing American Literary History,* ed. Sacvan Bercovitch (Cambridge, Mass., 1986), 30, and C. Hugh Holman, "No More Monoliths, Please: Continuities in the Multi-Souths," in *Southern Literature in Transition: Heritage and Promise,* ed. Philip Castille and William Osborne (Memphis, 1983), xiii-xxiv.

56. For accounts that stress the barrenness of turn-of-the-century southern writing, see H. L. Mencken, "The Sahara of the Bozart," in Mencken, *Prejudices: Second*

The disregard of a writer like Rives involves much more than one author's reputation. Such neglect diminishes historical understanding itself by making it exclusive rather than inclusive.

Through her writing Rives encouraged the growth of an indigenous southern feminism, urging the region she loved so deeply to adapt to change that would make possible a fuller life for half of its population. To the best of her ability, she fulfilled the serious writer's duty to, in the words of Peter Gay, "make the comfortable uncomfortable." [57] In doing so she served her calling and her region admirably.

Series (New York, 1920), 136–54; Louis J. Budd *et al.*, "The Forgotten Decades of Southern Writing, 1890–1920," *Mississippi Quarterly*, XXI (Fall, 1968), 275–90; and Bruce Clayton, *The Savage Ideal: Intolerance and Intellectual Leadership in the South, 1890–1914* (Baltimore, 1972), 109.

57. Gay, *Tender Passion*, 146.

Toward a Marriage of True Minds

The Federal Writers' Project and the Writing of Southern History

Jerrold Hirsch

I f we admitted no impediments to a marriage of true minds between folklore and history, the product of their union would be folk history," B. A. Botkin, the Federal Writers' Project national folklore editor, declared before a 1939 meeting of the American Historical Association. In his role as director of FWP folklore programs and as chairman of the Joint WPA Folklore Committee, which linked all the WPA agencies that had any connection with folk arts, Botkin encouraged studies that sought to achieve that union. His approach to the study of folklore and his view of the relationship between folklore and historical studies were years ahead of scholars in either field. Only recently have some southern historians begun to employ the concepts of cultural anthropology and the methods of the ethnographer in their work, and to treat oral traditions and folkways as significant historical sources.[1] The FWP's guidebooks to the southern states in the American Guide

---

1. B. A. Botkin, "Folklore as a Neglected Source of Social History," in *The Cultural Approach to History,* ed. Caroline Ware (New York, 1940), 308. Lawrence Levine, *Black Culture and Black Consciousness: Afro-American Folk Thought from Freedom to Slavery* (New York, 1977) and Charles Joyner, *Down by the Riverside: A South Carolina Slave*

Series, the life histories of southern tenant farmers and millwork-ers, and the interviews with former slaves, are important sources for the study of southern folk history.[2]

Southern historians currently working toward the union of history and folklore that Botkin envisioned may want to claim Bot-kin and the FWP as precursors, but only in a roundabout way could anyone claim that Botkin and the FWP begot a group of his-torians using folklore materials and methods in their writings. The FWP southern studies did not develop in a simple linear fashion from state guidebooks to life histories and interviews with former slaves, culminating in a marriage between folklore and history. In-deed, it is important to understand that most of the Federal Writers in the South directly or indirectly rejected Botkin's approach to the study of southern culture.

The tensions within the FWP over the best approach to studying the South illuminate change and continuity in the ways white southerners have viewed their culture and adapted tradi-tional patterns of thought to new circumstances. Then and now, the meanings that those who study the South assign to the terms *folk* and *folklore* involve not only methodological issues, but also those students' cultural politics—their hopes and fears. Although they have begun to use the FWP southern life histories, interviews with former slaves, folklore studies, and guidebooks as historical sources, historians have largely ignored the intellectual and cul-tural climate in which the Federal Writers produced these works. It is necessary to place the FWP's southern studies in a broad intellec-

---

Community (Urbana, Ill., 1984) draw heavily on FWP materials and offer excellent examples of what a marriage between folklore and history can accomplish.

2. These materials are examined in detail in Jerrold Hirsch, "Portrait of America: The Federal Writers' Project in an Intellectual and Cultural Context" (Ph.D. disser-tation., University of North Carolina, 1984), 382–424, 534–48, 562–96; Jerrold Hirsch, "Federal Writers' Project," in *Dictionary of Afro-American Slavery,* ed. Randall M. Miller and John David Smith (Westport, Conn., 1988), 233–36; and Tom Terrill and Jerrold Hirsch, eds., *Such as Us: Southern Voices of the Thirties* (Chapel Hill, 1978), xi–xxvi.

tual context, for these programs developed in response to an inherited and contemporary dialogue about both southern history and folk culture.

The federal structure of the FWP led to a unique dialogue between national FWP officials—who for the most part were members of a nationally oriented, left-of-center, cosmopolitan, and ethnically diverse intellectual community (there were few southerners among them)—and locally oriented, mostly conservative, middle-class southern white Federal Writers. (The number of blacks on each of the southern state units could be counted on one hand except in Virginia, Louisiana, and Florida, which had separate black units. In any case, there were not enough blacks on the southern FWP projects to affect the dominant approach of the southern FWP units and the assumptions underlying most of the published work.)[3]

National FWP officials embraced cultural pluralism and egalitarian values as central to an understanding of American history and identity.[4] The vast majority of southern Federal Writers

3. Monty Penkower, *The Federal Writers' Project: A Study in Government Patronage of the Arts* (Urbana, Ill., 1988), 66–67. The FWP's Negro Studies File contains repeated queries from Sterling Brown (FWP Negro affairs editor) concerning black employment on the state FWP projects. Boxes 200, 201, Federal Writers' Project Files, Works Progress Administration Records, Record Group 69, National Archives (hereinafter cited as FWPNA). The Federal Writers' Project Papers of William Terry Couch, in Southern Historical Collection, University of North Carolina, Chapel Hill (hereinafter cited as FWP-Couch Papers) contain a series of letters written in the fall of 1938 from Couch to each of the state directors in the Southeast, asking about black employment on the FWP in their states. From these sources it is possible to estimate black employment on the FWP in the South.

4. On the relationship between pluralism and cosmopolitanism among American intellectuals, see David Hollinger, "Ethnic Diversity, Cosmopolitanism, and the Emergence of the American Liberal Intelligentsia," *American Quarterly,* XXVII (1975), 133–51. In trying to understand romantic nationalism in the United States, I have relied heavily on Charles C. Alexander, *Here the Country Lies: Nationalism and the Arts in Twentieth Century America* (Bloomington, 1980), esp. 1–71. I examine the background and outlook of key national FWP officials in Hirsch, "Portrait of America," 30–67.

rejected both pluralism and egalitarianism. On one level the discussion between these conflicting groups was about how to interpret southern folklore and history, how to explain change and continuity; on another level it revealed how national, regional, state, and local officials themselves responded to change or the possibility of change. In the broadest terms the issue was the relationship between tradition and modernity; in a southern context, that meant the dominant issues were the relationship between traditional agrarian folkways and industrialization, and the place of Afro-Americans in the social order.

Some Federal Writers were more conscious than others of the cultural politics of the FWP studies, which dealt with urban as well as rural Americans, ethnic and racial minorities as well as the white Anglo-Saxon Protestant majority, and regional diversity as well as the forces that contributed to national unity. And certainly all of the writers, albeit at different levels of consciousness, were aware that both literally (in the American Guide Series to every state in the Union and to many individual cities) and metaphorically, they were bringing private traditions into shared public spaces, that their studies offered road maps for exploring diverse American experiences, guides to help their readers rediscover America.

For national FWP officials the rediscovery of America meant readdressing inherited questions about American identity and culture, and developing more inclusive and democratic answers than those that were part of the dominant tradition. The FWP was part of the cultural component of the New Deal's program of political and economic reform. As romantic nationalists, FWP officials assumed that the study of the experience of ordinary Americans could provide the basis for a revitalized national culture. As cultural pluralists, they believed that all groups had to be taken into account and that the various groups that constituted America could benefit from learning about others different from themselves.

At the national level, cultural pluralism complemented New

Deal programs that sought to address the problems of industrial workers, farmers, and blacks and other ethnic minorities. There was an implicit liberal-reformist alliance between New Deal officials directing political and cultural programs at the national level. In contrast, conservative approaches to culture and politics went hand-in-hand in the South. Conservative white southern Democrats feared that the New Deal might reopen political questions about class and caste relations in the South—questions they preferred to regard as settled.[5] Local southern Federal Writers shared the dominant views of history and culture that prevailed in their region—views that helped legitimize the social and political structure of their society. Within the Federal Writers' Project these regional disparities often resulted in work pursued on the basis of different assumptions and values.

The various approaches that national, regional, state, and local Federal Writers advocated toward the study of the South reveal differing definitions of folklore and conflicting assumptions about southern folk culture. Similarly, the attitudes toward change exhibited by southern Federal Writers versus those held by national FWP officials reflect contrasting definitions of folk culture: the southern writers stressed a static, eternal southern culture; the national officials emphasized the dynamic, adaptive, acculturative processes that characterize subcultures in a pluralist society. These attitudes were clearly linked to larger values concerning race relations within the South, southern economic development, and the South's relation to the rest of the nation.

Whatever their orientation, southern Federal Writers and national FWP officials all addressed such questions as, Who should be included in talking about the southern folk? Could southern culture change and adapt to new developments and still remain dis-

5. Frank Freidel, *F.D.R. and the South* (Baton Rouge, 1965) and George B. Tindall, *The Emergence of the New South, 1913–1945* (Baton Rouge, 1967), 607–49, Vol. X of *A History of the South,* ed. E. Merton Coulter and Wendell H. Stephenson, 10 vols., are still good starting points for understanding the forces limiting New Deal reform in the South.

tinctive? When was it better to resist new developments, and when preferable to adapt to them? These questions link the work of the FWP to debates that have been at the heart of the way white southerners have thought about the South since the defeat of the Confederacy, for questions about defining southern folklore and the central themes of southern history have always been implicitly (and sometimes explicitly) about whether the South has a future as a distinctive culture.

For many twentieth-century students of southern culture, the very existence of a distinctive southern culture has been a major topic of debate, and positions taken on the issue often have reflected political agendas. Conservative white southerners have feared change would destroy southern culture and identity; their references to "tradition" often have commingled with talk about maintaining racial and cultural purity. Liberals, on the other hand, both southern and nonsouthern, have taken more ambiguous positions on these issues, although some liberals have tended to equate the disappearance of a distinctive southern culture with progress. Key Federal Writers' Project officials such as Botkin and the southeast regional director, W. T. Couch, arrived at their own positions on these issues partly in response to the discussion of the nature of southern identity that took place between the Nashville Agrarians and the Chapel Hill Regionalists. The Agrarians rejected industrialism and social change in favor of their version of the folkways of the agrarian past. The Regionalists, although favoring industrialism and social change, also sought to describe and maintain a distinctive southern folk culture—goals the Agrarians argued were irreconcilable.[6]

Botkin's appointment as national FWP folklore editor in 1938

6. For interpretations that stress the emergence of modern southern thought out of Victorianism and the relationship of the idea of the South to modern fragmented society and the heritage of romanticism, see Daniel J. Singal, *The War Within: From Victorian to Modernist Thought in the South, 1919–1945* (Chapel Hill, 1982), esp. xi–33, 198–260, 111–52, and Michael O'Brien, *The Idea of the American South, 1920–1941* (Baltimore, 1979), 2–59, 220–23.

was a turning point in the history of the Writers' Project. Folklore studies were an obvious and indispensable part of a romantic-nationalist program like the FWP. Until Botkin joined the project, however, it was unclear how folklore fitted into the FWP's efforts both to reconcile romantic nationalism and cultural pluralism and to study contemporary American life and culture.[7]

Like romantic nationalists elsewhere, national FWP officials undertook folklore studies as part of their effort to record and celebrate an indigenous culture that would provide the basis for a national identity and a national literature.[8] John Lomax, the first national FWP folklore editor, shared with his Washington, D.C., colleagues the conviction that there was a rich indigenous culture in the United States that had grown out of the experience and history of ordinary Americans. He rejected the views of the many folklorists who thought that the material they collected in the United States was merely the remnants of Old World cultures—folklore in America, not American folklore—mere survivals from elsewhere that were bound to disappear with the passage of time. Even so, Lomax's outlook meshed only partly with that of other national FWP officials. Although he argued that there was a distinctive American folklore and that folklorists should be more "interested in the mutations and developments wrought by transfer to a new and pioneer land" than in the European origins of American culture, Lomax also thought folklore was dying out, and he was determined to collect what he thought of as a distinctive American lore before modernity destroyed it. Lomax thus had arrived at the same conclusions as the culture evolutionists who regarded folklore as being only the surviving evidence of past ways of life, and doomed to disappear with progress. From that point of

7. Henry Alsberg to Lewis Mumford, October 4, 1938, Alsberg to Ellen Woodward (assistant WPA director), April 1, July 22, 1938, all in Box 195, FWPNA.

8. For an overview of New Deal folklore programs, see Jerrold Hirsch, "Cultural Pluralism and Applied Folklore: The New Deal Precedent," in *The Conservation of Culture: Folklorists and the Private Sector*, ed. Burt Feintuch (Lexington, Ky., 1988), 46–67.

view, folklore was a survival useful only in reconstructing earlier stages in human cultural evolution, not in understanding contemporary life; folklore had no future in the modern world. Some romantic folklorists—including Lomax—regarded modernity and pluralism as mortal threats to folklore, and they regarded isolated and homogeneous communities as the only places in which a pure and uncontaminated folklore could survive.[9]

Many of the traditional assumptions underlying romantic-nationalist and evolutionary approaches to folklore studies were compatible neither with the pluralistic and egalitarian values of national FWP officials nor with their ideal of America as an inclusive national community that recognized and encouraged differences. Lomax's approach to folklore did not help these officials reconcile romantic nationalism with cultural pluralism. Although Lomax, who was born in Goodman, Mississippi, in 1867 and raised in Texas, was a famous collector of the songs of southern Negroes, there was little in his approach that threatened the values of local white southern FWP fieldworkers. His emphasis on purity, homogeneity, and uncontaminated traditions was easily reconciled with a commitment to a segregated social order, as his own published writings indicate.[10]

Botkin was one of the first American folklorists who did not see a mortal combat between modernity and folklore; rather, he saw in that relationship the dynamics of cultural change in an in-

9. John Lomax, Supplementary Instruction No. 9 to the *American Guide Manual,* "Folklore and Folk Customs," March 12, 1936, and No. 9C, "Folklore and Folk Customs—Example," August 4, 1936, both in Box 69, FWPNA; John Lomax, *Adventures of a Ballad Hunter* (New York, 1947), 128–29; John Lomax and Alan Lomax, eds., *American Ballads and Folk Songs* (New York, 1934), xxvi, xxvii, xxx, xxxi.

10. See, for example, John Lomax, "Self-Pity in Negro Folk-Songs," *Nation,* CV (August, 1917), 141; John Lomax, " 'Sinful Songs' of the Southern Negro," *Musical Quarterly,* XX (1934) 177, 179, and Lomax, *Adventures of a Ballad Hunter,* 128–29. See also the discussion of Lomax in Hirsch, "Portrait of America," 30–66, 305–307, and Jerrold Hirsch, "Modernity, Nostalgia, and Southern Folklore Studies: The Case of John Lomax" (Paper presented at the annual meeting of the Southern Historical Association, Houston, 1985, in possession of the author).

creasingly integrated national economy and pluralistic society. Bot-kin's idea of "folklore in the making"—the continual creative re-sponse of various American subcultures to their world—made it possible to integrate folklore studies with the FWP's interview proj-ects involving racial, ethnic, and working-class groups.[11] In hiring Botkin as national FWP folklore editor, Henry Alsberg, the director of the FWP, envisioned him editing an "American Folklore Guide," contributing to "A Guide to Composite America," and editing a col-lection of former slaves' narratives. By focusing on folk expression, ethnic and occupational groups, acculturation, and racial minori-ties, Alsberg contended, these various guides would "fill in the cul-tural picture sketched in the American Guide Series."[12]

Botkin's background, experiences, perspective, and cultural and political commitments complemented those of his colleagues in the Washington FWP office, but they were very different from those of most white FWP southern fieldworkers, and they also dif-fered in significant ways from those of either John Lomax or W. T. Couch. Botkin, born in East Boston in 1901, the son of Lithuanian Jewish immigrants, was educated at Harvard, Columbia, and the University of Nebraska. He taught at the University of Oklahoma from 1921 to 1937 and was a participant in the Southwest Renais-sance in the 1920s. He took an active part in discussions in the 1920s and 1930s about regionalism. Like most national FWP offi-cials, he was a cosmopolitan, left-of-center intellectual interested in America's diverse traditions. His interest in the South was cul-tural and political; although this interest was intense, it was also detached and theoretical in a way rare among native southerners.[13]

11. For an overview of Botkin's career and ideas see: Jerrold Hirsch, "Folklore in the Making: B. A. Botkin," *Journal of American Folklore*, C (January–March, 1986), 3–38.

12. Alsberg to Woodward, July 22, 1938, in Box 195, FWPNA; B. A. Botkin, "Manual for Folklore Studies," August 15, 1938, in Box 69, FWPNA; B. A. Botkin, "Social Ethnic-Studies Manual," September, 1938, in Box 191, all in FWPNA.

13. See, for example, B. A. Botkin, "Folk and Folklore," in *Culture in the South*, ed. W. T. Couch (Chapel Hill, 1934), 578–93.

With the help of a Rosenwald fellowship, Botkin went to Washington in 1937 to study southern and Negro folklore at the Library of Congress. The relationship of the South to the rest of the nation and the relationship between whites and Negroes in the region posed challenges to Botkin's view of a democratic, egalitarian, and pluralistic society. By stressing change, process, adaptation, and acculturation, Botkin was urging historians and folklorists to move beyond static definitions of the folk and folk culture, beyond abstract juxtapositions such as agrarianism and industrialism, and beyond the search for reified eternal qualities that defined southerners, whether black or white. Botkin understood that the democratic and egalitarian thrust of his view of a diverse American folklore as a cultural asset had political implications, perhaps more for black Americans than for anyone else.[14]

Rather than seeing folklore as consisting merely in survivals reflecting earlier stages of civilization, Botkin thought the lore had to be understood in relation to the life of the folk who kept it alive. He moved beyond the pastoral vision of folklore as something associated with peasants, something being destroyed by modern life. He was receptive to the anthropology of Franz Boas emphasizing a plurality of historically conditioned cultures, culture as an integrative force, and a relativistic outlook in place of an evolutionary hierarchy. Thus, rather than talking about contamination, Botkin wanted to study the life and lore of Americans living in a state of transition—one definition of the modern condition—such as white and black southerners, and eastern and southern European immigrants and their children. Folklore provided insights into contemporary everyday life, into the ways ordinary people responded to their world.[15]

14. B. A. Botkin to Henry Alsberg, March 24, 1938, in FWPNA. See also, for example, B. A. Botkin, "Regionalism and Culture," in *The Writer in a Changing World*, ed. Henry Hart (New York, 1937), 140–57, and B. A. Botkin, "The Folk and the Individual: Their Creative Reciprocity," *English Journal*, XXVII (1938), 121–35.

15. B. A. Botkin, "The Folkness of the Folk," *English Journal*, XXVI (1937), 464–68.

Botkin's functionalism allowed him to see that folklore could be created in industrial and urban environments, that folklore could be found among the literate and educated as well as among the uneducated and illiterate. He thought that technological media did not destroy folklore but in complex new ways became part of the process of transmitting it; he was convinced that industrialism and the end of geographic isolation would not destroy folk traditions.[16] Given his assumptions, Botkin did not share the fears that many southern intellectuals held regarding the future of tradition in an industrializing and urbanizing world.[17]

Southern folklore, black and white, was central to Botkin's working out of his view of folklore and his view of American diversity as a cultural asset. In struggling to arrive at an understanding of the dynamics of folklore in a pluralistic society, he gave the South and its folk traditions, black and white, considerable attention. On the theoretical level the issue was whether folk traditions had a future in an industrializing society in which geographical isolation was breaking down. On the social and political levels the issues were racial and economic inequality. Botkin concluded that neither industrialization nor the end of segregation would threaten the existence of southern folklore.[18]

The Agrarians viewed tradition as a static inheritance that could be maintained only in a homogeneous rural society. Botkin saw tradition as dynamic and changing, adapting to new circumstances and thriving among factories and cities as well as in the fields. The pluralistic and relativistic anthropology that informed Botkin's view of the folk and their lore worked against the evolu-

16. *Ibid.*, 465, 467–68; B. A. Botkin, "The Folk in Literature: An Introduction to the New Regionalism," in *Folk-Say: A Regional Miscellany,* ed. Botkin (Norman, Okla., 1929), 12.

17. See Botkin, "Folklore as a Neglected Source of Social History"; Botkin, "The Folk in Literature," 9–10; Botkin, "The Folk and the Individual"; and B. A. Botkin, "We Called It 'Living Lore,' " *New York Folklore Quarterly,* XIV (1958), 197–98.

18. Botkin, "Regionalism and Culture," 141, 156–57; B. A. Botkin, "We Talk About Regionalism—North, South, East, and West," *Frontier,* XIII (1933), 286, 291–93; B. A. Botkin, ed., *A Treasury of Southern Folklore: Stories, Ballads, Traditions, and Folkways of the South* (New York, 1949), xxi–xxii, 479, 646, 729.

tionary anthropology that, as Daniel Singal has pointed out, was part of the Victorian intellectual inheritance that informed the thinking of the Agrarians. The Agrarians, the Chapel Hill Regionalists, and Botkin all inherited romantic-nationalist cultural notions and tried to use them as ways of resolving identity, imposing wholeness on a fragmented reality, and overcoming alienation. Both the Agrarians and the Regionalists thought that their ideas about the South gave unity to a fragmented modern society. Similarly, Botkin set himself the task of taking romantic-nationalist notions based on the assumption of the necessity of cultural homogeneity and reconciling these with his desire to embrace and celebrate America's cultural pluralism. For him, the idea of a pluralist America played the same role in translating the romantic tradition to fit modernity that the South played for the Regionalists and the Agrarians.[19]

Botkin was drawn to the Agrarian poet Allen Tate's idea that tradition was a set of manners and ways of feeling that one did not have to learn and that one took for granted. Tate thought such traditionalism would prevent "atrophy" of one's "power of contemplation." Botkin, however, finally rejected Tate's outlook because he was convinced that it was bound to lead to atrophy of one's power of social perception: that, indeed, Tate's view meant taking "a certain social order as final"—in this case, the southern caste system.[20]

In arguing that the southern Agrarians made the "mistake of identifying culture with a particular trait or complex, a particular way of life . . . of taking a certain background for granted, and a

19. Botkin, "Folkness of the Folk," 465–69. Perhaps the most moving expression of the Regionalists' desire to reconcile their southern and American identities is found in Howard Odum, *An American Epoch: Southern Portraiture in the National Picture* (New York, 1930).

20. Botkin, "We Talk About Regionalism," 291–92; B. A. Botkin, "*Folk-Say* and *Space*: Their Genesis and Exodus," *Southwest Review*, XX (1935), 330–31; B. A. Botkin, "Regionalism: Cult or Culture?" *English Journal*, XXV (1936), 182; Allen Tate, "Regionalism and Sectionalism," *New Republic*, LXIX (December, 1931), 159; Botkin, "Regionalism and Culture," 141.

certain social order as final," Botkin was using anthropological positions to make both theoretical and normative judgments. Few FWP southern fieldworkers would have understood or agreed with Botkin's argument that "cultural minorities and other nondominant groups . . . were not static but dynamic and transitional, on their way up." These fieldworkers' underlying assumptions about folklore and their view of southern society were fundamentally opposed to Botkin's. They regarded the southern caste system as a fixed and final solution to race relations in the South.[21]

In the summer of 1938, when W. T. Couch, as the FWP's southeast regional director, began his southern life-history project—an effort to collect the life histories of ordinary southerners—Botkin was working in the national office to develop ways to coordinate folklore studies with black and social-ethnic studies. Couch, however, successfully resisted attempts to coordinate his southern life-history program with these efforts. Both Botkin and Couch advocated collecting life histories, but there were substantive differences in the way each of them conceived of the purposes of the life-history interview. Botkin saw the life history as part of the folklore interview. In his view, the fieldworker merely began with the personal history of the informant—but if the interview went well, the fieldworker soon would be recording "folk knowledge and folk fantasy." At that point the interviewer would be tapping the folk experience and history of a group. Such interviews, Botkin argued, helped capture a sense of the tremendous historical changes many groups of Americans had experienced in only a few generations— the migration (often immigration) from a rural to an urban world, the transition from rural to urban patterns of work and play. The interviews documented the creative reciprocity between the individual and his folk group and illuminated the dynamics of the acculturative process. Taken together, Botkin thought, a collection of such accounts constituted a folk history.[22]

21. Botkin, "Regionalism and Culture," 141; Botkin, "The Folk and the Individual," 126.

22. Botkin, "We Called It 'Living Lore,'" 197; B. A. Botkin, "'Living Lore' on the New York City Writers' Project," *New York Folklore Quarterly,* II (1946), 252–63.

Couch, on the other hand, thought of life histories as primarily representing different social types and classes. His view of the life history was rooted in journalistic and sociological approaches to the social problems that modernity had exacerbated. He aimed to obtain material that had literary qualities sociological writing lacked, yet that did not present "the composite or imaginary character" of the fiction writer.[23] In part, the differences between Botkin and Couch reflected the differences between anthropology and sociology in the 1930s. Botkin emphasized the strength and adaptability of folk traditions in a modernizing society, the norms and patterns that gave coherence to group life; Couch focused on the problems created by the growth of a market-oriented agriculture and an industrial work force in a traditionally hierarchical and biracial society—the problems, in short, of the tenant farmer and the textile worker.[24]

Like the national FWP officials, Couch was a supporter of New Deal reforms, and as such he advocated examining and possibly reforming much that many white southern Federal Writers did not question. But there remained ways in which Couch was closer to the local southern Federal Writers than to the national officials, for many of his views were responses to inherited and contemporary southern folk, popular, and intellectual attitudes and ideas that were a part of his cultural background. His way of studying a changing South was itself an example of how southern intellectuals adapted to change.

Couch, the son of a Baptist country preacher, was born in 1901 in Pamplin, Virginia. During his undergraduate years at the University of North Carolina, he became widely known for his articles in the *Carolina Magazine* attacking southern conservatism. In

23. [W. T. Couch] to [?], "Memorandum Concerning Proposed Plans for Work of the Federal Writers' Project in the South," July 11, 1938, in FWP-Couch Papers.

24. On this point I have been influenced by Werner Sollors, "Anthropological and Sociological Tendencies in American Literature of the 1930s and 1940s: Richard Wright, Zora Neale Hurston, and American Culture" (Paper delivered before the European Association for American Studies, Berlin, March 31, 1988, Typescript in possession of Jerrold Hirsch).

1925, while still a student, he became assistant director of the University of North Carolina Press. In 1932 he was appointed director. He worked to publish books that he thought would help southerners develop a critical attitude toward the social problems they confronted, that would provoke debate, and that would explore the ways various groups of southerners lived. He was convinced that it was the duty of the University of North Carolina Press to publish studies that would help the South clarify, understand, and address its problems. Couch was also deeply concerned that knowledge and discussion of these problems not be confined to experts. Knowledge, he thought, was power. It could promote reform.[25]

When Couch joined the FWP, he began to consider the ways in which the Writers' Project could aid him in his plans to promote regional self-understanding—the programs it could develop that a financially insecure university press could not hope to undertake. Couch saw in the FWP a means of examining southern life in a way that upholders of the status quo in the region would not support. In turning to the FWP to gain leverage against those who approved of things as they were, Couch was willing to break with southern tradition and—in a sense—seek federal interference. He was one of a growing number of southern liberals who in the thirties found a supportive network in government programs developed under the New Deal.

Couch thought that by interviewing tenant farmers, textile workers, and members of other occupational groups, the Federal Writers could help move the discussion of southern reality beyond stereotypes and abstractions, beyond the conventional wisdom that helped rationalize the status quo. To argue, as so many southerners did, that "we are held down by the Negro" or that "the masses of white people are not particularly helpful material," Couch insisted, was to "help keep things as they are." Despite the novelist Erskine Caldwell's impassioned appeals for the reform of sharecropping, Couch regarded Caldwell's portrayal of Jeeter Les-

25. W. T. Couch to Mrs. Leonard K. Elmhirst, October 17, 1935, in Frank P. Graham Papers, Southern Historical Collection, University of North Carolina, Chapel Hill. See also the discussion of Couch in Singal, *The War Within*, 265–301.

ter and his family in *Tobacco Road* (1932) as reinforcing stereotypes about the southern poor. On the other hand, he rejected what he also saw as the abstract and unrealistic position of the Agrarians. In his view their rejection of industrialization and their idealization of a simpler agrarian society constituted a misreading of southern culture and history and offered no realistic hope for those at the bottom of southern society. The Agrarians, Couch contended, "assert that virtue is derived from the soil, but see no virtue in the Negro and poor white who are closest to the soil." And Couch insisted that "the South must recognize that the kind of evils Mr. Caldwell describes actually exist in this region, and must do what it can to correct them."[26]

If southerners were given a chance to speak for themselves, Couch thought, their accounts would move the discussion of southern social problems away from the vast body of oral and written tradition that attributed the plight of poor southerners, black and white, to their inferior character and heredity. In place of the sentimental antimodernism of the Agrarians and the bloodless statistical abstractions of the sociologists, readers of the southern life histories, Couch thought, would encounter the voices of specific individuals recounting from their own perspective the impact of the tenant farm system, industrialization, and the Great Depression on their lives.[27]

26. W. T. Couch, Speech delivered at South Georgia Teachers' College, Collegeboro, Georgia, March 12, 1937, Typescript in FWP-Couch Papers, W. T. Couch, "Landlord and Tenant," *Virginia Quarterly Review*, XIV (1938), 309–12; W. T. Couch, "The Agrarian Romance," *South Atlantic Quarterly Review*, XXXVI (1937), 429.

27. See Couch's preface to Federal Writers' Project, *These Are Our Lives* (Chapel Hill, 1939), ix–xx. The image of the poor white in southern literature is examined in Shields McIlwaine, *The Southern Poor-White: From Lubberland to Tobacco Road* (Norman, Okla., 1939) and Sylvia Jenkins Cook, *From Tobacco Road to Route 66: The Southern Poor White in Fiction* (Chapel Hill, 1976). The way in which common images that seem to be mainly the product of reading other books rather than of direct observation permeate the "social problem" literature on textile mill workers can be seen in Clare de Graffenried, "The Georgia Cracker in the Cotton Mills," *Century*, XIX (1891), 483–98; Lois McDonald, *Southern Mill Hills: A Study of Social and Economic Forces in Certain Textile Mill Villages* (New York, 1928); and Frank Tannenbaum, *Darker Phases of the South* (New York, 1924).

With the publication of *These Are Our Lives* (1939), a small sample of the life histories the southern Federal Writers collected, Couch succeeded in many of his goals. Nevertheless, the very sources of the strengths of the life-history project are the reasons it did not result in a marriage between folklore and history, in a folk history. Couch, for all his interest in the daily life and problems of ordinary southerners, was not particularly interested in their folk culture, and this was revealed in the life-history outline and in the stories themselves. Some folk material inevitably turns up in the southern life histories, but it was not sought out and the interviewers were not especially interested in learning about it. For example, the ways in which southern textile workers adapted old folkways to a new means of making a living as they creatively responded to new circumstances remained unexplored. The interviewers failed on numerous occasions to ask additional questions when interviewees referred to their folk culture. To a significant degree the explanation lies in the southern context within which Couch formulated his outlook.

Couch not only made analyses that blamed the social and economic system rather than individuals for their plight, but he also worked within the context of an inherited set of regional attitudes about the character of the poor. The life histories in *These Are Our Lives* demonstrate his desire both to blame the system and to show the strength of character of ordinary southerners. On the whole, the inherited southern dialogue (which, ironically, had a significant folklore component) about the poor had more influence on how the southern life-history project was conducted than did anthropological approaches; therefore, the southern life histories did not pursue southern folk history and culture to the extent they could have. Traditional southern attitudes about character could be reconciled with a sociological approach, but such an approach prevented a deeper anthropological examination of culture.

In a review of *These Are Our Lives*, Allen Tate insisted that, given the absence of an underlying formal structure to lend them enduring significance, these interviews conveyed only information, not knowledge. Tate, however, found most satisfying two stories that he thought reflected the imaginative qualities of fiction. "Tore Up and Movin'" and "On the Road to Sheriff," he argued, exhibited "the qualities of two very old types of literature, the medieval exemplum and another form of medieval expression best known in 'Piers Ploughman,' a late development of the early mystical vision into an allegory of social protest." Tate found underlying allegory, myth, and vision in the life histories only by comparing them to earlier forms of literature from the culture of another time and place. It does not seem to have occurred to him that the interviewees, drawing on their folk culture, might have given narrative pattern to their stories and filled them with visual imagery and metaphoric language. It did not occur to Couch either.[28]

Couch's problem-oriented view of southern social needs remained within the bounds of a very old southern tradition; at the same time, it caused him to miss the opportunity more fully to explore change and continuity in the culture of ordinary southerners, white and black. Botkin's focus on what were widely regarded as erroneous and irrational folklore materials, mere survivals of a vanishing way of life, could have provided a view of the impact of change on the traditions of ordinary southerners that Couch's rational, problem-oriented approach could not. Like Couch, however, Botkin was limited in what he could do by the perspective brought to FWP projects by the middle-class white southerners employed on them.

Local southern Federal Writers, for the most part, shared a view of southern culture and folklore that differed from either Couch's or Botkin's. They accepted many of the traditional beliefs about poor whites and Negroes that Couch thought stood in the way of the South's addressing its economic and social problems. In trying to secure life histories of Negroes, Couch discovered that project workers not only found the assignment difficult, but were

28. Allen Tate, "Knowledge and Reporting in the South," *Free America*, III (1939), 18–20.

also reluctant to attempt it. They had to be reminded that "we must have life histories that reveal the way people in the South live, and Negroes and members of other racial groups are people just as well as whites." [29]

Given their assumptions, southern Federal Writers easily echoed the views of traditional folklorists who regarded industrialism and pluralism (in a southern context, racial equality) as enemies of folk culture—a view of folklore Botkin had rejected. The traditional assumptions underlying conservative romantic-nationalist and evolutionary approaches to folklore studies proved compatible with these writers' commitment to a racial caste system and a nostalgic view of agrarian folkways. Romantic-nationalist definitions of folklore had stressed the importance of homogeneity, isolation, and an agricultural way of life. Folklorists working within an evolutionary framework regarded folklore as being composed of survivals from an earlier stage in the progress of human beings. It was easy for white southerners to develop variations on these themes, adapting them to their determination to maintain a segregated society and to their anxiety about industrialism.

The determination of most southern Federal Writers to make the former slaves' narratives confirm the white South's traditional view of Negroes and slavery is one of the limitations of these interviews as a source on Afro-American slavery. Yet what in one context is a limitation in the sources is a strength in another. The reaction of white southerners to the assignment to interview former slaves reveals much about their outlook, about what can be called their white folk-view of black folklore. Chalmers S. Murray, a South Carolina Federal Writer, confided to his state director that he "thought from the first it was rather a mistake to write these ex-slave stories. . . . The general run of negro is only too glad of opportunity to record his grievances"—grievances Murray dismissed as either unfounded or exaggerated. [30] In many of their interviews

29. "Memorandum: From William T. Couch to All State Directors, Federal Writers' Project, Subject: Answers to Frequent Queries on Life Histories," n.d., in FWP-Couch Papers.

30. Chalmers S. Murray to Mabel Montgomery, July 8, 1937, in Box 192, FWPNA.

with former slaves, white southern fieldworkers strove to confirm the image of plantation slavery familiar to them from white southern folklore, popular culture, and the novels of writers such as Thomas Nelson Page.[31] The FWP guidebooks to the southern states reveal that local Federal Writers and most of the other southerners asked to contribute to the guides as specialists worked within a conservative, antimodern, hierarchical, romantic southern plantation tradition that viewed the past with nostalgia, served to rationalize the status quo, and looked at folklore as material endangered by change. In many ways, this view constituted a mirror image of Botkin's liberal-radical romanticism, which looked forward to change; which envisioned a more inclusive, democratic, and egalitarian community than what had existed; which sought to document the ways in which folklore demonstrated how people adapted their traditions to a changing world; and which regarded folklore as an important source of social history. Although the national FWP officials wanted to produce encyclopedic guides that would "introduce" Americans to the diverse traditions that existed in their country, the guides never completely transcended the tourist mode.[32] The southern guides presented folklore and life within the limits of a plantation tradition that patronized black folkways and many white folkways as merely exotic and quaint.

The guidebooks to the southern states represented not only an outgrowth of the plantation tradition, but also, in part, a contribution to it. For white southerners the plantation tradition was an

31. Anyone dipping into both the FWP former-slave interviews and Page's work will be struck immediately by the frequent similarities. Graduate papers in David Donald and Syd Nathans' Harvard seminar helped call my attention to this fact. The dominance of the white South's view of slavery in popular culture, literature, and history had profound cultural and political consequences. In Francis Pendleton Gaines, *The Southern Plantation Tradition: A Study in the Development of the Accuracy of a Tradition* (New York, 1924) and Paul Buck, *The Road to Reunion, 1865–1900* (Boston, 1937), scholars close to the plantation tradition, and unembarrassed by and sympathetic to the assumptions underlying it, have offered insights into the tradition's pervasiveness that less sympathetic students of the subject need to understand.

32. "The American Guide and the American Guide Series: Their Task to Introduce America to Americans," n.d., in Box 74, FWPNA.

important discourse about their relationship to the past, to the former slaves and their descendants, and to the new nation that emerged from the crucible of war. Its mythic description of a lost idyllic world of friendship and affection between master and slave, of devoted, contented, and comic darkies, helped rationalize a caste system in the New South. Through repetition and variation, white southerners molded the plantation tradition to reflect and fulfill the purposes of the white community. The portrayal of blacks in the plantation tradition tells more about white southern folklore about blacks than about the folklore of southern blacks, more about how whites wanted blacks to function in society than about the functions of folklore and oral tradition in black culture.[33]

The plantation tradition glorifying the Old South had developed in tandem with a New South creed that advocated industrialization and urbanization under the guidance of a conservative southern elite determined to maintain a traditional social and racial hierarchy.[34] In the guidebooks to their states, southern Federal Writers linked discussions of the New South that they saw developing around them with references to the Old South and the Negro. According to the Alabama guide, "the ante bellum mansion and the towering steel mill still symbolize Alabama's dual personality." The writers welcomed industrialization, but with mixed feelings. For example, the Louisiana guide writers insisted that "while Monroe is [an] essentially modern and semi-urban [city] in aspect, its people cherish many old southern traditions, especially as regards relations between whites and Negroes, hospitality, and a chivalrous attitude toward the ladies."[35]

33. Gaines's *Southern Plantation Tradition* can be treated as both a secondary source indirectly supporting my analysis and a primary source providing evidence for my interpretation. Among more recent works, see Paul Gaston, *The New South Creed: A Study in Southern Mythmaking* (New York, 1970) and Charles Reagan Wilson, *Baptized in Blood: The Religion of the Lost Cause* (Athens, Ga., 1980), 177–202.

34. Gaston, *New South Creed*, 167–86.

35. Writers' Program, *Alabama: A Guide to the Deep South* (New York, 1941), 184; Writers' Program, *Louisiana: A Guide to the State* (New York, 1941), 292.

The southern guides are full of traditional pictures of black folklife that draw on the plantation tradition and portray Negroes as an unchanging folk element linking white southerners of the New South to their Old South ancestors. The Texas guide tells readers about Negroes spending their days "chopping and picking cotton," noting that "their faded jeans and bright sunbonnets are part of the southern tradition," that "old customs of the golden age of cotton survive," and that while the tenant houses of these Negroes constitute a "squalid scene," their "usually smiling faces . . . lend cheer."[36]

Throughout the southern guides, southern Federal Writers offer traditional images of the Negro as reassuring signs of stability amidst change. As the muckraking journalist Ray Stannard Baker had pointed out earlier in his *Following the Color Line: Negro Citizenship in the American Democracy* (1908), "Many southerners look back wistfully to the faithful, simple, ignorant, obedient, cheerful, old plantation Negro and deplore his disappearance. They want the New South, but the old Negro."[37] Baker focused on how a segregated society worked, reported on lynchings, and described white-initiated riots that resulted in attacks on Negroes and their property. In the FWP southern guides there are only passing references to these matters.

The guides also contrast the Old and New South by the use of adjectives like *slow* and *swift*, reflecting what southern Federal Writers perceived as traditional versus modern concepts of time and space—and acknowledging change in their world. The Mississippi guide writers noted that Laurel presented a sharp contrast to "many Mississippi towns richly flavored with the essence of the ante-bellum South." Rather, Laurel "reveals in a few fast-moving chapters a swift transition from forest through lumber camp to a stable industrial city in the course of fifty years." In Selma, Ala-

36. Writers' Program, *Texas: A Guide to the Lone Star State* (New York, 1940), 570, 631.

37. Ray Stannard Baker, *Following the Color Line: An Account of Negro Citizenship in the American Democracy* (New York, 1908), 44.

bama—and throughout the South—"Negro and white citizens have lived in an atmosphere of sympathetic understanding, tinged by a friendly paternalism on the part of whites." The repeated use of the same picturesque scenes takes the place of direct observation; indeed, it is substituted for any knowledge of the black perspective, of black folklore and ways.[38]

The guidebooks portray white and black southerners as separate groups, each with its distinctive folklore. They explain any similarities within an evolutionary framework, not as the product of acculturation. Southern Federal Writers portray the interaction between these two folk groups as unidirectional, from white to black, from higher to lower levels on the scale of cultural evolution. Georgia Federal Writers working on the study that became *Drums and Shadows* (1940) argued the Negro has "innate instincts stronger than the new civilization," which even in the educated members of the race constitutes only a "thin veneer." Reconstructing folk history along evolutionary lines, which was still common in American folklore scholarship in the 1930s, white southerners could recount the "history" of Afro-American folklore without relating it to a southern historical experience shared by blacks and whites, and without acknowledging the active role of blacks in helping shape a distinctive southern folklore.[39]

In the essay "Negro Folkways" in the Mississippi guide, the writer makes clear his distance from his subject (always referred to as "him," so that the subject turns into an object). That space makes possible a patronizing tone characteristic of the southern guides: "Those who know him well enough to understand something of his psychology, his character, and his needs, and like him well enough to accept his deficiencies, find him to be wise but credulous—a superstitious paradox." The writer found both amusement

38. FWP, *Mississippi: A Guide to the Magnolia State* (New York, 1938), 223; FWP, *Alabama*, 184.

39. See draft "Stories of Negro Survival Types in Coastal Georgia," n.d., in Box 201, FWPNA.

and reassurance in the Mississippi Negro, "a genial mass of remarkable qualities . . . carefree and shrewd. . . . As for the so-
called Negro question—that, too, is just another problem he has
left for the white man to cope with." The third-person description
effectively silences the black subject; its use in this context links the
guides to the southern plantation tradition. As Francis Pendelton
Gaines pointed out in his study of the southern plantation tradition, "A popular literary device, repeated again and again, was to
hand down the legend of splendor and joy through the mouths of
the slaves themselves." By casting blacks in the role of clown, court
jester, guardian of the tradition, "sable curator of folk-lore," the
plantation tradition tried to make a racist world view appear benign. It employed the stereotyped portrait of the Negro as humorous primitive to make the ideal of the blissful race relations of the
plantation believable; it used the Negro's own folklore, as interpreted by whites, to justify slavery in the past and the creation of a
caste system to replace it.[40]

In part the plantation tradition was a deeply conservative
form of antimodernism that profoundly influenced the way southern black folklore and life were presented to a national audience.
In a clear but subdued form, the FWP southern state guides embody variations on the genre. According to Gaines, the "genuine
darkey" of the plantation tradition, "the folk figure of a simple,
somewhat rustic, character, instinctively humorous, irrationally
credulous, gifted in song and dance, interesting in spontaneous
frolic, endowed with artless philosophy," represents the romantic
longings of the "public."[41] Implicitly, the public is white America.
These qualities of the "folk figure" draw on a long-standing conservative European romantic-nationalist tradition as well as on indigenous racist traditions. In the South, however, the folk/nonfolk
dichotomy is also a white/black dichotomy, and the allegedly positive qualities of the "folk" Negro win black Americans no status;

40. FWP, *Mississippi*, 76–86; Gaines, *Southern Plantation Tradition*, 63.
41. Gaines, *Southern Plantation Tradition*, 3.

rather, they serve to rationalize inequality. These "folk" qualities appear frequently in the work southern Federal Writers submitted to their superiors.

Southern Federal Writers, like other white southerners, used the plantation tradition to dichotomize past and present, to offer a view of a lost world deemed superior in many ways to modern circumstances. Their approach was a variant on a conservative European romantic interest in folklore that saw in the folk and their lore survivals from a past world free of the ills of modern life. The working out of the question of race relations within a tradition that could capitalize on nostalgic reactions to the stresses of modernity helped gain the plantation tradition a national audience. The plantation tradition also gained popularity "as a kind of American embodiment of the golden age," allegedly fulfilling the need of a youthful nation for "a misty, heroic long ago." [42]

As a conservative romantic-nationalist myth, the plantation tradition worked against every goal that national FWP officials hoped to achieve. At the same time that those officials were seeking to reconcile romantic nationalism and pluralism and to redefine American identity and nationality along more inclusive, egalitarian, and democratic lines, the southern Federal Writers' use of the plantation tradition conveyed the message that a racially diverse society could only work when one group dominated. This message's implicit criticism of the present offered no program or hope for change; it was an accommodation to a form of modernization that exacerbated inequality. It wrote blacks out of the national culture except as subordinates confined to white-defined roles. It celebrated a slave society and helped justify a system that denied black Americans their rights as citizens. In this national myth about the southern past, the black point of view was excluded.

The FWP studies of the South embody the conflicting visions of national FWP officials and local southern Federal Writers.

42. *Ibid.*, 4.

That conflict makes the materials a difficult, but nevertheless valuable, source for southern folk history—and an especially rich source for studying how white middle-class southerners adapted their folk traditions to change even while trying to limit and deny the impact of change.

Southern Federal Writers either ignored or rejected Botkin's approach to the study of folklore as a neglected source of social history. Questions of methodology were only the tip of the iceberg; it was the cultural and political implications of different approaches that led national FWP officials and local southern Federal Writers each to object to the approach of the other. Southern Federal Writers, unlike national FWP officials, had no desire to reconcile romantic nationalism with cultural pluralism. Couch's reformist approach to the study of ordinary southerners was no more helpful than that of local southern FWP fieldworkers when it came to understanding the way southern tradition adapted to change, especially as seen in the relationship between changing ways of living and ways of making a living. Working within the plantation tradition, southern Federal Writers sought to celebrate a static southern folklore in an unchanging social structure; in doing so they were contributing to that same nostalgic tradition—a tradition that helped accommodate economic development even while serving as a barrier against political and social change. The writers' assumptions made it impossible for them to study and understand the ways in which white and black southerners adapted their folklore to a continually changing world—to an emerging industrial order and an increasingly market-oriented agriculture—within a paternalistic and hierarchical society. The writers treated both black and white folk cultures as homogeneous wholes. They largely ignored the impact of class divisions on folkways. They denied and left unexplored the evidence that a dynamic acculturative process affected the lore of both blacks and whites, although often they recorded the evidence of this very process.

Nevertheless, despite the aims of southern Federal Writers and the resulting limitations in the material they collected, their work can make a contribution both to scholarship and toward realizing the vision that guided the national FWP officials. Two works that Botkin later edited, both drawing on FWP southern studies, offer powerful examples of his vision of the role of folklore in studying social history; both meet what he called "the tremendous responsibility of studying folklore as a living culture and of understanding its meaning and function not only in its immediate setting but in progressive and democratic society as a whole."[43] Using excerpts drawn from the FWP interviews with former slaves, Botkin edited *Lay My Burden Down: A Folk History of Slavery* (1945), a volume that sought to bring the black oral tradition into a public forum and that allowed the generation of blacks who had experienced slavery and freedom, Civil War and Reconstruction, to present a history that questioned every assumption of the plantation tradition.[44] In *A Treasury of Southern Folklore* (1949) Botkin did not simply stick to traditional and safe topics—agrarian lifestyles and the beliefs of isolated mountaineers—but instead emphasized the folklore that emerged from the interaction between cultures. Labor conflicts, such as those between mill owners and textile workers, he maintained, "created a new folklore-in-the-making."[45]

Botkin's emphasis on folklore as a process kept him from searching for fixed southern qualities—personalism, the love of the concrete, hierarchy, biracialism. In his view, external and concrete measurements did not adequately define the region. He was interested in consciousness. He insisted that folklore as a living tradition, which together the individual and the folk group molded and *remolded*, offered insights into areas of culture to which traditional historical sources provided only limited access. Botkin's

43. B. A. Botkin, "WPA and Folklore Research: 'Bread and Song,'" *Southern Folklore Quarterly,* III (1939), 14.

44. For a fuller analysis of this point and a reconsideration of the historical, literary, and moral value of *Lay My Burden Down,* see Jerrold Hirsch, "Foreword to the Brown Thrasher Edition," in *Lay My Burden Down: A Folk History of Slavery,* ed. B. A. Botkin (1945; rpr. Athens, Ga., 1989), ix–xxx.

45. Botkin, ed. *Treasury of Southern Folklore,* xxi.

methodology embodied values he wished to promote, and he found a happy congruence between his scholarly positions and his values as a citizen.

Ironically, the attitude of local southern Federal Writers toward folklore was also an example of one of the dynamic ways in which southerners adapted their traditions to change. While the local Writers' theoretical view is less helpful than Botkin's to historians today trying to understand southern social history, his methods can be employed to understand their folklore. Botkin attacked the theoretical approaches to folklore that ignored tradition as part of the process of adapting the past to the present; he also rejected the views of white southerners who held such theories much more for political and social reasons than for scholarly ones. In effect, Botkin argued that the demise of the caste system, the growth of a more democratic social order, and the spread of industrialism would not mean the demise of southern identity if southerners worked to adapt what was valuable in their traditions to the world he and other New Deal liberals envisioned. The history of the Federal Writers' Project, however, indicates that the demise of a particular theoretical perspective among folklorists and historians is no guarantee that conservative southerners will not find new ways to meet, and sometimes to promote, change within a conservative framework.

Frank Graham and the Politics of the New South

Julian Pleasants

In 1949, V. O. Key, Jr., described Frank Porter Graham as "by all odds the South's most prominent educator and versatile public servant." Placing Graham "in the forefront of American progressivism," Key further observed that "it is significant that Dr. Graham is indigenous to North Carolina and himself a product of the University."[1] Writing in a similar vein, W. J. Cash also grasped the quality of Graham's contribution to progressivism in the South. Cash believed that southerners of sense and decency felt themselves bound to respect such men as Frank Graham even when they were opposed to Graham's views.[2]

Frank Graham was a figure of great significance in the transition from Old South to New South, grappling as he did with the forces of change and their impact on such sensitive and emotional issues as race relations, the rights of southern workers, public education, and the related issue of academic freedom. Especially important was the fact that Graham's views of life were grounded in

1. V. O. Key, Jr., *Southern Politics in State and Nation* (New York, 1949), 206.
2. W. J. Cash, *The Mind of the South* (New York, 1960), 349.

southern tradition; and when he proposed reforms for the South, he could not be attacked as an outsider.

Graham's life symbolized the South in transition. To understand the man and his ideas, therefore, is to capture the essence of the struggle between those values of southern life that Graham cherished and seldom questioned and the ethos of the rapidly approaching New South, part of which Graham embraced. Perhaps no other twentieth-century southerner better exemplified the South's attempt to adapt to the changing social and economic realities of the period from 1930 to 1950. Graham's patient persuasion and unwavering faith in mankind helped many southerners, even those who rejected his social values, come to grips with the problems of integration of the races and accept a new era.

In his nineteen years (1931–1949) as president of the University of North Carolina, Graham won great recognition and notoriety as the champion of numerous liberal and radical causes. Francis Butler Simkins wrote that Graham "signed enough liberal manifestoes to put the South in the reformer's paradise." Simkins knew, however, that Graham's "simple manners and deep human sympathies made him immensely popular" in spite of the fact that some of the groups he joined were later classified as Communist front organizations. People seemed to realize "that a disarming generosity rather than a rational understanding had made him a radical and that despite his utterances he was a member of an old family with friends among the rich and politically powerful."[3]

Graham was a native southerner, and it is instructive to look at his early life and background. He was born in Fayetteville, North Carolina, on October 14, 1886. From his stern Presbyterian father and his sensitive, caring mother, Graham developed a Calvinistic religious intensity and a strong moral drive that became integral and immutable features of his character.[4] Matriculating at the University of North Carolina in the fall of 1905, he began a warm and

3. Francis Butler Simkins, *A History of the South* (New York, 1958), 607.
4. Warren Ashby, *Frank Porter Graham: A Southern Liberal* (Winston-Salem, 1980), 5–7.

intimate relationship with the university that would last for the rest of his life. During his four undergraduate years, Graham was twice president of his class, was president of the YMCA, served as editor in chief of both the *Tar Heel* (the student newspaper) and the school yearbook, and earned membership in Phi Beta Kappa. According to the school yearbook, Graham left the university as a man characterized by idealism, fair play, integrity, and the belief that others were trustworthy as well. His naïveté and his puritanical behavior (he never smoked, drank, or cursed) were well known to all his friends, but Graham was rarely judgmental or critical of people with different ideas and values.[5]

After a stint as a high-school teacher and as secretary of the university YMCA, Graham gained a master's degree in history at Columbia University, intending to return to teach at Chapel Hill. Before he could fulfill his professional goal, the United States entered World War I. Graham decided that it was his duty to fight for his country. Although he was too small at five feet six inches and 145 pounds to qualify for the marines, he was so determined to serve that he hounded the recruiters until they finally accepted him. He served two noncombat years in the Marine Corps. Upon release from service, he accepted an offer to be dean of students and teach history at Chapel Hill.[6]

After an additional year studying at the University of Chicago and the London School of Economics, Graham became fascinated with economic ideas, especially as they concerned the coming of the industrial revolution to the South. Graham believed his task was to find a true balance between material and human values—property rights versus human rights—as well as to assist the South in achieving greater economic wealth while avoiding the industrial dilemmas of the North. Warren Ashby, Graham's biographer, presents him as a person who understood that man's overwhelming desire for material riches and success were in direct

5. *Yackety Yack* (Yearbook of the University of North Carolina), 1909, p. 40; Ashby, *Frank Porter Graham*, 27–31.

6. Ashby, *Frank Porter Graham*, 32–43.

conflict with the teachings of Jesus. Thus, Graham concluded, the supreme task of modern man was to overcome greed and build a society in the light of Christian standards.[7] Graham lived his own life in service to others and believed that the Sermon on the Mount was sound social and economic doctrine.

With the goal of economic equality in mind, Graham embarked on a series of activities designed to improve the conditions in the South and in his home state of North Carolina. Graham knew that politics in the South were a natural outgrowth of social and economic conditions and the South's political problems could be solved only by modifying the economy and changing the racial attitudes of the region. Graham was no rural visionary; he felt that industrialism could help the South significantly by making the region less poor. As a step toward that end he helped organize the Citizens Library Movement to improve libraries and combat illiteracy in the state. Graham fought for a workman's compensation law and advocated the improvement of working conditions. In a 1927 address entitled "The Old South and the New Industrialism," he called for advances in race relations and for improved roads, mental institutions, and colleges. He pleaded with citizens to overcome the barriers to economic success, including racial stereotypes that would block the improvement of living conditions for a large segment of the population, white as well as black.[8]

Graham's advocacy of significant reforms in working conditions, combined with his strong belief in the right of labor to organize and bargain collectively, led him into involvement in several labor strikes. In 1929 he supported an effort to secure a fair trial for Communist party member Fred Beal and fourteen other strikers. Graham wired the Raleigh *News and Observer:* "We owe it to the most despised of those accused in this case that they be tried by due process of law without regard to their economic or religious views."[9] Textile manufacturers criticized Graham for supporting a

7. *Ibid.*, 55–59.
8. *Ibid.*, 66–69.
9. Raleigh *News and Observer,* July 28, 1929.

Communist, but Graham did not fear identification with an unpopular cause if he perceived the cause to be just.

In 1934 there was another bitter textile strike in North Carolina, and a former University of North Carolina student, Alton Lawrence, was arrested in High Point for forcible trespass. Lawrence was secretary of the state Socialist party and secretly a member of the Communist party. Lawrence received an unexpected telegram from Frank Graham: JUST HEARD OF YOUR ARREST. GLADLY GO YOUR BOND. CONFIDENT YOU HAVE COMMITTED NO CRIME. Graham's telegram made front-page news all over the state and resulted in an immediate outcry from the conservative element.[10] Some critics believed that since he had tried to bail out a Socialist, Graham must be a Communist or the next thing to it.[11] Others saw him as sympathetic to violence-prone strikers rather than the beleaguered and respected mill owners. One enemy particularly disliked the fact that Graham, as president of the university, had publicly agreed to pay Lawrence's bond: it would have been bad enough for a private citizen to question the integrity of the officers of the law; for a public official to do so was intolerable.[12]

Graham justified his defense of Lawrence in a letter to a friend. He said that he did not stop to analyze his action when he learned that Lawrence was in jail. "The picture of the boy as I knew him in Chapel Hill came into my mind. The thought of his being in jail was intolerable to me. . . . The fact that we disagree about some things is not pertinent in a situation like this."[13] Or as Graham explained to another correspondent: "I would do it again and for any other person, Democrat or Republican, Socialist or Communist, white or black. I did it simply and will stand on the simple act itself, I trust, with humility and without bravado, retraction or apology."[14]

10. Greensboro (N.C.) *Daily News*, September 8, 1934.

11. Winston-Salem *Journal*, September 12, 1934.

12. O. K. Merritt to Frank P. Graham, September 8, 1934, in Frank P. Graham Papers, Southern Historical Collection, University of North Carolina, Chapel Hill.

13. Frank P. Graham to Dr. George Critz, September 17, 1934, in Graham Papers.

14. Frank P. Graham to Otho Ross, September 17, 1934, in Graham Papers.

After Alton Lawrence wrote Graham to thank him for his help and to praise Graham's fearlessness and courage, Graham replied that he had been glad to stand by Lawrence as Graham believed that Lawrence had not intentionally committed any crime. Graham admitted that the criticism and denunciation heaped on him (Graham) had been hot and widespread, but such opposition was all in a day's work. Graham, in fact, had no resentment for those who denounced him. "I hope I will always try to understand those who misunderstand me." Graham thought that the most important fact was that Lawrence was deeply enough interested in his fellow human beings to stand by them in their struggle for the recognition of the democratic principles of collective bargaining.[15]

For Graham the issue was not that Lawrence had broken the law or that he was a Socialist, but that he was a compassionate individual working for the betterment of society. In his innocent and moralistic way, Graham felt honor-bound to protect and nurture those who, regardless of political affiliation, joined him in his search for a balance between property rights and human rights. He ended his part in the controversy with a final letter reiterating that he would always stand by a friend in a time of misunderstanding and bitter antagonism. "If being President of the university could ever come to mean that I am not free to be a human being according to the lights of my own conscience, I, of course, do not want to be President."[16] The Raleigh *News and Observer,* in an editorial praising Graham's decision, commented that government was more concerned with property rights than the rights of man, and that because of this narrow view by government, liberals everywhere could "thank God that the courage of one great liberal gleams in the present darkness."[17]

Frank Graham had been chosen as president of the University of North Carolina in 1931. From the start he wanted to use the resources of the school in his fight for economic and social reform.

15. Alton Lawrence to Frank P. Graham, September 14, 1934, Graham to Lawrence, September 27, 1934, both in Graham Papers.

16. Frank P. Graham to T. G. Elliott, September 29, 1934, in Graham Papers.

17. Raleigh *News and Observer,* September 10, 1934.

He believed that the university was not an isolated tower of academe. In addition to the education of the state's citizens, the university also had a responsibility for serving the welfare and protecting the rights of all the people.[18] Under Frank Graham, the university made a moral commitment to assist in breaking the social and economic shackles that meant poverty and ignorance to many in the South. The university would be both teacher and citizen. It would stand for increasing the opportunities for human beings to work honorably, live decently, and enjoy personal dignity.[19]

Graham thought the most important feature of the university was academic freedom:

> Freedom of the university means the freedom of the scholar to report the truth honestly without interference by the university, the state or any interests whatever. . . . It means freedom from the prejudices of section, race or creed; it means a free compassion of her sons for all people in need of justice and brotherhood. It means freedom of the liberated spirit to understand sympathetically those who misunderstand freedom and would strike it down. It means consideration for the plight of the unorganized and inarticulate people in an organized world. . . . In the university should be found the free voice not only for the unvoiced millions but also for the unpopular and even hated minorities.[20]

An example of his unwavering belief in academic freedom and humanity came in 1936 when a white University of North Carolina English professor, E. E. Ericson, dined at a black hotel in Durham with James W. Ford, the Negro candidate for vice-president of the United States on the Communist party ticket. The Raleigh *News*

18. *Ibid.*, February 17, 1972.
19. Charlotte *Observer*, February 17, 1972.
20. Frank P. Graham, "The University Today" (Inaugural address as president of the University of North Carolina, November 11, 1931, Typescript in Graham Papers).

and Observer accused Ericson, a Socialist and Communist party member, of engaging in purely personal practices that offended the conventions of the people. The paper further criticized him for violating southern racial integrity and for disregarding the interests of the university. Ericson must have known his act would subject the university to unpleasant attacks. Jonathan Daniels, writer of the denunciatory editorial, demonstrated his respect for the southern custom of strict segregation by denying that the Ericson incident was an issue of academic freedom.[21]

Spurred on by the attack from the *News and Observer* and by other critical statements, several alumni of the university called for the removal of Ericson from the faculty. Graham refused to yield to the insistent demands for Ericson's ouster; he praised Ericson as an excellent scholar, a distinguished teacher, and a man of unimpeachable character. Graham said that Ericson had the meal in Durham "with no conscious attempt to affront the sensibilities of our people," especially since Ford and Ericson had been in graduate school together and were old friends. Graham would not fire Ericson. Graham later told the university trustees: "If Professor Ericson has to go on a charge of eating with another human being, then I will have to go first."[22]

In this case, Graham clearly went against the cultural traditions of the South. For him, the principle of academic freedom took precedence over social custom and narrow prejudice. Graham did not go so far, however, as to advocate the mixing of the races. He simply did what he thought was morally right in this particular case. Gerald Johnson, an old friend, understood that Graham, because of his early conditioning and his Christian belief in human relationships, could not have acted differently.[23]

Another racial incident, in 1931, demonstrated the extreme

21. Raleigh *News and Observer*, October 26, 27, 30, 1936.

22. Frank P. Graham to Kemp P. Lewis, November 25, 1936, in Graham Papers; Greensboro (N.C.) *Daily News*, February 20, 1972.

23. Gerald Johnson to Howard W. Odum, June 15, 1936, in Howard W. Odum Papers, Southern Historical Collection.

sensitivity of such problems in the South and also revealed the difficult choices facing a liberal university president like Graham. Graham's dilemma resulted from an appearance by Langston Hughes, the Negro poet. *Contempo*, an off-campus literary magazine, published some of Hughes's poetry, including "Black Christ," which featured the line "Christ is a nigger on the cross of the South." Graham's office was flooded with mail critical of the university. The letters denounced Graham's willingness to allow the publication of sacrilegious poetry and to allow disrespectful individuals such as Hughes to speak on the campus. One alumnus, Kemp P. Lewis, wrote that Graham's acceptance of free assembly and free utterance would result in great abuses of the privilege of free speech. Lewis had never read anything any worse than the material printed in *Contempo*, he said. "It is enough to make the blood of every Southerner boil to have a man like this Hughes given any attention by decent white people." [24]

Graham replied to Lewis that he never had the slightest disposition to deny an invitation to Langston Hughes, who, he pointed out, had been invited to speak by the YMCA and by a university professor who taught a course on the Negro. Privately, however, Graham was extremely angry with the editors of *Contempo* for having taken advantage of the situation to publish a sacrilegious poem calculated to offend religious sensibilities and to inflame racial hatred. [25]

Graham defended Hughes's right to speak and *Contempo's* right to publish, but he knew that such incidents led to increased opposition from intransigent whites, and he regretted the entire controversy. He wrote a scathing letter to Milton A. Abernathy, one of the editors of *Contempo*. Graham chastised Abernathy for being irresponsible and reckless in inflaming racial prejudices, which might lead to harm for innocent colored people. Graham explained that black and white proponents of better relationships between

24. Kemp P. Lewis to Robert W. House, December, 1931, Lewis to Frank P. Graham, December, 1931, both in Graham Papers.

25. Frank P. Graham to Kemp P. Lewis, December 15, 1931, in Graham Papers.

the races greeted the *Contempo* issue with scorn as they were patiently and sympathetically trying to build a commonwealth that would be more just to all human beings, regardless of race, creed, or social position. "I have no jurisdiction over your private publication," continued Graham, "and it is not my policy to set up a censorship of any publication. . . . Yet I think you have a moral responsibility as a human being to have a decent regard for honest religious convictions and better interracial relations."[26]

In this incident and others similar in nature, Graham demonstrated a moderate stance on racial issues. He feared the exacerbation of racial prejudice by aggressive and deliberately provocative acts, but he believed that race relations in North Carolina were on a sound enough basis to survive the sensationalism of a few isolated incidents. For Graham, the best way to end segregation was to raise the educational level of all the people of the state and to get southerners, both black and white, to understand the importance of democracy and religious teachings about human brotherhood.[27] Graham truly believed that racial interaction would lessen racial hostility—but in the North Carolina of the 1930s that was an arguable proposition.

Graham's way was, of course, evolutionary and extremely slow. It would take at least one generation before white attitudes in regard to black equality would be changed. Graham and other liberals, if not the blacks, were prepared to wait until society, on a rational basis, decided that integration was the correct course of action. Graham did not want the federal government to force the issue. He believed that Negro violence or legal challenges or confrontations would simply lead to a stiffening resistance to integration, as well as trigger white retribution. Since whites had to be educated to understand the sensitivity of the race issue, the only way for Graham was the peaceful and gradual way of education

26. Frank P. Graham to Milton A. Abernathy, n.d., in Graham Papers.

27. Washington *Post*, February 17, 1972; Interview with Charles Jones by Joe Herzenberg, November 8, 1976, in Southern Oral History Collection, B-41, University of North Carolina (hereinafter cited as Jones interview), 2–3.

and religion.[28] Graham, of course, would have been considered a moderate and gradualist on race by national standards, but by southern standards in the 1930s he was a radical and dangerous man.

Despite strident opposition from conservatives, Graham continued to pursue his paternalistic, middle-of-the-road course on race. An exchange of letters with Pauli Murray, a black woman who desired to attend the segregated University of North Carolina, aptly illustrates Graham's attitudes. Graham wrote Murray that it would not be possible for her to attend the university since the clear intent of the United States Supreme Court, the North Carolina legislature, and the constitution of the state was to continue segregated educational facilities. Graham, therefore, had a lawful responsibility to accept these decisions. The admission of Negro students to white universities would unleash consequences not in the interests of either race. Unlike most of his contemporaries, however, Graham wanted more money and a higher standard for Negro undergraduate colleges to make them more nearly equal. He also favored the beginning of graduate and professional work in Negro colleges. Graham admitted to Murray that the improvement of Negro education in North Carolina might seem inadequate and minimal, but it was a formidable task that could be achieved only with the cooperation and struggle of both races. Graham had been doing all he could to promote Negro education. Indeed, he often had been criticized for going too far. On the other hand, he was also attacked by some blacks and liberals for understanding and accepting the limitations under which he had to work in order to make the next advance possible.[29]

Publicly Graham paid allegiance to the laws and mores of society, but he was obviously more committed to black leaders and opportunity than most North Carolinians. Many black leaders

28. Jones interview, 2–3.

29. Pauli Murray to Frank P. Graham, January 17, 1939, Graham to Murray, February 3, 1939, both in Graham Papers.

understood that Graham had to compromise his goals while facing the entrenched beliefs of white supremacy, but they also knew that his basic sympathies were with them. Walter White, executive secretary of the NAACP, admired Graham's honest and direct letter to Pauli Murray. White wrote that the spirit of the letter was "magnificent not only for what it actually says, but in what, knowing you as I do, I can read between the lines." Graham, in fact, thought privately that Negroes should be admitted to the graduate schools at UNC since Negro colleges did not have equal courses or facilities. He recommended that the board of trustees admit qualified applicants since the Supreme Court ultimately would rule in favor of Negroes' right to admission. The trustees responded that they were officials of the state and, regardless of their personal opinions, were obligated to obey the laws of the state regarding segregation. Graham accepted this situation and did not push for admission of Negroes, but continued his sympathy for Negro rights and demands. When the Supreme Court ruled in 1944 that Negroes could not be barred from Democratic primaries, Graham called the decision "a fine thing." [30]

Graham frequently came under attack in North Carolina for his efforts in behalf of workers, the underprivileged, and blacks. His liberal economic and social views offended some wealthy and influential alumni of the university, and some of these continually criticized his actions and demanded his ouster. Their anger reached a fever pitch after a concert given in Chapel Hill on January 19, 1947, by Dorothy Maynor, a black singer. The Fellowship of Southern Churchmen, a regional interracial group, in cooperation with students at the university, had invited Maynor and had secured the use of a university auditorium for her performance. Since there had never been an unsegregated public concert at the university, the sponsors needed approval from the president of the uni-

---

30. Walter White to Frank P. Graham, February 11, 1939, in Graham Papers; Ashby, *Frank Porter Graham*, 229; Frank P. Graham to Frederick B. Patterson, April 18, 1944, in Graham Papers.

versity. Although an integrated concert was a delicate and potentially disruptive issue, Graham quickly agreed to allow it. He even
went so far as to write the press release, in which he referred to
Maynor as a distinguished artist and invited both races to hear her.
The seating, he wrote, would "be without discrimination in line
with the practices of interracial assemblies long observed here and
in many other communities in the South." Graham clearly had
overstated the circumstances, since there was no tradition of unsegregated assemblies in Chapel Hill except at some churches or at
professional meetings where invitations were sent.[31] Graham's
willingness to accept an integrated activity in 1947 demonstrated
his belief that both races would comport themselves with dignity
and revealed his faith in the ultimate benefit of integrated activities.

An anonymous letter written to the board of trustees of the
university complained about the integrated concert and blamed
Graham for beginning a movement to trample southern traditions
underfoot. The author thought that the next move would be to admit Negroes to the Carolina Inn (a university-owned hotel on campus) on an equal basis with whites.[32] Graham simply ignored the
attack and continued to seek equal treatment for all races.

The Reverend Charles Jones, chairman of the Fellowship of
Southern Churchmen, admired Graham for his stand on the Maynor concert. Jones called Graham "the great encourager" as well as
"the great protector." Graham inspired others to act on their beliefs, and when they did so he never criticized their decision, regardless of the consequences for the university or for Graham personally. He himself never took the initiative to become involved in
a direct confrontation, but once the event transpired, as with the
Maynor concert or the Alton Lawrence affair, he supported the participants with all his influence and eloquence. If Graham had been
the radical and the initiator, believed Jones, then there would have

31. Ashby, *Frank Porter Graham*, 230–33.
32. [?] to University of North Carolina Board of Trustees, n.d., in Graham Papers.

been no one to turn to for practical help and support. Progress in race relations needed the nurturing, protective presence of someone like Frank Graham. What made Graham unique was that despite his great love for the South and its culture, he was not bound by his past and could look to the future.[33]

In 1938, Frank Graham read President Franklin Roosevelt's *Report on Economic Conditions of the South.* This report confirmed Graham's belief that poverty in the South was the nation's number one economic problem. In response, Graham helped organize the Southern Conference for Human Welfare. This organization grew out of liberal and radical desires for a general reform group in the South that would advocate greater political and economic opportunities for blacks. The SCHW called for a campaign against segregation, demanded federal aid to education, housing, and medical clinics, and favored abolition of the poll tax as well as recognition of labor unions and collective bargaining. The conference was open to southerners of all political parties, races, and creeds who would work with devotion and good will to build up the South.

Graham became the first chairman of the SCHW and was the keynote speaker at the initial meeting of the organization in Birmingham, Alabama, in 1938. The theme of his address was equal justice for all. He spoke for the underprivileged groups in society and wanted the kind of government that rested on the dignity of the common man. Graham saw the treatment of the Negro as the true test of the reality of democracy and Christianity. He proposed building a new South rather than tearing down the old one. Ironically, conflict already was at hand. Denouncing Birmingham's system of forced segregation of the races, the SCHW had integrated its first meeting. Eugene "Bull" Connor and the Birmingham police, upset with this violation of city law, descended upon the city auditorium in force, threatening to arrest the entire group if they did not immediately impose segregated seating. Graham, acting as peacemaker, convinced the SCHW to accept local law, but

33. Jones interview, 5, 6, 7, 25, 37.

the delegates resolved never to convene again in a city where segregation would be imposed on their meetings.[34]

Gunnar Myrdal, the Swedish sociologist, attended the first meeting and felt that the real importance of the initial convocation was that for the first time in the history of the region, lonely southern liberals met in great numbers and experienced a taste of the freedom and power that organization and concerted action provided. Myrdal also offered a perceptive assessment of the southern liberalism he observed first hand. Myrdal thought southern liberalism was a unique species unlike liberalism elsewhere in America or in the rest of the world. He pointed out that southern liberalism lacked mass support, dealt primarily with regional as opposed to national issues, depended on funds and political power from groups outside the South, and emphasized "the cautious approach, the slow change, the organic nature of social growth."[35]

Charles Martin, in an article on the SCHW, agreed that Myrdal accurately described the traditional form of twentieth-century southern liberalism. Martin argued, however, that in the late 1930s and the early 1940s southern liberalism began to change and to reject the older gradualistic approach; partly because of the New Deal, it assumed a more assertive stance, even endorsing the principle of federal intervention in some southern affairs.[36]

Southern liberalism did not achieve its immediate goals through the SCHW in 1938. At the end of the first meeting, several prominent politicians withdrew from the group because of its integrationist position. Graham intended to decline an offer to be

34. Frank Graham, Opening address, Birmingham Proceedings of the Southern Conference for Human Welfare, 1938 (MS in Socialist Party Papers, Duke University, Durham, N.C.), 29; Thomas A. Kreuger, *And Promises to Keep: The Southern Conference for Human Welfare, 1938–1948* (Nashville, 1967), 26–39.

35. Gunnar Myrdal, *The Negro in a White Nation* (New York, 1964), 466–73, Vol. I of Myrdal, *An American Dilemma*, 2 vols.

36. Charles H. Martin, "The Rise and Fall of Popular Front Liberalism in the South: The Southern Conference for Human Welfare, 1938–1948," in *Perspectives on the American South*, ed. James C. Cobb and Charles R. Wilson (4 vols.; New York, 1985), III, 119.

chairman for the following year since he had numerous other commitments, but when he heard the attacks on the SCHW he felt
honor-bound to accept the post in order to insure the survival of
the organization. His decision to stay was sufficient to persuade a
number of other prominent individuals to remain, and this gave
the SCHW badly needed respectability.[37]

The SCHW had achieved, in many parts of the South, a reputation as a radical organization. Harry Ashmore, a southern editor, did not agree with this assessment. Ashmore pointed out that
Frank Graham, "a remarkable combination of Christian charity, old
shoe back-country charm, sheer guts, and unswerving devotion to
academic excellence," had stuck to the *traditional* southern liberal
line on segregation by asserting that SCHW's purpose was to promote social justice for blacks, but not social equality.[38] Nonetheless,
the mass of conservative southerners considered the SCHW a
crackpot group run by Communists with the avowed purpose of
mixing the races. Because of the outcry from conservatives, many
liberals became disaffected. They thought that racial problems in
the South could better be solved by a research and public-
information organization such as the Southern Regional Council.
They also feared that the SCHW would do more harm than good
and would destroy those associated with it.

These southern liberals and other friends consistently urged
Graham to sever his ties with the SCHW. Barry Bingham, the publisher of the Louisville *Courier Journal* and a long-time associate of
Graham, wrote his old friend in May, 1940, asking him to resign
from the SCHW. Bingham understood that Graham was a man
who had "a great responsibility and a great work to perform in the
South. That work is too important to be jeopardized by your running unnecessary risks with public opinion." Bingham thought

37. Krueger, *And Promises to Keep*, 38–39; Martin, "Rise and Fall of Popular Front
Liberalism," 124; Frank P. Graham to Mark Ethridge, December 20, 1938, in Graham
Papers.
38. Harry S. Ashmore, *Hearts and Minds: The Anatomy of Racism From Roosevelt to
Reagan* (New York, 1982), 77.

that the SCHW gave little promise for future usefulness in its present form, so that the stake did not seem high enough for the risk involved. Bingham was more concerned with Graham's prestige and the maintenance of Graham's full usefulness in the area of southern reform than in the survival of the SCHW. "The South cannot afford to lose one whit of your leadership."[39]

Many citizens of North Carolina—and much of the state's press—excoriated Graham for his membership in the SCHW, but to no avail. R. D. Douglas, Jr., upset by Graham's affiliations with Communists, wrote: "I know it is said of him that he has a heart so big that he can't think there's anything wrong with anybody, but I just don't see how anyone can be so blind." The High Point *Enterprise* held Graham in high esteem as far as his intentions were concerned, but regretted that his naive views had caused him to lend his name to the SCHW without ever suspecting that there were ulterior motives involved. The newspaper referred to Graham as "a perfect, ready-made stooge for any organization which gives a little attention to pulling the wool over his eyes."[40]

Graham ignored the press criticism and the advice of friends, and steadfastly maintained his ties to SCHW. He tried to explain to friends and critics alike why he remained in the SCHW even after it had fallen into disrepute and had lost any real hope of obtaining its objectives: although he did not think that the Communists controlled the organization, he understood the devious ways in which the Communist party worked and felt obligated to protect Negroes and the underprivileged from falling prey to Communist propaganda. According to one black leader, blacks trusted Graham, and if he left, black youth would listen to the Communists. Thus, Graham believed that by leaving he would be a traitor to the black youth as well as to the principles for which he had been fighting all these years. He wanted to remain in the SCHW to help

39. Anne Brackinridge to Frank P. Graham, October 25, 1946, Barry Bingham to Graham, October 25, 1946, both in Graham Papers.

40. Winston-Salem *Journal*, March 19, 1947; High Point (N.C.) *Enterprise*, June 15, 1947.

millions of blacks who were not raising questions of social equality, but wanted only social justice. Graham thought that the vicious attacks had been directed at the SCHW not because it was 1 percent Red, but because it was 50 percent black.[41]

Graham also favored admitting avowed Communists to membership in the SCHW because it was the democratic way. He did not want to drive the Communists underground, but to meet them and defeat them in an open, free, and democratic struggle with such weapons as education, rational discourse, and humane good will. "We should give them the fair open chance of a democratic way by holding our own ground as believers in liberty and democracy."[42]

Frank Graham was not a deep thinker and he often failed to understand the consequences of his actions. Nor did he understand the ideas and trends that characterized left-wing politics in America in the 1930s. He simply allied himself, without assessing the potential risk to his reputation and his credibility, with any group who claimed concern for the disinherited. Thus, Graham willingly lent his name and support to literally hundreds of organizations that were involved, or so Graham believed, in the cause of improving human welfare. He was committed to justice and opportunity regardless of the unpopularity or the controversial nature of the organization. He was a sponsor for such groups as the National Committee to Abolish the Poll Tax, the American Committee for Peace and Democracy, and the Committee to Free Earl Browder (the head of the Communist party in the United States). Several of the organizations to which Graham belonged were later placed on the attorney general's list of subversive organizations, and these developments hurt his reputation. His critics often pic-

41. Frank P. Graham to Hobart A. McWhorter, December 1, 1939, in Graham Papers; Interview with Frank Graham by Jonathan Daniels, Mrs. W. Kerr Scott, and Kate Humphries, June 10, 1962, in Southern Oral History Collection, B-4-2, p. 50.

42. Frank Graham to Joseph Leib, April 19, 1941, in Graham Papers; Interview with Clark Foreman by Jacquelyn Dowd Hall and Bill Finger, November, 1974, in Southern Oral History Collection, B-3.

tured him as a romantic, inept idealist, easily deceived by Socialists and Communists. Thus, even when they conceded his good intentions, Graham's enemies considered him a dangerous person.

Graham joined many national organizations about which he knew little, often partly because he simply wanted people to know that he was on the right side. His support for many of the causes he favored was essentially verbal and symbolic. He talked about reform, but as with the SCHW, very little was actually done to implement reform measures. Graham's decisions to stay in these organizations and his lack of judgment on certain issues not only concerned his adversaries, but created a continuing problem for his friends as well.

Graham shifted his public service from regional to national organizations during World War II, when he accepted an appointment to the National War Labor Board. Graham wrote the opinions in several significant cases, including the Southport Petroleum case. In a decision called by Oregon's liberal senator Wayne Morse "one of the great decisions in the annals of American law," the board ruled that all workers on government projects, regardless of color, were to receive the same rate of pay—in other words, equal pay for equal work.[43] The classifications "colored laborer" and "white laborer" were to be abolished. In his summary of the decision, Graham praised Negroes as loyal citizens who had made great progress. The United States, he continued, needed the Negro in order to win the war, and if the democracies were to be victorious over totalitarian powers, then the Negro must be given the freedom to struggle for equality of opportunity.[44]

In December, 1946, President Harry Truman appointed Graham as one of two white southerners on a Committee on Civil Rights that was to study the condition of the Negro in America and recommend social policies. The commission included prominent citizens from the fields of law, education, industry, and labor.

43. Ashby, *Frank Porter Graham*, 187.
44. Frank Graham, "Southport Petroleum Company," June 5, 1943, *National War Labor Board Reports* (n.d.), VIII, 2898.

The commission rendered its report, "To Secure These Rights," on October 29, 1947. This powerful document was a political bombshell. It thrust the civil rights question to the forefront of American politics and served as a point of departure for the modern era of race relations in the United States. "To Secure These Rights" denounced all private and government support of segregation and proposed the elimination of segregation based on color, creed, or national origin. The report presented thirty-five recommendations for action, including the use of federal laws to end segregation in the armed services, housing, public schools, public conveyances, and public accommodations. Also included were an antilynching law, an anti-poll-tax law, the protection of the right of all qualified citizens to vote, and the establishment of a permanent Fair Employment Practices Commission (FEPC) with the power to penalize employers who discriminated in hiring. The report also advocated a permanent Commission on Civil Rights to search out violations of the civil rights of minorities. The authors urged the use of coercion, where necessary, to enforce its recommendations, and asked that federal funds be denied to public or private agencies practicing racial discrimination.[45]

Truman greeted the report as a charter for human freedom, and black spokesmen hailed it as the beginning stage on the long road to equality. The South, however, was outraged at the threat to its traditional way of life. Some irate southerners offered Truman physical violence, and the Democratic party in the South threatened to bolt the national party if the recommendations were carried out.

Frank Graham agreed with the basic recommendations for eliminating segregation in America and accepted most of the specific proposals for action. He endorsed the elimination of segregation in interstate travel and the armed forces, the creation of greater economic opportunity for blacks, an end to the poll tax, the

45. Robert J. Donovan, *Conflict and Crisis: The Presidency of Harry S. Truman, 1945–1948* (New York, 1977), 332; U.S. President's Committee on Civil Rights, *To Secure These Rights: Report of the President's Committee on Civil Rights* (1947), 151–78.

establishment of a Civil Rights Commission, and the admission of qualified blacks into white graduate schools when there were no comparable schools for blacks. But he vigorously disagreed with the report's recommendations regarding enforcement. Graham especially opposed the use of federal monetary sanctions against states that maintained segregation. He knew that federal sanctions would merely strengthen the southern will to resist the use of such arbitrary power. "In the long run, religion and education are to work this difficult, delicate matter out, not federal power and financial sanction." Graham felt so strongly about his position that he authored a dissenting minority statement, included in the body of the report, which reaffirmed his belief that his way of freedom and equality achieved by education and religion would be "a more solid basis for a genuine and lasting acceptance by the people of the states."[46]

Graham saw his views on race as typically southern, and thought that if people understood his beliefs, they would agree with him. At first glance, his views seem similar to the states' rights position of most southern conservatives. On closer examination, however, it is clear that Graham favored eventual integration of the races, whereas the states' righters used their arguments to prohibit or delay integration. Graham, of course, was no wild-eyed radical demanding an immediate end to segregation, and he did oppose federal coercion in racial matters, but his views on race were unacceptable to many North Carolinians. A large number of people were opposed to racial integration at any time whatsoever. The die-hard segregationists admired Graham as a good Christian but viewed him as a liberal idealist whose ideas threatened the status quo.

Frank Graham finally had to face the reality of racial attitudes in the South in March, 1949, when he left the university for the bruising arena of politics. On March 22, 1949, Governor Kerr

46. Frank P. Graham to Gerald W. Johnson, August 6, 1948, in Graham Papers; President's Committee on Civil Rights, *To Secure These Rights*, 166–67.

Scott, in a move that stunned political observers all over the state, appointed Graham to the United State Senate to fill the unexpired term of the recently deceased J. Melville Broughton. Reluctant to enter politics, Graham turned down the appointment three times before he finally was persuaded that duty required his acceptance.[47]

The Negro press in North Carolina hailed Graham's appointment and believed him to be a man of destiny who would hasten the death of the old order in the South. Yet friends and critics alike recognized that Graham, owing to his liberal stance on issues, would have a difficult time if he ran for election in 1950. The Montgomery (Alabama) *Journal* thought that Graham's membership on Truman's civil rights committee would insure that he would be badly defeated in a bid for election in 1950. One old friend advised Graham to compromise on his civil rights views immediately: should he vigorously back an early end to segregation or a federally mandated FEPC he would imperil his political future.[48]

Graham's political advisers, including Jonathan Daniels, editor of the Raleigh *News and Observer,* understood early that the most critical issue facing Graham was Truman's civil rights program. Graham's opponents hoped to embarrass him by highlighting his past racial views. Daniels wrote Eleanor Roosevelt that the only possible way that the popular and respected Graham could be defeated in an election would be in "a horrible nigger-Communist campaign." Daniels, like Graham and other southern liberals, believed that the citizens of the state were too intelligent to allow such a campaign to succeed.[49]

47. New York *Times,* March 23, 1949; Raleigh *News and Observer,* March 23, 1949; Author's interview with Frank P. Graham, July 1, 1969, Chapel Hill, N.C.

48. *Carolina Times* (Durham, N.C.), March 19, April 2, 1949; Montgomery (Ala.) *Journal,* March 28, 1949; Nere E. Day to Frank P. Graham, March 27, 1949, in Graham Papers.

49. Jonathan Daniels to Eleanor Roosevelt, December 20, 1949, in Jonathan Daniels Papers, in Southern Historical Collection.

North Carolina, as Daniels indicated, had indeed acquired a national reputation as a progressive southern state. V. O. Key, Jr., writing in 1949, observed that North Carolina was known for progressive action and outlook in education, race relations, and industrial development. The prevailing mood in the state, according to Key, was energetic and ambitious, and its citizens were determined and confident—making North Carolina the most moderate and "presentable" state in the South. The state had developed a political leadership described by Key as a "Progressive Plutocracy"—an elite group of business leaders whose control had provided numerous benefits to its citizens, namely, very few scandals in government, no demagogues, fairer treatment of blacks (although segregation still existed), a balanced and virile economy, and a state university system famed for academic freedom and tolerance. Despite his glowing remarks, Key recognized that the comfortable picture of progress, tolerance, and enlightenment was clouded by the rough and difficult struggles to come—especially the bitter conflicts over the Negro question and the rights of organized labor. North Carolinians knew from their long history, concluded Key, that "every liberation from ancient taboo is bought by shrewdness and hard work and endless patience."[50]

Indeed, in their *Transformation of Southern Politics* Jack Bass and Walter DeVries claimed that the progressive image that North Carolina had acquired in the 1940s had evolved into the "Progressive myth" by 1950. When Key wrote about the state, the race issue had been suppressed for nearly fifty years by politicians of distinction who agreed to an unspoken code that barred the arousal of race antagonisms. Blacks had been allowed marginal participation in politics and had been given a degree of paternalistic protection, but once political appeals on race were unleashed in the 1950 Senate race, the momentum for progressive reform in North Carolina slowed significantly.[51]

50. Key, *Southern Politics*, 205–206.
51. Jack Bass and Walter DeVries, *The Transformation of Southern Politics* (New York, 1976), 219.

The race issue exploded in 1950 partly because North Carolina blacks had been achieving a growing voice in both state and national politics owing to the reforms of the New Deal and the Fair Deal, the egalitarian propaganda of World War II, and a series of federal court decisions that augured ill for the long-term survival of the separate but equal concept. Blacks were obviously moving away from paternalistic control by whites, but it took whites in the South a long time before they recognized the significance of the black emergence. When southern whites finally realized that blacks were about to get out of "their proper place" in society, conservative whites launched a desperate, back-against-the-wall resistance.

The mass political and social protests by whites in the 1950s, although focusing on the race issue, resulted from circumstances other than race. Southerners were also expressing their fears and resentment over being rapidly propelled into an urbanized and industrialized age they did not understand. Southern whites feared the abolition of the poll tax, an FEPC, the destruction of the white primary, and the desegregation of their graduate schools because all of these changes would lead to the destruction of the southern way of life. These tensions and fears produced political uncertainty, which in turn reinforced the rapidly developing southern conservatism and stimulated a longing for traditional values and symbols. The immediate threat of integration stirred up memories of earlier resistance to forced changes, and it heightened feelings of racial prejudice that had been relatively dormant over the years. More than any other issue, the possibility of mixing the races caused southerners to rally in massive numbers to the faded values of the Old South.[52]

Senator Frank Graham, in his bid for the full six-year Senate term, expected the good and intelligent people of his state to accept his views on race and return him to his post in Washington. Gra-

52. Lewis M. Killian, *White Southerners* (New York, 1970), 7; Dewey Grantham, Jr., "The South and the Politics of Sectionalism: The Sectional Theme Since Reconstruction," in *The South and the Sectional Image*, ed. Grantham (New York, 1967), 49.

ham, however, soon found himself confronted with a major political problem. Truman's proposal for a permanent FEPC with coercive powers was before the Senate for consideration. Graham restated his oft-repeated position: he favored the principle of fair employment through voluntary cooperation but opposed a compulsory FEPC, which he believed would do more harm than good because it would arouse strong reactions from whites and set back racial progress.[53] Even so, Graham refused to join a southern filibuster against the FEPC, and this caused some political repercussions back in North Carolina. Aware of the fear of an FEPC and the racial unease among whites, a supporter warned the Graham forces about the type of opposition they could expect in 1950. "The low-class white mob, nigger-hating, Communist yelling wool hats" would follow the nod of the Ku Klux Klan and fight Graham tooth and nail.[54]

On the other hand, a Winston-Salem newspaper supported Graham's decision not to filibuster against the FEPC; the editor thought that Graham would now be a far more effective spokesman for the South on race relations, in that the North would be more receptive to the idea of achieving reasonable civil rights legislation through a gradual effort.[55]

Graham was not seriously worried about the possibility of a direct confrontation over the race issue until late February, 1950. On February 24, 1950, Willis Smith, a prominent, conservative Raleigh attorney, announced as a candidate for the Senate seat occupied by Graham. Smith, financed heavily by large corporations in the state, immediately went on the offensive. Smith charged, unfairly, that Graham favored an FEPC as he was a member of the Civil Rights Committee that had approved an FEPC in its final report. Graham claimed, continued Smith, that he had signed a minority plank that opposed federal sanctions, but readers of the fi-

53. Greensboro (N.C.) *Daily News,* January 4, 1950.
54. John B. Palmer to Gladys Tillett Coddington, February 6, 1950, in Gladys Tillett Papers, Southern Historical Collection.
55. *Twin City Sentinel* (Winston-Salem, N.C.), January 5, 1950.

nal document would search in vain for any minority report. With this charge, Smith had implied that Graham had once been for an FEPC but had changed his position in order to get elected. This sort of frontal attack put Graham on the defensive from the beginning and prompted the Raleigh *News and Observer* to come to his aid. The *News and Observer* explained that Graham's opposition to the FEPC was as clear as it could be and that Smith's only purpose in bringing up the question was "to stir up the furies of racial prejudice as a means of getting votes."[56] Graham himself chose not to respond to the charges since he had stated his position on race and the FEPC so often that he assumed the voters understood his position.

Instead of attacking his opponent or answering Smith's charges, Graham preferred to speak about world peace and the future of America. Gentle and soft-spoken, he simply presented his views to the public; if the listener, after hearing his policies, decided not to vote for him, so be it. Graham, in his innocence and pristine morality, was not primarily motivated by the possibility of victory, but was propelled by an ethical imperative to do the right thing and abide by his Christian upbringing. This was a phenomenon rarely seen in North Carolina politics—or politics anywhere, for that matter. Drew Pearson, the columnist, said that Graham was simply too nice and too honest to be elected in the cutthroat vote-getting game.[57]

Jeff Johnson, Graham's campaign manager and a seasoned politician, knew that he had to respond quickly to the assault on Graham even if the candidate himself did not take the charges seriously. Johnson accused Smith of a vicious smear campaign based on innuendo and the repetition of catch phrases designed to appeal to ignorance and prejudice. Johnson also took out a series of newspaper ads praising Graham's service to his state and

56. Raleigh *News and Observer*, February 25, 1950; Asheville (N.C.) *Citizen*, March 23, 1950; Raleigh *News and Observer*, March 24, 1950.

57. Charlotte *News*, May 1, 2, 1950; Author's interview with R. Mayne Albright, November 30, 1984.

country while denouncing the scandal mongers and bigots who besmirched Graham's good name. The "loose-lipped character assassins" were going up and down the state distributing hate literature and whispering foul words. These "messengers of deceit" would not be able to fool the citizens of North Carolina, who knew from many years of experience about the great character and stature of Frank Graham.[58]

Near the end of the first primary, Willis Smith saw that the Communist-Socialist attack on Graham was not working as well as he had hoped, so he shifted his emphasis to the most controversial and emotional issue of the campaign—race. Smith stepped up his charges that Graham was for an FEPC and that his position on race was inconsistent with that of the North Carolina electorate. These tactics quickly began to bear fruit: Graham campaigners found that voters were beginning to turn against Graham in droves. As one man said, "I ain't voting for no Red and no Nigger Lover."[59]

Graham's political future now depended on how well he could parry the thrusts from Smith and how effectively he could present his southern progressivism to the Tar Heel voters. He was fighting not only for his political life, but also, "in effect, for the emergence of the South from its long dark era of representation by Rankins and Byrds."[60] The Graham forces struck back against the racial charges with an attack of their own. A newspaper ad proclaimed that the Smith backers "MUST NOT CRUCIFY NORTH CAROLINA and its half century of progress in economics and racial amity on the cross of bigotry, hate, and greed." Hiden Ramsey, another Graham stalwart, said that Smith had run an entirely negative campaign, the sole appeal of which was to the fears of the voters. Graham was a better choice than Smith because he was a kindly, compassionate man who would wittingly do no man the slightest

58. Charlotte *Observer*, April 28, 1950; *The Pilot* (Southern Pines, N.C.), April 28, 1950; Newspaper ads and pamphlets, n.d., in Gladys Tillet Papers.

59. Charlotte *Observer*, April 8, 1950; Mary Coker Joslin, "Precinct Politics in North Carolina: The Red and the Black" (Pamphlet in possession of the author).

60. Tom Schlesinger, "Frank Graham's Primary Election," *Nation*, April 22, 1950, p. 368; Robert Bendinger, "Maytime Politics," *ibid.*, April 29, 1950, pp. 389–90.

injustice. Governor Scott, who had campaigned heavily for his nominee, said that the United States Senate needed a man who would concern himself with the hopes and aspirations of all the people rather than just the corporate interests.[61]

A black newspaper, the *Carolinian,* came to Graham's assistance with a plea to vote for him because his view of progressive gradualism in segregation was better than the traditional southern position of maintaining the status quo. Graham's plan fell short of the goal of equality for blacks and was much too slow, but Graham was the best that blacks could hope for. At least he could be counted on to support human rights and oppose unconstitutional discrimination.[62]

The fight over the FEPC bill in the United States Senate came up immediately prior to the first primary, but Graham was ill with pneumonia and did not take part in the debate. If he had joined the southern filibuster against the passage of the FEPC bill—if he had even indicated that he would have voted against any attempt to cut off the southern filibuster—he would almost certainly have won the election. Senator Clyde Hoey told Graham that if he had indicated that he would have voted against cloture (cutting off debate), it would have been worth 50,000 votes. Since Graham had not been present for the debate on the bill, however, he felt that he could not make a proper decision; therefore, he refused to say how he would have voted on FEPC or on cloture.[63] Eventually, long after he had lost the election, Graham voted against the cloture motion to cut off debate on FEPC. He had refused to make the same vote in May, 1950, even though it would have insured his election, simply because he felt such a vote would have smacked of political expediency and a desperate attempt to get votes.[64]

61. Charlotte *Observer,* May 22, 1950; Radio address by D. Hiden Ramsey, May 16, 1950, Typescript in D. Hiden Ramsey Papers, Southern Historical Collection; Greensboro (N.C.) *Daily News,* May 23, 1950.

62. *Carolinian* (Raleigh, N.C.), May 13, 20, 1950.

63. Paul H. Douglas, *In the Fullness of Time* (New York, 1972), 240–41.

64. Author's interview with Frank P. Graham, July 1, 1969; Author's interview with R. Mayne Albright, November 30, 1984.

In the final week of the first primary, the racial invective became ugly and vicious. Smith supporters claimed that Graham was trying to tear down the traditions of the South by mixing the races in schools and factories. Pictures of the black members of South Carolina's Reconstruction state legislature of 1868 were distributed throughout the state with the caption, "Will history repeat itself?"[65]

Other anonymous handbills had pictures of black G.I.'s dancing with white women in World War II England; the implication was that Graham favored such activities for North Carolina.[66] There were also bogus postcards sent to white voters all over the state bearing the signature of Walter Wite [*sic*], secretary of the National Society [*sic*] for the Advancement of Colored People, soliciting votes for Frank Graham. These unauthorized and inflammatory cards were designed to make it appear that Walter White and the NAACP were ardently campaigning for their friend Frank Graham.[67]

The most effective flyer bore the picture of a young black man named Leroy Jones. The handbill announced, incorrectly, that Senator Graham had "appointed a nigger to West Point." This charge created a sensation throughout the state and unquestionably cost Graham votes in the black belt of eastern North Carolina, where the flyers were prominently displayed within view of many polling places on election day.[68]

The actual circumstances of the Jones case point up the chicanery and deviousness of the anti-Graham forces. North Carolina had previously appointed several young men to the service acade-

65. Charlotte *Observer*, May 23, 1950; Laurinburg (N.C.) *Exchange*, n.d., clipping in papers of Donald McCoy, Fayetteville, N.C.

66. Raleigh *News and Observer*, May 24, 1950; *Newsweek*, May 29, 1950, p. 16.

67. Walter Wite [*sic*] to Joe W. Grier, May 22, 1950, in Dan Powell Papers, Southern Historical Collection.

68. Harry Golden, *The Right Time: The Autobiography of Harry Golden* (New York, 1969), 271; C. C. Burns to Jeff Johnson, May 22, 1950, in Jeff Johnson Papers, Manuscript Division, Duke University, Durham, N.C.

mies who had done poorly academically. In order to provide a better-quality appointee and give all the young men in the state an equal opportunity for admission, Graham instituted an open, competitive, state-wide examination. Leroy Jones placed fifth in this examination, and Graham appropriately designated him the second alternate to West Point. Since the first choice, William Hauser of Fayetteville, attended West Point instead of Jones, Graham had not actually appointed a black to West Point. Nonetheless, the Gastonia *Gazette* praised Graham for his courage in picking Jones, the first southern Negro ever named as a principal or alternate to West Point.[69]

Graham stated that there was such an uproar over making Jones a second alternate that "you would have thought that I had made him commandant." Graham congratulated Jones on the excellent grade he had achieved and released the names of all appointees to the press. Graham knew the release of Jones's name would be politically inexpedient, but decided to do so to call attention to the fact that a black student educated in the schools of Kinston could do as well as whites on a competitive exam.[70]

The Jones issue became a volatile one only in the context of the emotional racial oratory of the first primary—and only because Smith backers were desperate to head off an apparent victory by Graham. The tactics of the Smith campaign paid off as Graham was denied a clear-cut majority in the first primary. Graham received 48.9 percent of the vote and had a margin of 53,373 votes over Willis Smith, but failed by 11,921 votes to win the primary outright.[71]

The significance of the first primary was not that Graham failed to win a majority of the votes cast, but that he came so close.

69. Greensboro (N.C.) *Daily News*, September 21, 1949; Gastonia (N.C.) *Gazette*, n.d., clipping in Graham Papers.

70. Author's interview with Frank P. Graham, July 1, 1969; John D. McConnell to Leroy Jones, September 20, 1949, in Graham Papers; Author's interview with William L. Hauser, October 23, 1989.

71. Charlotte *Observer*, May 28, 1950; *North Carolina Manual, 1951* (Raleigh, 1951), 237–38.

The Graham supporters were disappointed that a second primary was necessary, but were elated at Graham's large plurality. Immediately after the vote Smith, convinced that his chances for success in the second primary were remote, decided not to call for a run-off.

At this critical point, the United States Supreme Court handed down three highly significant decisions, striking down segregation as practiced by two southern universities and as practiced on interstate railroad cars. In the most important of the cases, *Sweatt* v. *Painter,* the Court ruled that the University of Texas had to admit Heman Sweatt to its all-white law school since the black law school in Texas was not equal to the white law school.[72] The Supreme Court decisions did not actually overturn *Plessy* v. *Ferguson* and the separate but equal concept, but they represented a definite threat to the survival of segregation. The adverse reaction in North Carolina was loud and angry, but Senator Graham took a more moderate tack. He reiterated his unalterable opposition to the federal government's forcing integration on the states and praised the North Carolina way of "mutual understanding, respect, and cooperation between the races." Graham said the decisions would have no effect on North Carolina because the state, in "good faith," was maintaining equal educational facilities for blacks.[73]

The Supreme Court decisions gave Willis Smith the issue—integration of the schools—and the impetus he needed to call for a second primary. Although Smith weighed other factors, it is more than coincidence that the Court's decisions were handed down on June 5 and he asked for a run-off on June 7.[74]

In the second primary, Smith's supporters immediately revived the Leroy Jones issue and forced Graham to stump the state explaining his earlier action. Graham, by now somewhat desperate

72. Asheville (N.C.) *Citizen,* June 6, 1950; Richard Kluger, *Simple Justice: The History of* Brown v. Board of Education *and Black America's Struggle for Equality* (New York, 1976), 281–82.

73. Greensboro (N.C.) *Daily News,* June 7, 1950.

74. Raleigh *News and Observer,* June 8, 1950.

206

to win the second primary, pointed out that Jones had not attended West Point. To prove his point, Graham presented, in person, William Hauser, the young man who did get the appointment. Graham's tactics failed. For one thing, his attempt to demonstrate to the voters that a Negro did not attend West Point made it appear that he was ashamed of his role in the matter. For another, some members of Graham's audiences, already conditioned by race hatred and voluminous racial literature, simply refused to believe him. One man asked: "Why didn't he bring the nigger he appointed? Who is he trying to fool, showing us that white boy?" Another observer, after seeing Hauser, remarked, "My ain't he light?"[75]

Graham, who had lived a life of honesty and integrity, was surprised by his failure to convince his fellow Tar Heels that he was telling the truth. Unfortunately for him, his troubles were just beginning. His opponents spread rumors that if Graham were elected, mixing of the races in public schools and interracial marriages were just around the corner.[76] Smith, whose theme song was "Dixie," assailed the bloc voting for Graham by Negroes in the first primary. Since Graham received an overwhelming majority of the black votes (newspaper ads listed the returns from such predominantly black precincts as Hillside in Durham, which voted 1,514 for Graham and 7 for Smith), Smith said there must have been a deal between Graham and the Negro voters, and eventually the Negroes would control the Democratic party. Since the Negroes had voted for Graham in such large numbers, continued Smith, they were the racists and were the ones who had raised the race issue. The bloc-voting ads were accompanied by other misleading advertisements claiming that the FEPC Graham favored would force whites to hire Negroes, and then whites would have to work next to Negroes and share toilet facilities. As for handbills, the most incendiary was one entitled "White People Wake Up," distributed

75. Samuel Lubell, *The Future of American Politics* (New York, 1951), 105; Author's interview with William L. Hauser, October 23, 1989.

76. Nathan M. Johnson to Mattie Gaines, June 21, 1950, in Jeff Johnson Papers.

two days prior to the second primary vote. The flyer warned that if North Carolinians wanted a mixing of the races in hotels, schools, hospitals, restaurants, etc., they should vote for Graham.[77]

As the emotional level of the contest peaked, voter reaction to the racial attacks became hostile—in some cases, violent. Mill-workers refused to shake hands with Graham and on occasion spat on him. Graham's followers were called "nigger lovers," were threatened with harm, and in many cases were so intimidated that they were afraid to go to the polls on election day.[78]

The racial attacks worked. On election day, Smith defeated Graham by 280,798 votes to 262,126, turning a deficit of 53,000 votes in the first primary into a majority in the run-off.[79]

According to most observers, Graham was defeated mainly by the most bitter racial invective seen in North Carolina in fifty years. One journalist wrote that Graham had lost because of a hate campaign that could not be met by turning the other cheek and because Smith had succeeded in making Graham a personal devil on the race issue.[80] One issue seemed to dominate: which candidate would defend southern traditions more vigorously?

Jeff Johnson saw his candidate's defeat as the result of a tidal wave of race hatred stirred by false charges and distortions of the grossest sort. The New York *Herald Tribune* noted that the unleashing of antiblack prejudice in North Carolina made it clear how difficult it would be to free southern politics from the fearful nightmare of the race issue. Graham represented a broad, gradual, humane liberalism, but when the forces of racial hatred were loosed, his prestige and a devoted personal following were not enough.[81]

77. Raleigh *News and Observer*, June 22, 1950; Asheville (N.C.) *Citizen*, June 21, 1950; "White People Wake Up" (Flyer, n.d., in Dan Powell Papers).

78. Lubell, *Future of American Politics*, 102–104.

79. Charlotte *Observer*, June 25, 1950; *North Carolina Manual*, 1951, pp. 237–38.

80. Washington *Evening Star*, June 29, 1950.

81. Jeff Johnson to Sam Lubell, July 18, 1950, in Jeff Johnson Papers; New York *Herald Tribune*, June 27, 1950.

As long as the prospect of integration was abstract, southerners could accept Graham's liberalism, but when the Supreme Court decisions made integration seem imminent, North Carolinians panicked and rejected him. Numan Bartley and Hugh Graham, in *Southern Politics and the Second Reconstruction*, explained the result as owing also to the fact that rural and lower-class whites, who had provided much of the impetus for New Deal reform politics, now felt threatened by black advancement and wanted to reestablish the solidarity of southern customs on race.[82] The Senate race had become a symbol, a metaphor for racial change.

Letters of condolence poured into Graham's office from all over the country. A great majority of the writers praised Graham as a man of dignity and a great humanitarian. The labor leader Walter Reuther said that he had been proud to be associated with Graham in the fight for basic human and democratic values. Graham's speeches, wrote Reuther, stood as a monument to tolerance, understanding, and human decency. Governor Scott wrote to the defeated candidate that he had no regrets about appointing him. Scott knew that in time the public would realize the mistake that had been made and history would record that a "distinct gesture was made for representation in behalf of the masses in North Carolina."[83]

In later years, Graham was asked repeatedly if he was bitter about the attacks and smears that marred the 1950 campaign. He was not, he insisted. He never denounced those who attacked him. He understood that the race issue was incendiary—once ignited, it would rage. People feared racial change as they feared little else and on that subject were easily misled. Were he required to exploit the race issue in order to win Senate election, he would rather lose. Hence, in the campaign he had merely tried to do the right thing—

82. Numan V. Bartley and Hugh D. Graham, *Southern Politics and the Second Reconstruction* (Baltimore, 1975), 53.

83. Walter P. Reuther to Frank P. Graham, December 19, 1950, W. Kerr Scott to Graham, December 8, 1950, both in Graham Papers.

to prepare for the day when blacks would have a fairer deal in America—and for that he had no apologies.[84]

Despite his protestations, there can be little doubt that Graham's rejection by the voters of his native state marked the deepest disappointment of his life. Loved and respected as few people ever are, Graham for the first time had been rebuked and scorned by the very people—textile workers, farmers, and small businesspeople—for whom he had labored so diligently. He expressed no public bitterness at his treatment by the state's voters, but the experience menaced his most cherished assumptions. He had to be deeply distressed that he had failed to articulate his position in a way that convinced people of the basic goodness and rightness of his cause. His defeat perhaps suggested to him that he was not the saint that others had made him out to be. Although he believed himself to be nonjudgmental, his postelection statement that he would never use race to get elected was quintessentially judgmental.[85] He did judge others who did not share his faith and beliefs, and he was inwardly angry that they would not accept his guidance on these issues. Secure in his own sense of rightness, he resented the voters' repudiation of that rightness. Objectively analyzed, Graham had not been a radical on race. He had, in fact, been true to his past and his southern heritage in his advocacy of gradualism. The final tragedy for Graham was his realization that his fellow southerners perceived him as a threat to their way of life—and that he could not persuade them otherwise.

In the moment of defeat in 1950, a small-town newspaper in eastern North Carolina commented that Graham was a man of high ideals who was just too far ahead of his time; it predicted that despite the electoral setback, all that Graham had stood for would come to fruition within twenty years.[86] In time, many others would

84. Interview with Frank Graham by Legette Blythe, June 9, 1970, in Special Collections, University of North Carolina–Charlotte; Author's interview with Frank P. Graham, July 1, 1969.

85. Raleigh *News and Observer*, February 17, 1972.

86. Washington (N.C.) *Daily News*, June 26, 1950.

concur. Despite Graham's failure in the political arena, former governor Terry Sanford understood his importance for the region and the nation, praising Graham for his influence in bringing the South into the mainstream of the nation, for his sensitivity toward the disadvantaged, and for his battles for justice and humanity.[87] A gentleman and a scholar, Frank Potter Graham forged a path into the future. In time, his people would follow.

87. Author's interview with Terry Sanford, December 3, 1984.

From Shotguns to Umbrellas

The Civil Rights Movement in
Lowndes County, Alabama

Charles W. Eagles

I n six short years of intense and courageous struggle, the civil rights movement produced a revolution in Lowndes County, Alabama. For example, though no black could vote in the county at the start of 1965, in 1970 Lowndes blacks elected a black sheriff. To achieve such dramatic results, the movement had to overcome among blacks a pervasive and intimidating fear of whites that had resulted from "bloody" Lowndes's long history of oppressive violence.[1] Whites routinely had employed violence to intimidate blacks, enforce segregation, and insure white supremacy. In fact, whites seeking to forestall racial change in 1965 killed two white civil rights workers in the county. White resistance, however, proved unsuccessful in the face of organized local blacks, assistance from outside activists, and intervention by the federal government. The changes produced by the civil rights movement, though

1. For an example of the term *bloody Lowndes*, see Washington *Post*, May 9, 1965. Innumerable people used the term in my interviews with them. For a black man's first-person account of violence in Lowndes County in the 1920s and 1930s and of race relations generally in the Alabama Black Belt, see Charles Denby, *Indignant Heart: A Black Worker's Journal* (Boston, 1978), 1–86.

revolutionary, were also limited. Among other things, severe economic problems continued to plague the county. Though Lowndes had distinctive characteristics—its overwhelming black majority, its extreme poverty and isolation, and its tradition of violence—its experience in the 1960s demonstrated that southerners could rapidly overcome some of their racial fears and adjust to sweeping changes in race relations.

Fear and oppression began in the antebellum era, when cotton dominated the Black Belt county. Though outnumbered more than two to one by black slaves, Lowndes whites held all the economic, political, and social power; backed by the state's slave code, they easily dominated and exploited their slaves.[2] When the slave system ended with the Civil War, the white minority used tenancy, peonage, segregation, disfranchisement, and violence to continue the repression of blacks and to retain white supremacy.

The post–Civil War system of tenancy bound the landless freedmen to the whites' land and capital, and black tenants found their new lot of debt and drudgery little better than slavery. An even harsher form of oppression soon snared many tenants: debt peonage. To live through the growing season, tenants borrowed money at high interest rates from creditors; to repay the loans, they increasingly turned to the cash crop of cotton. A poor crop meant more borrowing and more debts. Tenants, who could not leave until they repaid all their debts, often found themselves caught under crushing debts. A 1903 report by a United States district attorney in Alabama argued that the center of the South's peonage system was Lowndes County: "This county, it is claimed, is just honeycombed with slavery."[3]

2. J. S. Gibson, "The Alabama Black Belt: Its Geographic Status," *Economic Geography,* XVII (January, 1941), 1–23; James M. Richardson, ed., *Alabama Encyclopedia* (Northport, Ala., 1965), 285; Charles S. Davis, *The Cotton Kingdom in Alabama* (Montgomery, 1939), 7, 11–12; James Benson Sellers, *Slavery in Alabama* (University, Ala., 1950), 332–60; *Eighth Census, 1860: Population,* 8; *Eighth Census, 1860: Agriculture,* 3.

3. On tenancy, see Roger L. Ransom and Richard Sutch, *One Kind of Freedom: The Economic Consequences of Emancipation* (Cambridge, Mass., 1977). Although Ran-

Compounding the oppression of peonage was racial segregation, which whether enforced by law or backed only by customs, dominated Lowndes after the Civil War. In such a rural area, racial segregation resulted more from the daily habits and routines of the people than from legislation, but it existed nonetheless. Disfranchisement supplemented peonage and segregation. Blacks in Lowndes County voted for years after the end of Reconstruction, but in 1903 a new state constitution effectively stripped them of the vote and of any possible political power; Lowndes County, which had had 5,500 black voters in 1900, had only 44 after the first registration period under the new laws.[4]

Perhaps the most effective means to instill fear in blacks was overt violence, which was a routine part of life in Lowndes. Violence included intraracial clashes as well as white violence against blacks. Perhaps in frustration at their lack of autonomy, blacks frequently fought other blacks. On the other hand, whites—accustomed to using violence to deal with troublesome blacks—often resorted to similar methods to solve disagreements with fellow whites. Even in the post–World War II era, whites frequently took the law into their own hands. In one well-known incident, a white man in a Hayneville barbershop took exception to another white man's profanity in the presence of his young daughter. The offended party announced that he intended to settle the matter after he went home to get his gun. Shortly thereafter, the two men con-

som and Sutch's findings may be applied to most regions of the South, their work is particularly appropriate for Lowndes County because they included it in their sample of representative counties of the cotton South (see p. 291). On peonage, see Pete Daniel, *The Shadow of Slavery: Peonage in the South, 1901–1969* (Urbana, Ill., 1973), esp. 19–21, 59–60.

4. No work has been done specifically on segregation in Lowndes or in Alabama, but see generally C. Vann Woodward, *The Strange Career of Jim Crow* (3d rev. ed.; New York, 1984). On voting and disfranchisement, see Loren Schweninger, *James T. Rapier and Reconstruction* (Chicago, 1978) and Malcolm Cook McMillan, *Constitutional Development in Alabama, 1789–1901: A Study in Politics, the Negro, and Sectionalism* (Chapel Hill, 1955).

fronted each other on a downtown street and engaged in an old-fashioned shoot-out. Both died.[5]

White violence against blacks, however, played the important role in Lowndes race relations. Outnumbered nearly eight to one by blacks by 1930, whites believed violence was essential to the maintenance of their supremacy. Blacks faced physical retaliation if they so much as irritated or annoyed whites, sometimes merely by failing to be sufficiently obsequious and subservient. According to one native of the county, right after World War I a local white planter killed a Negro soldier just because the white man "couldn't stand the sight of a Negro in uniform and shot him." Later, in the 1930s, a black woman from Lowndesboro admitted that the county "had a terrible reputation" for violence. "You can't mess around in Lowndes," she observed. "Better stand back."[6] Blacks in Lowndes learned early to "stand back" and avoid confrontations or even misunderstandings with whites. Nevertheless, whites sometimes turned to the ultimate form of violence—lynching.

Though Lowndes whites killed untold blacks in the obscurity of the rural county's fields, forests, and swamps, three lynchings received publicity in the first decades of the twentieth century. One week before Christmas in 1914, a white mob lynched a black man near Fort Deposit after an alleged attempted attack on a white girl. In broad daylight, an unmasked mob hanged the man from a telegraph pole and then "riddled the body with bullets." After a short investigation the very day of the lynching, a coroner's jury reported that the Negro had died at the hands of a "party or parties

---

5. Author's interviews with Tom L. Coleman, June 6, 1984, July 25, 1986, September 16, 1989, and Virginia Varner and John Robert Varner, September 15, 1989.

6. Jonathan Worth Daniels, Notes on trip through Alabama in mid-1930s, in Jonathan Daniels Papers, Southern Historical Collection, University of North Carolina, Chapel Hill; Marie Reese, "A Near Miracle" (Interview with Bettie D. McCall, January 1, 1939, in papers of Works Progress Administration Federal Writers' Project of Alabama, Alabama Department of Archives and History, Montgomery); Denby, *Indignant Heart,* 19. Numerous Lowndes natives referred to the violent ways of Robert S. Dickson, the planter mentioned by Daniels.

unknown."[7] In 1917 two Negroes died at the hands of another white mob, ostensibly for threatening a white man, who happened to be the son of the Letohatchie justice of the peace. News stories reported that "the lynching is shrouded in mystery. Where the mob came from is not known."[8] Newspapers protested the outrage, but no white was ever punished for the murders. In a third example, in 1931, no arrests were made for the lynching of a sixteen-year-old black boy for allegedly accosting an eleven-year-old white girl. After his investigation the sheriff claimed to have no idea who had killed the boy.[9] Other, unpublicized examples of white mob violence in Lowndes County reinforced in the minds of Lowndes blacks the reality of the unrestrained power exercised over them by the white minority.

In the first half of the twentieth century, the county's severe and continuous economic decline exacerbated the fearful plight of its black population. Cotton production continued to lag behind antebellum levels and prices remained low. Though farmers tried to diversify, cotton was still the main crop. Lowndes farmers suffered in the 1910s and, like the larger South, entered an agricultural depression in the 1920s, only to join the rest of the nation in the Great Depression in the 1930s.[10] Hard times in agriculture contributed to a population decline: the white population dropped from 4,762 in 1900 to 3,214 in 1950, and the black population fell

7. Atlanta *Constitution*, December 19, 1914, January 7, 1915; New York *Times*, December 19, 1914; Montgomery *Advertiser*, December 31, 1914. Denby comments on two other, unreported lynchings of the period in *Indignant Heart*, 40–43.

8. For accounts of the lynchings, see Montgomery *Advertiser*, July 24, 25, 26, 1917; Montgomery *Journal*, July 26, 1917; Birmingham *Weekly Voice*, July 28, 1917; Mobile *Register*, July 26, 1917; and Birmingham *Age-Herald* quoted in Birmingham *Weekly Voice*, July 28, 1917.

9. Atlanta *Constitution*, August 31, 1931; New York *Times*, August 31, 1931.

10. *Twelfth Census, 1900: Agriculture*, Pt. 2, p. 430; *Thirteenth Census, 1910: Agriculture*, 50; Glen M. Sisk, "Alabama Black Belt: A Social History, 1875–1917" (Ph.D. dissertation, Duke University, 1951), 435–38, 455–75; Gilbert C. Fite, *Cotton Fields No More: Southern Agriculture, 1865–1980* (Lexington, Ky., 1984), 6–7, 48, 94–95.

from more than 30,000 at the turn of the century to fewer than 15,000 in 1950.[11]

During and after World War II, changes in Lowndes County farming continued, as did the shifts in the county's population. By 1964 cattle yielded 35 percent of the county's farm income, timber produced 20 percent, and both exceeded cotton's value to the economy. Between 1940 and 1960, the number of farms declined by two thirds and the average farm size exploded from 79 acres to more than 250 acres. Consolidation of agriculture and the shift to cattle and timber eliminated the need for many black tenants; economic opportunities in urban industry in the North and South lured many away.[12] Thousands of blacks, nevertheless, remained mired in poverty in Lowndes.

Adjacent to the more populous and more developed Selma and Montgomery, Lowndes County in 1960 remained isolated and backward. Of Lowndes's 3,414 households, 58 percent lacked any automobile, so even Selma and Montgomery were distant to them. Only one house in five in Lowndes had a telephone, and whites undoubtedly owned most of them. The county's weekly newspaper, the *Lowndes Signal*, with a circulation of about one thousand, carried only news pertaining to whites and ignored the lives of the county's huge black majority. Lowndes had no radio station, no local television station, and no free public library service.[13]

By modern standards the daily lives of most people in Lowndes County in 1960 remained backward. Seven out of ten

---

11. *Twelfth Census, 1900: Population*, Pt. 1, pp. 9, 529; *Seventeenth Census, 1950: Population*, Vol. VII, Pt. 2, p. 87.

12. Bureau of the Census, *Census of Agriculture, 1964*, Vol. I, Pt. 32, pp. 259, 275, 283, 291, 307, 321, 339, 345, 351, 373; *Sixteenth Census, 1940: Population*, 238; *Seventeenth Census, 1950: Population*, Vol. VII, Pt. 2, p. 87; *Eighteenth Census, 1960: Population*, Vol. I, Pt. 2, p. 193.

13. Bureau of the Census, *Census of Housing, 1960*, Vol. I, Pt. 2, p. 78; *Alabama Official and Statistical Register, 1963* (Montgomery, 1963), 497; Richardson, ed., *Alabama Encyclopedia*, 503, 924, 936–43.

homes did not have any kind of washing machine. A mere 2 percent had clothes dryers, only 8 percent had food freezers, and just 5 percent had air conditioning to moderate the hot summers of the Black Belt. Without piped water, more than half of all the occupied residences in Lowndes County lacked bathtubs or showers, flush toilets, and sewers or septic tanks.[14] The county had no hospital, nursing home, or ambulance service; it had just two doctors and two dentists, and three of the four practiced in Fort Deposit, at the county's southern edge. The county health department had an officer present only one day each week.[15]

Lowndes was without a doubt a poor county, but the poverty fell unevenly on its citizens. Four out of every five of Lowndes's black families in 1959 had incomes of less than $3,000, whereas less than 20 percent of the white families in the county and under 40 percent of all Alabamians had incomes that low. Conversely, only about 4 percent of black families had incomes above $5,000, whereas more than 40 percent of the white families did.[16]

In spite of the county's decline, the dominant whites were committed to maintaining their power, often at any cost. They followed, according to one observer, "a century-old Lowndes County tradition—unquestioned, unbending white supremacy." In 1960 whites controlled Lowndes County as thoroughly as they had in 1860. Not only did whites own most of the land, but they also ran the entire local government. Blacks had no political power because, as late as the beginning of 1965, not one of the nearly six thousand eligible blacks was registered to vote. Blacks had no influence on public officials or policies and could not serve on local juries. Even blacks who wanted to vote were afraid to try to register.[17]

A decade after the Supreme Court's *Brown* decision,

14. Bureau of the Census, *Census of Housing, 1960*, Vol. I, Pt. 2, pp. 83, 78.

15. *Hearing Before the United States Commission on Civil Rights, Montgomery, Alabama, April 27–May 2, 1968* (Washington, D.C., 1968), 255–65.

16. *Eighteenth Census, 1960: Population*, Vol. I, Pt. 2, pp. 140–42, 233–35.

17. *Alabama Official and Statistical Register, 1963*, pp. 468–69; New York *Times*, May 3, 1965; Washington *Post*, March 23, 1965; Chicago *Sun-Times*, March 3, 1965; *Wall*

Lowndes County whites continued to maintain strict racial segregation. Black and white students and teachers were completely segregated in the public schools, and the quality of the black schools fell far short of the white schools. Segregation, however, extended far beyond the classroom. As one man said early in 1965: "I was raised in Mississippi and always thought we were segregated there. But it's not like here—we got no integration—and what's more, we won't." Even after passage of the 1964 Civil Rights Act insuring equal access to public accommodations, blacks faced rigid segregation in Lowndes County. In 1965 the courthouse in Hayneville still had three rest rooms—White Women, White Men, and Colored. A receptive federal court in Montgomery would have supported any Lowndes black in a constitutional challenge to segregated facilities, but one local white explained to a visiting journalist the improbability of a lawsuit: "You don't get the point. He [a black complainant] would never make it to Montgomery."[18]

When the civil rights movement gained momentum in the late 1950s and early 1960s, Lowndes County had a wide reputation among Alabamians and civil rights workers alike as a bastion of white racial prejudice in which whites would readily resort to violence to protect their segregated way of life. It seemed to symbolize Black Belt resistance to racial change. According to one report, some local whites even expected "Congo-like violence," referring perhaps inaptly to the bloody civil war in what had been the Belgian Congo.[19] Lowndes whites did worry for their safety and security if blacks ever challenged white supremacy, for the whites knew that they would not yield to blacks without a fight.

Street Journal, January 20, 1965; Morton Rubin, *Plantation County* (Chapel Hill, 1951), 96–100.

18. *Southern Courier* (Montgomery, Ala.), February 19–20, 1966; Andrew Kopkind, "The Lair of the Black Panther," *New Republic*, August 13, 1966, p. 10; *Wall Street Journal*, January 20, 1965. The quotations come from Kopkind. See also author's interview with Hulda Coleman, June 20, 1984.

19. Washington *Post*, March 23, 1965; Chicago *Sun-Times*, March 3, 1965; New York *Times*, March 23, 1965.

In spite of white intransigence, a few brave blacks began in the late 1950s to confer quietly around the county about trying to pay their poll taxes and attempting to register to vote, but no organized action ever resulted from the meetings. In late 1964 another group met secretly and discussed going to Hayneville to register to vote. Hopeful but apprehensive, they decided to work seriously toward registering. The group soon got vital support from the Student Nonviolent Coordinating Committee (SNCC) and the Southern Christian Leadership Conference (SCLC). In February, 1965, as the voting rights campaign started in Selma, James Bevel of the SCLC staff ventured into Lowndes to recruit blacks for a voter registration effort. Bevel found "quite a lot of fear among the Negro people in the county, particularly among those who are dependent upon the white people for employment," including not just sharecroppers, but even schoolteachers. Encouraged by SNCC, the Lowndes blacks decided to try to register to vote. Local white authorities had announced that they could register blacks as individuals but not as part of any organized campaign. Wary of going singly, the blacks went as a group anyway.[20]

On March 1, thirty-seven blacks went to the county courthouse on the town square to register. The registrars turned all thirty-seven away. Later the same day, the Reverend Martin Luther King, Jr., went to Hayneville to protest the complete absence of registered blacks in the county. In the hallway of the courthouse, King confronted Carl Golson, a member of the board of registrars. Golson was a wealthy landowner and businessman in Fort Deposit and a former state senator. "There is a better relationship between the Negroes and whites here than anywhere in the world," Golson told King. "If you folks would stay out of Lowndes County, we can take care of the situation."[21]

20. Author's interviews with John Hulett, June 18, 1984, December 7, 1986, and Robert L. Strickland, December 8, 1986; Clayborne Carson, *In Struggle: SNCC and the Black Awakening of the 1960s* (Cambridge, Mass., 1981), 162–64; Kopkind, "Lair of the Black Panther," 11; Selma *Times-Journal*, January 1, February 26, 1965.

21. Birmingham *News*, March 2, 1965; New York *Times*, March 2, 1965; Baton

Two weeks after King's visit and the refusal of Lowndes authorities to consider registering blacks, Lowndes blacks discovered that the registrars had moved a few blocks away to the old county jail to consider black applicants, while whites could still register in the courthouse. In their one concession to blacks, the registrars did not require a registered voter (necessarily a white because no blacks were registered) to vouch that each black was a resident of the county. Seventeen Negroes completed the registration forms and took the literacy test; two passed and became the first blacks to qualify to vote in the county in more than fifty years. The board rejected the others, reportedly because three had criminal records and twelve failed the literacy test. "Our policy on the board," Golson announced, "is just this: If they can qualify, we are going to put them on." As a Birmingham journalist commented, the registration of the first black constituted "a social and political revolution" in the county.[22]

Four days after the registration of the first two blacks, the civil rights activists took an unprecedented step. In the evening of March 19, a group of twenty-eight blacks met with SCLC representatives to consider how they should organize and what they should try to accomplish. Unanimously, the group adopted the name Lowndes County Christian Movement for Human Rights (LCCMHR) and decided to promote black voter registration and to voice the grievances of blacks in the county. As the first chairman of the LCCMHR, they chose thirty-eight-year-old John Hulett, one of the county's first registered black voters.[23]

Rouge *State Times*, March 24, 1965; Kopkind, "Lair of the Black Panther," 11; Charles E. Fager, *Selma, 1965: The March That Changed the South* (New York, 1974), 84.

22. Birmingham *News*, March 17, 1965, August 21, 1965; Baton Rouge *State Times*, March 24, 1965; Author's interview with John Hulett.

23. *Southern Courier* (Montgomery, Ala.), April 2–3, 1966; Author's interviews with John Hulett, Charles Smith, June 27, 1984, July 19, 1987, and Rosceno Haralson, July 25, 1986. The organization's name was clearly patterned after the Alabama Christian Movement for Human Rights, which Fred L. Shuttlesworth of Birmingham had started after the state of Alabama effectively barred the NAACP.

Three days after the formation of the LCCMHR, the Selma-to-Montgomery march led by King entered Lowndes County. A black Lowndes minister had warned the march organizers that his county was "worse than hell." Fearing assaults from angry and violent whites, the marchers met instead jubilant blacks; on the march's first day in the county, a group of local blacks waited patiently for four hours to greet the marchers. The marchers even spent two peaceful nights in the county as they walked along U.S. Route 80.[24]

The presence of the three hundred marchers inspired Lowndes County's blacks, only to have the slaying of Viola Liuzzo in their county later in the week shock them. On March 25, Mrs. Liuzzo had taken a carload of marchers back to Selma and returned along Route 80 to Montgomery for another group. Leroy Moton, a black teenager working with the SCLC, accompanied her on the trips. About eight o'clock that evening, on the edge of Selma, a carload of Ku Klux Klansmen from Birmingham spotted the white woman and black youth and knew immediately they were civil rights workers. Miles down the highway the Klansmen pulled alongside and fired at Mrs. Liuzzo's car. Moton was not hit, but two bullets killed Viola Liuzzo instantly. The Klansmen were arrested early the next morning after the Federal Bureau of Investigation received a call from an FBI informant in the Klan. The man had been in the car with the killers.[25]

The LCCMHR activists stood strong despite the murder. On the following Sunday night, one hundred people attended a mass

24. Washington *Post*, March 23, 1965; Chicago *Sun-Times*, March 3, 1965; New York *Times*, March 23, 1965; Houston *Chronicle*, March 23, 1965; Fager, *Selma, 1965*, 153–57; David J. Garrow, *Protest at Selma: Martin Luther King, Jr., and the Voting Rights Act of 1965* (New Haven, 1978), 69; Author's interview with Gardenia White, July 25, 1986.

25. Fager, *Selma, 1965*, 159–64; Garrow, *Protest at Selma*, 117–18; Jack Mendelsohn, *The Martyrs: Sixteen Who Gave Their Lives for Racial Justice* (New York, 1966), 176–95.

meeting at the Mount Gillard Baptist Church in Trickem. They protested the murder of Mrs. Liuzzo and reinforced their own courage in challenging the control of local whites.[26] By the time of the meeting, however, they had been joined by a leader from the Student Nonviolent Coordinating Committee.

Stokely Carmichael, a full-time organizer with SNCC, came to Lowndes County the day after the shooting of Mrs. Liuzzo. Carmichael had resigned his post with Mississippi's Freedom Summer to work in the rural areas of Alabama. During the protests in Selma in the early spring of 1965, he learned of the racial situation in Lowndes County and decided to work there. According to one scholar, he "combined astute political awareness with an ability to communicate with less-educated people on their own terms." In the spring and early summer of 1965, other SNCC workers joined Carmichael in Lowndes. Most of them were black college students from the South and experienced as civil rights workers, but they had never encountered an area as difficult to organize as bloody Lowndes.[27]

The campaign to organize blacks and get them to register to vote was a quintessentially grass-roots effort, and progress in Lowndes came slowly. Even with the assistance of LCCMHR, Carmichael and his SNCC co-workers had to move about the county carefully, frequently at night, because they knew that local whites would resist their efforts to organize blacks and might resort to violence to stop the "outside agitators." The wary SNCC workers especially avoided the small towns of Hayneville, Fort Deposit, and Lowndesboro during daylight and worked primarily along the

26. *Southern Courier* (Montgomery, Ala.), April 2–3, 1966; New York *Times,* March 29, 1965.

27. Carson, *In Struggle,* 162–63; Milton Viorst, *Fire in the Streets: America in the 1960s* (New York, 1979), 361–62; and Stokely Carmichael and Charles V. Hamilton, *Black Power: The Politics of Liberation in America* (New York, 1967), 96–101; Author's interviews with Bob Mants, July 21, 1986, Stokely Carmichael, March 7, 1990, and Ruby Sales, August 11, 1986.

county's unpaved rural roads. SNCC could depend, of course, on the LCCMHR members for support, but many other leaders in the black community hesitated to join or help them.[28]

On April 4, the day after a mass meeting organized by SNCC and LCCMHR, 50 blacks went to Hayneville to register at the old county jail. Two weeks later more than 60 Lowndes blacks filled out the application and took the tests to register to vote. Finally on the first Monday of May, the registrars announced the results of the tests. The registrars accepted only three of the applicants. Out of 5,922 voting-age blacks, therefore, merely 5 had become registered voters. Comparable figures for the white population revealed the level of corruption and discrimination in the process: the voter rolls included 2,314 white names—even though fewer than 2,000 whites of voting age lived in the county.[29]

Although they made progress very slowly, blacks finally had broken what one observer called "the stalemate of fear" in Lowndes County. A popular saying among whites in the county had been that no black had tried to register and that the first one who did try would be dead by sundown. Blacks, who all their lives had been well aware of the white attitude, had in the spring of 1965 at last overcome their fears and joined the civil rights movement. Still apprehensive, and sometimes even scared, they had begun to push for change.[30]

The killing of Mrs. Liuzzo occurred in Lowndes County, so the trial took place in the county courthouse in Hayneville. The first defendant, Collie Leroy Wilkins, came to trial for first-degree manslaughter early in May. Local whites seemed resentful that outsiders—Klansmen from Birmingham as well as Detroit's Liuzzo—and the trial brought so much attention to their community and upset their peaceful lives. Satisfied with the status quo and appre-

28. Author's interviews with Stokely Carmichael, Bob Mants, Ruby Sales, and John Hulett.

29. Lowndes County WATS Report, April 4, 1965, in SNCC Papers, King Center, Atlanta; New York *Times*, May 3, 4, 1965; Houston *Chronicle*, March 15, 1965.

30. Chicago *Sun-Times*, March 3, 1965.

hensive of any change, most denied any racial problems in Lowndes County. One woman declared: "We grew up with the Negroes and played with them as children. We have never had any trouble getting along. Up until the recent agitation began, there was the best of feeling between the races." Even the county solicitor said, "I was born and reared in Lowndes County, and I'd say the spiritual kindness that has existed here cannot be surpassed." Most local whites did not expect an all-white Lowndes jury to convict Wilkins, even though the defendant was not from Lowndes County. Contradicting his neighbors, a local official did admit that "it can't be a real trial. There has been too much racial conflict, too much hate, too much bitterness."[31]

Wilkins' prosecutors urged their neighbors on the all-white jury to convict the Klansman from Birmingham. Arthur Gamble, the circuit solicitor, admitting he did not agree with Liuzzo's activities, nevertheless argued strongly for a conviction: "She was here, and she had a right to be here on our highways without being shot down in the middle of the night." Imploring the jury to muster their courage, Gamble said, "Don't put the stamp of approval on chaos, confusion, and anarchy." Matt Murphy, the Klan lawyer defending Wilkins, harangued the jurors in his one-hour summation. Frequently shouting, Murphy denounced "niggers" and "the black race" and tied the civil rights movement to the worldwide Communist conspiracy. "The Communists are taking us over," Murphy cried. "I say never! gentlemen. We shall die before we lay down and see it."[32]

After ten hours of deliberation, the white Lowndes jury reported a deadlock.[33] As most local whites apparently expected and as most observers had predicted, the all-white Lowndes jury had refused to convict Wilkins for killing a civil rights worker. Even though he was a known Klansman and from Birmingham, the

31. Selma *Times-Journal*, May 2, 1965; Chicago *Sun-Times*, May 2, 1965.

32. New York *Times*, May 7, 1965; Birmingham *News*, May 7, 1965.

33. New York *Times*, May 8, 1965; Birmingham *News*, May 9, 1965. The jury reported a 10–2 split in favor of conviction.

Lowndes jury would not convict a white man for protecting their way of life. The jury upheld the tradition of "bloody Lowndes" as a place where whites could brutalize blacks and their white allies without fear of punishment in the halls of justice.

Throughout the early summer of 1965, Lowndes blacks continued to try to register. On May 3, the opening day of the Wilkins trial, 150 blacks organized by SNCC went to the old jail in Hayneville to register during the board's regular session. Of the first 15 applicants processed by the board, 11 could not fill out the required forms and 1 of the remaining 4 could not pass the literacy test. The board examined 60 blacks during its five-hour session. Eventually the board approved only 6 additional black voters, for a total of 11 registered black voters in the Black Belt county.[34]

Each applicant had to pass a literacy test (questions might include, how many congressional districts are there in North Carolina?). Blacks protested that the test was administered unfairly. One story heard frequently in the Black Belt in 1965 told of a Negro with a doctor's degree going to register in Lowndes County. After he finished the lengthy questionnaire, as part of the qualification test administered by the registrar he recited the Gettysburg Address, told the number of congressional districts in each state, and repeated the preamble to the Constitution. Finally the registrar asked, "What does the Ninth Amendment mean?" The black man smiled and said, "It means no Negro is goin' to vote in Lowndes County." Under pressure from the pending SNCC lawsuit, the board of registrars on July 6 agreed with representatives from the United States Justice Department to suspend the use of the literacy test for forty-five days. In addition, the registrars agreed to keep their office open every day that week so blacks could take advantage of the new rules and procedures.[35]

34. New York *Times*, May 4, 1965; Lowndes County WATS Report, May 20, 1965, in SNCC Papers.

35. Donald Strong, *Registration of Voters in Alabama* (University, Ala., 1956), 25–34; Houston *Chronicle*, March 15, 1965; *Southern Courier* (Montgomery, Ala.), July 16, 1965.

The changes elated SNCC workers. In an unusual move, civil rights activists held mass meetings every night to organize a massive registration drive. Scores of blacks continued to go before the board of registrars during its regular sessions on the first and third Mondays in July and August. In the meantime Congress passed legislation to protect the rights of blacks to vote. Even though Lowndes blacks fully expected federal registrars to be in their county within a week or two as provided for by the new civil rights law, on August 2 more than one hundred blacks filed applications to vote with the local registrars. Within days, as many as twelve hundred blacks had attempted to register. Only two hundred had succeeded, but whites could see that black voters might soon be in the majority.[36]

While campaigning for the right to vote, Lowndes blacks also challenged school segregation. In the spring of 1965, under pressure from the federal government, the county school board had accepted a plan to desegregate grades nine through twelve at the two white schools. The "freedom of choice" plan gave each student the right to ask the school board for permission to switch to another school. If no black students requested transfers to the white schools, then no desegregation would occur. The plan gave final authority to the local, all-white school board to approve or deny all transfers. Although blacks disliked the freedom of choice plan because of the burden placed on them to achieve what should have been their right, thirty-five black students did apply in July for transfers to the white Hayneville School instead of returning to the Lowndes County Training School.[37]

The county's white community reacted with hostility to the attempt to end school segregation and threatened to retaliate

36. Lowndes County WATS Reports, May 20, July 6, 7, 9, 26, August 3, 1965, SNCC news release, July 8, 1965, Lowndes County weekly report, August 5, 1965, Transcript of recorded interview with Stokely Carmichael, April [?], 1965, all in SNCC Papers; *Southern Courier* (Montgomery, Ala.), July 16, 1965.

37. Author's interview with Hulda Coleman; *Southern Courier* (Montgomery, Ala.), August 13, 1965, February 19–20, 1966.

against blacks seeking to desegregate schools. Despite white intimidation, few blacks withdrew their applications to transfer to white schools. A group of whites, therefore, formed the Lowndes County Private School Foundation and planned to open a private white high school in the fall of 1965. Even more effectively, the school board simply rejected all but five of the applications for transfer.[38]

With the increasing black voter registration and with the applications of black students to attend the white schools, the pressures for change in Lowndes County mounted rapidly that summer, and white resistance intensified. As one sympathetic Birmingham newspaperman remarked: "The white people in Lowndes County have been living with and under a set of guidelines handed down from grandfathers and great-grandfathers. It has been an accepted way of life. And when things have 'always' been one way it does not come easy to have a stranger come in to disrupt things." The local whites stoutly opposed school desegregation because, as one of them argued, "Niggers in our schools will ruin my children morally, scholastically, spiritually, and every other way if the number [of blacks in the schools] is too high."[39]

Particularly ominous to whites was the prospect of black political power that could yield blacks as sheriff, superintendent of schools, probate judge, voter registrars, and other public officials. "It's just inconceivable," declared a white storekeeper, "that white landowners are going to surrender control of the county to the nonlandowners—you know what I mean?" Everyone knew. If blacks gained control of the local government, many whites said they would leave the county. "I would [leave] if I was living," said

38. Lowndes County WATS Report, July 26, 1965, Lowndes County weekly report, August 5, 1965, SNCC Papers; *Southern Courier* (Montgomery, Ala.), August 13, 1965; Author's interview with Hulda Coleman; Author's interview with Sarah B. Logan, June 25, 1984.

39. Walling Keith, "In Hayneville's Roots," Birmingham *News*, August 26, 1965; *Southern Courier* (Montgomery, Ala.), August 13, 1965.

Carlton Perdue, the county solicitor. "I wouldn't live here under no Negro."[40]

On Tuesday, August 10, Lowndes County became one of four Alabama counties to get federal examiners under the new Voting Rights Act. The Justice Department selected Lowndes because only 3.8 percent of the blacks of voting age were registered, and all of them had registered since March. Just as the federal registrars set to work in Lowndes, some of the whites' worst fears of black violence seemed to be confirmed when on August 11, the Watts section of Los Angeles exploded as mobs in the black ghetto clashed with police and later National Guard troops in rioting that lasted six days and spread over forty square miles. Thirty-four people were killed, more than nine hundred injured, and about four thousand arrested in the Watts riot.[41]

In the middle of the momentous, tense summer of 1965, a white seminarian from New Hampshire entered Lowndes to help SNCC in registering black voters. Jonathan Myrick Daniels had been working in Selma since the Selma-to-Montgomery march. In Lowndes he encouraged blacks to register, attended mass meetings, and generally provided a Christian witness in support of the movement.[42] The presence of a white civil rights worker irritated Lowndes whites.

On August 14, Daniels and the Reverend Richard Morrisroe, a white Catholic priest from Chicago whom Daniels had just met at an SCLC meeting in Birmingham, participated in a SNCC demonstration in Fort Deposit. The demonstration protested what local blacks considered the dishonest and discourteous treatment of black customers by white storekeepers. A couple of dozen

40. Miami *Herald*, June 20, 1965.

41. Birmingham *News*, August 10, 1965; Selma *Times-Journal*, August 10, 1965. On the Watts riots, see David O. Sears and John B. McConahay, *The Politics of Violence: The New Urban Blacks and the Watts Riots* (Boston, 1973).

42. Mendelsohn, *Martyrs*, 196–218; Author's interviews with Judith Upham, June 2, 3, 1982, Ruby Sales, Stokely Carmichael, Bob Mants, and John Hulett.

protestors, including Daniels and Morrisroe, were immediately arrested and taken to the county jail in Hayneville. Suddenly released with all the others after six days in jail, Daniels, Morrisroe, and two young black women then walked to a nearby store to buy soft drinks. At the door of the store, a white man armed with a shotgun told them to leave; when they did not, he opened fire at point-blank range and shot the two white men. Daniels died instantly, and Morrisroe was seriously wounded.[43]

The assailant, Tom L. Coleman, an employee of the state highway department and a Lowndes native, turned himself in at the courthouse. Charged initially with first-degree murder, Coleman was indicted by a Lowndes grand jury for manslaughter. Less than six weeks after the shootings, a jury of twelve white Lowndes County men heard the evidence against Coleman, including testimony from two of Coleman's friends that Daniels and Morrisroe had been armed. Accepting the defense contention that Coleman had acted in self-defense, the jury acquitted him. The verdict, common in civil rights cases at the time, demonstrated the intransigence of white supremacy in bloody Lowndes. The next year the court dismissed the charge against Coleman for shooting Morrisroe.[44]

The Daniels case did have some positive results. The American Civil Liberties Union and friends of Daniels won a major federal lawsuit challenging the exclusion of blacks and women from Lowndes juries, but their victory came after the trial of Coleman. More immediately, Daniels' witness inspired blacks to continue their struggle for equal rights, although many despaired of work-

43. *McMeans* v. *Mayor's Court, Fort Deposit,* Alabama 247 F. Supp. 606 (1965); *State of Alabama* v. *Tom L. Coleman* (Transcript in possession of author); Author's interviews with Richard Morrisroe, May 17, 1985, Ruby Sales, Joyce Bailey Dozier, June 1, 1985, Gloria Larry House, June 2, 1985, and others.

44. Selma *Times-Journal,* August 22, September 15, 1965; New York *Times,* August 22, September 16, 1965; Los Angeles *Times,* September 29, 30, October 1, 1965; *State of Alabama* v. *Tom L. Coleman;* Author's interview with Tom L. Coleman. See also Marshall Frady, "A Death in Lowndes County," in Frady, *Southerners: A Journalist's Odyssey* (New York, 1980), 138–56.

ing with local whites. Blacks continued to register to vote, and four black students did desegregate the white Hayneville School in late August, 1965.[45]

Increasingly, Lowndes blacks challenged white political dominance directly. In December, 1965, with the help of SNCC, blacks in the LCCMHR started to form their own independent political party, based in part on the Mississippi Freedom Democratic party established the previous year. The independent black party, which would operate as the Lowndes County Freedom Organization, expected to nominate candidates in May for tax assessor, sheriff, tax collector, and two seats on the county school board.[46]

Early in January, blacks sued in federal court to invalidate the election of all officials in Lowndes County because the constitutional rights of blacks had been violated in those elections. Recognizing the connections between economic and political power, they also sued white landowners for evicting black tenants who participated in the civil rights movement; black activists started a tent city to provide for the homeless blacks. Additional impetus for a new party came in February when the local Democratic Executive Committee suddenly raised the qualifying fees from $50 to $500 for candidates for sheriff, tax assessor, and tax collector. Candidates for the county board of education faced an increase in filing fees from $10 to $100. Poor blacks who could least afford the higher fees found their own independent party attractive.[47]

While Lowndes blacks began to organize politically, the federal government provided some support for them on the broader front. Not only did a federal court rule in their favor in *White* v.

45. *White* v. *Crook*, 251 F. Supp. 401 (1966); Selma *Times-Journal*, August 30, 31, 1965; *Southern Courier* (Montgomery, Ala.), September 4–5, 1965; Author's interviews with Charles Morgan, April 2, 1989, John Hulett, Stokely Carmichael, Bob Mants, and Hulda Coleman.

46. *Southern Courier* (Montgomery, Ala.), January 1, 2, 1966; *Hearing Before the United States Commission on Civil Rights* [Montgomery, Ala., April 27–May 2, 1968], (Washington, D.C., 1968), 655–87; New York *Times*, December 10, 1965.

47. *Southern Courier* (Montgomery, Ala.), January 1–2, 1966; New York *Times*, January 6, February 5, April 1, 1966.

Crook, but the Justice Department brought suit against the Lowndes County schools for failing to create and implement a desegregation plan. In February, Judge Frank M. Johnson, Jr., ordered Lowndes to eliminate its segregated public school system over the next two years. A few weeks later, however, joined by two other judges, Johnson dismissed the challenge to the county's elected officials. Blacks also lost their suit against white landowners for evicting black tenants.[48]

On April 2, 1966, blacks officially organized the Lowndes County Freedom Organization (LCFO). The LCFO elected John Hulett as president and, as required by state law, selected a party symbol. They chose a black panther, and the LCFO soon became known as the Black Panther party. On May 3, the day of the Democratic primary, about 1,400 blacks attended a LCFO nominating convention at a Hayneville church in spite of their fears of violence. Nearly 900 black voters nominated candidates for tax assessor, tax collector, coroner, the school board, and sheriff—all the offices that were open in the fall election. During a summer and fall of controversies connected with the increasingly radical Stokely Carmichael and his calls for "black power," the LCFO worked to elect its candidates. They all lost. The margins of defeat ranged from 273 to 677 votes out of fewer than 3,900 cast. Two years later the LCFO ran three candidates in county elections and lost each contest by at least 500 votes. Although they constituted a majority of the county's registered voters, blacks simply failed to support the LCFO candidates—several hundred did not even vote, some black tenants protected their jobs by voting for white candidates, and illiteracy prevented other blacks from voting properly.[49]

48. New York *Times,* January 11, February 12, April 1, 1966; *Southern Courier* (Montgomery, Ala.), April 9–10, 1966.

49. *Southern Courier* (Montgomery, Ala.), April 9–10, May 7–8, 1966; David Campbell, "The Lowndes County (Alabama) Freedom Organization: The First Black Panther Party" (M.A. thesis, Florida State University, 1970), 43–77; Hanes Walton, Jr., *Black Political Parties: An Historical and Political Analysis* (New York, 1972), 138–49; Steven F. Lawson, *In Pursuit of Power: Southern Blacks and Electoral Politics, 1865–1982*

In 1969 the nearly collapsed LCFO or Black Panther party became part of the National Democratic Party of Alabama (NDPA), a statewide black political organization formed the year before. With more black voters than ever, the NDPA in Lowndes County won several crucial victories in the 1970 elections. Blacks were elected coroner and circuit clerk. Most important, John Hulett was elected sheriff.[50] Barely five years after the first blacks registered to vote in Lowndes County, they had succeeded in electing a black sheriff.

The election of a black sheriff brought a new pattern in race relations. Taking control of law enforcement away from oppressive whites signaled a significant shift in the safety and security of Lowndes's black citizens. Without a friendly sheriff who would condone their violence, whites could no longer freely harass and beat blacks. At the same time whites, initially fearful of a black sheriff, soon adjusted to Sheriff Hulett because they discovered that he did a good job; if anything, trouble with blacks in the county decreased under the black sheriff. Some whites even grew to like and respect Hulett. In the evening Tom Coleman, for example, often listened to his police scanner and helped Hulett by contacting him when he heard of trouble. Though he could never bring himself to address him as Mr. Hulett, Coleman thought of the sheriff as his friend.[51]

By the end of the 1970s, blacks effectively controlled the Lowndes County government, but the civil rights movement in Lowndes involved more than political action. For example, organized blacks sought federal funds to help them improve their com-

---

(New York, 1985), 109; Author's interviews with John Hulett and Charles Smith. Campbell's thesis is the only significant secondary source on the Lowndes County Freedom Organization.

50. Walton, *Black Political Parties*, 148–49; Andrew Kopkind, "Lowndes County: The Great Fear Is Gone," *Ramparts*, April, 1975, p. 12; Author's interviews with John Hulett and Charles Smith.

51. Author's interviews with Tom L. Coleman and John Hulett.

munities by building better housing, paving streets, installing water and sewer systems, and upgrading the schools. In 1966, the LCCMHR received a $240,000 federal antipoverty grant to fund literacy programs and vocational training in Lowndes County. The largest project came in 1969 when the Office of Economic Opportunity established a million-dollar community health center next to the county jail. Also, the public schools gained a Head Start program.[52]

Local community action and federal spending brought impressive changes in the lives of blacks. The more visible improvements included restoration of the antebellum courthouse—where many blacks now worked—and miles of new paved roads, including many in Hayneville. By 1980 more than 70 percent of the county's residences had complete bathrooms (compared with less than 50 percent in 1960), 80 percent of the residences had a motor vehicle (compared with only 42 percent twenty years earlier), and most homes had telephones (in 1960 only 20 percent had phones). Blacks participated in many of the gains. In part the improvement resulted from higher income levels in the county. The median black family income rose from $935 in 1960 to $7,493 in 1980, while comparable white incomes rose from $2,624 to $18,350. Thus, the median black income in Lowndes moved only from 36 percent to 41 percent of the median white income.[53]

The small comparative gain in black income over two decades betrays the persisting economic problems in Lowndes County. The county continued to be fifth poorest in the nation in 1980. In 1983 the staff of the United States Civil Rights Commission concluded: "Political gains have yet to translate into economic gains. Blacks in Lowndes County have little reason for optimism." Even the arrival of major industry could not alleviate Lowndes's

52. Kopkind, "Lair of the Black Panther," 13; Kopkind, "Lowndes County," 53; *Southern Courier* (Montgomery, Ala.), July 16–17, 1966.

53. Bureau of the Census, *1980 Census of Housing*, Vol. I, chap. B, 125; Margaret Edds, *Free at Last: What Really Happened When Civil Rights Came to Southern Politics* (Bethesda, Md., 1987), 83.

problems of unemployment and poverty. In the late 1980s, General Electric opened a $350 million plastics plant in the northwestern part of the county, near Montgomery, but it had little impact on the county because it demanded skilled workers unavailable among the Lowndes population. Furthermore, few GE employees moved to Lowndes County, partly because the still almost totally segregated schools were inferior; GE's employees instead commuted to work each day from outside of Lowndes. In addition, tax waivers meant that GE paid no county taxes. Even after the arrival of GE, a solution to Lowndes County's economic woes seemed as distant as ever. Faced with such bleak prospects, many residents simply moved away: between 1960 and 1980 the population declined from 15,417 to 13,253.[54]

As a result of the civil rights movement, Lowndes County experienced dramatic, if uneven and incomplete, progress. With many outward manifestations of white supremacy and black oppression eliminated, the two races lived together more comfortably and peacefully than ever before. Rapid political change in the late 1960s gave blacks the right to vote and the power to control their local government; court decisions insured their right to serve on juries and protect themselves in the courts. They also freely entered all public facilities, though the county's schools remained segregated, whites attending private schools, blacks the public schools. Local churches and other aspects of private life continued segregated too. More significantly, poverty persisted and whites retained their economic dominance of the county. Yet even though the efforts of local activists assisted by outside civil rights workers and the federal government achieved only limited successes in the county, at least Lowndes was no longer bloody; at least the great fear was gone.

John Hulett saw concrete evidence of the most important

54. Edds, *Free at Last,* 80, 85, 96; *Twentieth Census, 1980: Population,* Vol. I, Pt. 2, chap. B, p. 130.

change in his county shortly after his election in 1970. He looked at the gun racks in pickup trucks. Before Hulett's election, a white man's gun rack usually brandished an intimidating shotgun visible in his truck's rear window; blacks, fearful, seldom displayed a weapon. After Hulett became sheriff, he noticed that some blacks began to exhibit shotguns in their trucks just as the whites did. Gradually, as the number of black shotguns grew, whites displayed fewer in their trucks. Eventually, the number of shotguns in pickup-truck gun racks began to decline among both whites and blacks, to be replaced by fishing rods and umbrellas. For Hulett, the shift from shotguns to fishing rods and umbrellas symbolized a major change in power and in community peace in Lowndes County.[55]

55. Author's interview with John Hulett.

Jimmy Carter

A Southerner in the White House?

Robert C. McMath, Jr.

> *The time is coming, if indeed it has not already arrived, when the Southerner will begin to ask himself whether there is really any longer very much point in calling himself a Southerner.*
>
> — C. Vann Woodward, 1958

> *I am a Southerner and an American. I am a farmer, an engineer, a father and husband, a Christian, a politician and former governor, a planner, a businessman, a nuclear physicist, a naval officer, a canoeist, and among other things, a lover of Bob Dylan's songs and Dylan Thomas' poetry.*
>
> — Jimmy Carter, 1975

During his marathon quest for the presidency, Jimmy Carter made a litany of the autobiographical statement that began, "I am a Southerner." Like so much of his campaign, this affirmation defied conventional wisdom. C. Vann Woodward was by no means the only expert to have announced the impending irrelevance of southern identity, only the most self-conscious southerner to do so.

Candidate Carter's confession of southernness was heartfelt, but its meaning and implication were not self-evident. What kind of a southerner was he, anyway? (As early as 1977 one Carter watcher published a piece entitled "Jimmy Carter Is a Closet Yankee" and forwarded a copy to the White House.)[1] And if elected, what difference would his southernness make in the way he governed and in the image he presented to the American people? Answers to these questions will not only shed light on the public career of the thirty-ninth president, but they also may illustrate how his native region has adapted to change in the late twentieth century.

To begin with the question of Carter's pedigree, just what kind of a southerner was he, culturally and politically? There was never any doubt about Carter's ancestry or place of residence, but for many Americans he was, as a fellow Georgian said of him, "hard to figure."[2] Jimmy Carter provided a version of his own story in a campaign autobiography, *Why Not the Best?*, and in the testimonial campaign speech he repeated in living rooms and at political rallies across the land from 1974 to 1976. It was the stuff of which presidential images have been made ever since William Henry Harrison's "Log Cabin" campaign of 1840: humble beginnings in a remote corner of the South, a promising career in the elite nuclear submarine corps, responsiveness to the call of family after the death of his father, and finally a career of public service grounded in all those attributes he listed after proclaiming himself a southerner and an American.

Once Carter became visible (had appeared, that is, on the

1. William Lee Miller to President Jimmy Carter, May 10, 1977, Jody Powell to William Lee Miller, July 11, 1977, both in White House File, Central File (hereinafter cited as WHCF), Name File (William Lee Miller), Carter Presidential Library, Atlanta. Miller subsequently sent the president a copy of his book *Yankee from Georgia: The Emergence of Jimmy Carter* (New York, 1978). The book found its way to a member of Mrs. Carter's staff, who reported to Miller that she was "dazzled by your insights." Mary Finch Hoyt to William Miller, February 26, 1979, WHCF, Name File (Miller).

2. Roy Blount, Jr., *Crackers: This Whole Many-Angled Thing of Jimmy, More Carters, Ominous Little Animals, Sad-Singing Women, My Daddy, and Me* (New York, 1980), 77.

cover of national magazines), journalists and academicians conducted a brisk trade in commentary on his "character" and the exotic culture from which he sprang. Enterprising writers added to Carter's self-told story and even challenged it at certain points, but Carter watchers still had difficulty fitting the pieces together. The celebrated *Playboy* interview containing the simple statement, "I've looked on a lot of women with lust," further confused many Americans, although to Southern Baptists and their fellow travelers Carter's public confession was not remarkable.[3]

Academicians also took up the challenge. Political scientist James David Barber, who had already demonstrated an uncanny ability to predict presidential behavior in *Presidential Character,* now turned his attention to his fellow southerner Carter. Barber's task was complicated by the fact that his subject had read the book—thus raising the specter of life imitating social science. Among the other professors who stalked the elusive Carter were a duo from MIT (a psychohistorian and a journalist) who together wrote a credible "character portrait" despite such lapses as quoting as an authority on the southern family the "English traveler, Francis Butler Simkins."[4]

The essays on Carter depicted him as at once rooted in and at variance with familiar types of southernness. Thus, while fellow southerner Bill Moyers could evoke from Carter a fondness for the land and the rhythms of rural life, other analysts noted that the Carters of Sumter County were neither beleaguered dirt farmers nor stereotypical planters. Mr. Earl Carter, and after him his sons and daughters-in-law, were rather of that new breed of agribusinessmen to which magazines like *Progressive Farmer* pointed with

3. "Jimmy Carter: Candid Conversations with the Democratic Candidate for the Presidency," *Playboy,* November, 1976, p. 86.

4. James David Barber, *The Presidential Character: Predicting Performance in the White House* (3d ed.; Englewood Cliffs, N.J., 1985), 401–402; Bruce Mazlish and Edwin Diamond, *Jimmy Carter: A Character Portrait* (New York, 1979), 20. See also Mazlish and Diamond, "Thrice-Born: A Psychohistory of Jimmy Carter's 'Rebirth,' " *New York,* August 30, 1976, pp. 27–33.

pride. The Carters were "sometimes a little more eager to be up and doing than some of their neighbors considered comfortable." At home, at school, in the navy, and in the family business, Jimmy stood out as one inclined toward hard work and self-improvement: "a Georgia Ben Franklin," one observer called him.[5] Among good ol' boys, real and affected, that is no compliment.

Roy Blount, Jr., a southern urbanite who has won fame and fortune by affecting the old ways, wrote of Carter while he was still in the White House: "He don't look like much of a redneck, I know. Most of the time he looks, and sounds, like a man who's come down from a slightly higher level of church administration to give a talk to your congregation on good sound business reasons why you ought to tithe."[6]

This Blount caricature, although not flattering to a head of state, suggests characteristics that are to be found among real people in the towns, cities, and suburbs of the modern South: a certain purposeful evangelicalism, belief in the value of hard work and self-improvement, and faith in human progress. These traits are not the stuff of traditional stereotypes about southern white males. "The fact is," sociologist John Shelton Reed reports, "that the Carters are middle class, *upper* middle-class Southerners, and old stereotypes of Southerners don't fit such folks comfortably."[7]

Reed has had some interesting things to say of late about the southern middle class, beginning with the observation that there now *is* one of sizable proportions. Reed's proposal for an ethnography of this newly emergent group begins with study of the read-

5. Interview with Jimmy Carter by Bill Moyers, PBS series "USA: People and Politics," May 6, 1976 (Transcript in *The Presidential Campaign, 1976* [Washington, D.C., 1978], Vol. V, Pt. 1, pp. 163–68); William Greider, "A Carter Album," Washington *Post*, October 24, 1976, Sec. A, p. 16; Miller, *Yankee from Georgia*, 70.

6. Blount, *Crackers*, 84.

7. John Shelton Reed, *One South: An Ethnic Approach to Regional Culture* (Baton Rouge, 1982), 124; John Shelton Reed, *Southern Folk, Plain and Fancy: Native White Social Types* (Athens, Ga., 1986), 64.

ership of *Southern Living* magazine, until recently a subsidiary of the aforementioned *Progressive Farmer.* Reed's new southern middle class seems to have more in common with the national norm than with traditional southern social types, but they are, he insists, still southerners—more likely to be church members and to take religion seriously, and still wanting to think of themselves as southerners, at least in the appropriate social settings. Magazines like *Southern Living* instruct them in half-remembered southern traditions of manners, hospitality, and above all, eating and drinking.[8]

Reed's southern baby boomers are close to Carter's social type, but not exactly it. The baby boomers, in fact, are the *children* of the first substantial cohort of middle-class white southerners, the sons and daughters of Jimmy and Rosalynn Carter's generation.

The Carters' was the first generation to benefit on a large scale from the southern crusade for public education. They witnessed as teenagers and young adults the last desperate years of the old agricultural South and the abrupt transformation of the southern countryside. And they escaped the region's historic cycle of poverty, many by means of that great engine of southern economic progress—the federal largess that began with the New Deal, increased through World War II, and has never stopped. This generation achieved a level of economic independence and absorbed habits of mind that would mark them as "middle class," but they needed neither slick magazines nor history books to tell them about the South.

For Jimmy and Rosalynn Carter this blending of southern and middle class identity is strikingly illustrated in the book that they jointly wrote in "retirement," *Everything to Gain: Making the Most of the Rest of Your Life.* The dust jacket photograph, a natural for *Southern Living,* features Mr. and Mrs. Carter at ease in the den

8. Reed, *Southern Folk, Plain and Fancy,* 64–65.

of their comfortable but not palatial home in Plains. The text, like their earlier autobiographical writing, evokes the continuities of small-town southern life.

Theirs is not, however, a book about "gracious living" but about self-improvement, and the maxims are those of the Carters' youth. Compare, for example, the Carters' nine rules for "preventing unnecessary sickness and premature death" with young Jimmy Carter's school report "Healthy Mental Habits." And note the attitudes toward work and progress embedded in their recollection: "During our school years we were taught at home and in the classroom to strive and compete, and that any limitations on our lives were self-imposed. We memorized the names of artists and their famous paintings, listened to scratchy recordings of symphonies and operas, and were publicly rewarded for reading great books. . . . We studied the lives of great men and women, and pondered their high ideals, a closeness to God, and hard work."[9]

Such words from the Carters may draw faint smiles, and cosmopolitan analysts had such in mind when they observed that Jimmy read literature, theology, and Scripture "for self-improvement" rather than for aesthetic or abstractly intellectual gratification. These experts may imagine they have thereby delivered a devastating critique, but in the world of the Men's Sunday School class or Miss Julia Coleman's English class self-improvement was, without apology, the object of it all.[10]

The Carters' experience confirms John Reed's conclusion that middle-class southerners are more likely than their northern counterparts to take religion seriously. Much has been written already about Jimmy Carter's faith.[11] Suffice it here to say that Jimmy

9. Jimmy and Rosalynn Carter, *Everything to Gain: Making the Most of the Rest of Your Life* (New York, 1987), 62, 71–72; Greider, "A Carter Album," 16.

10. Mazlish and Diamond, *Jimmy Carter,* 163; James Fallows, "The Passionless Presidency: The Trouble with Jimmy Carter's Administration," *Atlantic,* May 1979, p. 42.

11. All the biographical studies of Carter cited thus far include treatment of his religion. See also Betty Glad, *Jimmy Carter: In Search of the Great White House* (New

Carter's evangelical piety was not remarkable among people of his time and place, nor was there any serious question of its genuineness, regardless of the political benefit he reaped from it in 1976. And the juxtaposition of pietism, social action, and serious theological study in Carter's religion is not incongruous. Southern evangelicals have had their own prophetic strand of the social gospel, and Jimmy Carter was by no means the first southerner to find wisdom and cultural resonance in the writing of Reinhold Niebuhr.[12]

For Jimmy and Rosalynn Carter's generation of middle-class southerners, youthful habits of mind would be filtered through the experiences of a Great Depression and the wrenching transformation of the rural South. The book about the South that Jimmy Carter called his favorite, the one that he took with him from Plains to the White House, was James Agee's *Let Us Now Praise Famous Men*. Agee's text and Walker Evans' photographs were powerful reminders of the collapse of an old way of life on the land, as C. Vann Woodward also was moved to note: "I saw all that he [Agee] saw, but it was Agee and Evans who brought it all home to me later in the pit of my stomach by means of their book."[13]

Jimmy Carter, like Woodward, witnessed that great rural transformation in his own time and place. In a little more than a decade, farming in his native southwest Georgia was altered beyond recognition, not just by the depression, but also by a revolu-

York, 1980) chap. 17, and E. Brooks Holifield, "The Three Strands of Jimmy Carter's Religion," *New Republic*, June 5, 1976, pp. 15–17.

12. See, for example, Anthony Dunbar, *Against the Grain: Southern Radicals and Prophets, 1929–1959* (Charlottesville, Va., 1981); and James R. Green, *Grass-Roots Socialism: Radical Movements in the Southwest, 1895–1943* (Baton Rouge, 1978), chap. 17. C. Vann Woodward's classic essay "The Irony of Southern History" was heavily influenced by Niebuhr's *The Irony of American History*, published in 1952.

13. Barber, *Presidential Character*, 418; Walter Winfred to Herbert Mitgang, in WHCF, Box 83 [January 20, 1977–January 20, 1981]; C. Vann Woodward, *Thinking Back: The Perils of Writing History* (Baton Rouge, 1986), 12.

tion in agricultural technology.[14] Years later President Carter recalled that moment of change during the historic reconciliation between the United States and China, a nation that, like Carter's impoverished South, was trying to hoist itself into modernity. At a White House dinner for Deng Xiaoping, Carter toasted the architect of China's "four modernizations" (before Tiananmen Square it was possible to think of Deng as the Henry Grady of the New China) with this reflection on the changing South:

> Like you, Mr. Vice Premier, I am a farmer; and like you, I am a former military man. In my little farming community, when I grew up, our agricultural methods and way of life were not greatly different from those of centuries earlier. I stepped from that world into the planning and outfitting of a nuclear submarine. When I returned to the land, I found that farming had been transformed in just a few years by new scientific knowledge and technology. I know the shock of change, and the sometimes painful adjustment it can require—as well as the great potential for good that change can bring to individuals and nations. I know, too, that neither individuals nor nations can stifle change. It is far better to adopt scientific and technological advances to our needs—to learn to control them—to reap their benefits while minimizing their potential adverse effects.[15]

Technology changed the southern landscape of Carter's youth, and it changed Jimmy Carter: engineering was the focal

14. Students of agricultural mechanization in the South have used the diffusion of tractors as a measure of technological change. Two years before Jimmy Carter left for college and naval duty, only 14 percent of all farms in Sumter County had tractors. The year after he returned, there were more tractors than farms. *Sixteenth Census, 1940: Agriculture,* Vol. I, Pt. 3, pp. 513, 631; Bureau of the Census, *1954 Census of Agriculture,* 72, 125.

15. Press release, Jody Powell Files, Press, Powell, Box 81, "Visit to U.S. by China's Vice-Premier Deng Xiaoping 1/29/79/–2/5/79" (CF, O/A 587) (2), in Carter Presidential Library.

point of his chosen profession and his ticket out of south Georgia. His initiation into the world of the technologist (at Georgia Tech, at Annapolis, and in postgraduate studies associated with the nuclear submarine program) would define Carter's approach to whatever task lay before him, much as it had for the first engineering president, Herbert Hoover. In tandem with his drive for self-improvement, these experiences left him with a positive attitude toward technical innovation and a belief that change need not be culturally disruptive. In Deng's China and in Carter's South, adaptation was both possible and desirable.

The "shock of change" would also confront Jimmy Carter's generation in the form of a revolution in race relations. During the 1976 campaign Theodore White asked all the presidential aspirants this question: "Where did modern American history really begin?" Carter named first the civil rights movement, which in the course of redirecting American history had also radically altered his native Southland.[16]

Segregation was not exactly the word for the rural world in which Carter grew up (the necessities of farm life dictated otherwise), but racial control was the rule there until the system began to unravel in the 1950s. Jimmy Carter cultivated a version of his own family history that identified the Carters as participants in Sumter County's racial reconciliation, but not as radical proponents of change. Carter also echoed a familiar refrain of southern white "moderates" on desegregation: the white South was forced to do what it knew was right, and in that moment the suffering of black southerners and the "trauma" of whites were finally redeemed.[17]

16. Theodore H. White, *America in Search of Itself: The Making of the President, 1956–1980* (New York, 1982), 198–99.

17. Numan V. Bartley, "Jimmy Carter and the Politics of the New South," in *The Forum Series* (St. Louis, 1979), 11–12. Bartley suggests an ironic twist on George Tindall's idea of a southern dialectic. In the 1950s and 1960s, blacks and federal authorities had demanded an end to segregation; much of the southern political establishment resisted, but in the end the civil rights movement and the federal government

Talk like that made it difficult for Americans to fit Jimmy Carter into standard southern categories. If he did not fit the stereotypes, it was in part because the South had changed so radically during his own lifetime. If he was acutely aware of those changes, it was in part because he had been away. At Annapolis and on sea duty Carter, like generations of expatriates before him, had confronted his own southernness. Jimmy Carter was no Quentin Compson at Harvard, but his dormitory bull sessions, his refusal as a plebe to sing "Marching Through Georgia" for the amusement of upper classmen, and his enduring of shipmates' taunts about his Bible Belt origins all tended toward the affirmation that began, "I am a Southerner."

Just as the American people had difficulty locating Jimmy Carter within a taxonomy of southern social types, so too they puzzled over how he fit into a recognizable *political* framework. The confusion in this case stemmed more from Carter than from the taxonomy. The triad of Bourbonism, Populism, and Progressivism has provided a serviceable framework for the study of southern politics, even though scholars continue to squabble about how the three connect. George Tindall has suggested a "dialectic" relation: "The Bourbons supplied a thesis, the Populists set up an antithesis, and the Progressives worked out a synthesis which governed southern politics through the first half of the twentieth century."[18]

---

prevailed and the old leaders were discredited. The political beneficiaries were not, with a few exceptions, the participants in the civil rights movement, but rather the new generation of southern business progressives, including Carter. Although this analysis may underestimate the resilience of some of the older generation of southern political leaders (Strom Thurmond, John Stennis, and Herman Talmadge come to mind) and overestimate the differences between Carter and, say, George Wallace, it nevertheless provides a useful framework for viewing southern politics in the 1970s.

18. George B. Tindall, *The Persistent Tradition in New South Politics* (Baton Rouge, 1975), xii. See also Dewey W. Grantham, *Southern Progressivism: The Reconciliation of Progress and Tradition* (Knoxville, 1983), esp. chap. 9.

The Carters of Sumter County represented all three strands of this tradition. First, Earl Carter's farming, processing, and mercantile interests located him in the category of what Ralph McGill called the "small-town rich man," who was the twentieth-century version of the Bourbon. Second, Jim Jack Gordy, Lillian Carter's father and Jimmy's maternal grandfather, had been a southwest Georgia Populist and confidant of Tom Watson. And finally, in the state house and in the White House, Jimmy Carter's approach to governance was squarely within the progressive tradition.

In his first presidential campaign Carter appropriated the populist label as part of his "outsider" appeal and affected a certain populist style as a counterpoint to the imperial presidency of Richard Nixon. Programmatically, as well as stylistically, Carter identified himself with populism, of sorts: "Among the most important goals in the Southern brand of populism," he later wrote, "was to help the poor and aged, to improve education, and to provide jobs. At the same time the populists tried not to waste money, having almost an obsession about the burden of excessive debt." Carter identified as populists the southern political leaders Huey Long and Richard Russell, both of whom were in fact babes-in-arms when the genuine Populist movement briefly flourished and then collapsed.[19] Although both men—Long in particular—conducted themselves in a style reminiscent of the Populists, the *program* that Carter identified with them (and with himself) more nearly fits the third element of the triad.

For the sake of argument, recall the *actions* of Huey Long as governor of Louisiana, rather than his flamboyant rhetoric; then call to mind *young* Richard Russell, the reform governor of Georgia whose claim to fame was the reorganization of state government. Viewed in this light, Long, Russell, Carter, and the "populist" program that Carter articulated actually fit best in the tradition of

19. Jimmy Carter, *Keeping Faith: Memoirs of a President* (New York, 1982), 74, 104. In his memoirs, Carter identified as southern populists Richard Russell and Huey Long. The diary entry concerning Russell Long identifies the senator's father as "Huey Long, former populist governor of Louisiana."

southern *progressivism*—specifically, that variant which Tindall has labeled "business progressivism."

Since the 1920s southern state governments often have been managed by men who stressed efficiency and public service, who fostered a "scientific" approach to public administration, and who championed state-supported economic development rather than the redistributive programs of the Populists. These progressives were, with the exception of a few interesting characters like the Kingfish, men of steady, middle-class habits, "circumspect in demeanor, conservatively 'constructive' in their approach to public problems, storming no citadels of entrenched 'privilege,' but carrying forward the new public functions that had gained acceptance in the progressive era."[20]

They were, in short, men like Jimmy Carter, the pietist and engineer-businessman. From his emergence as a civic leader in Sumter County to his first campaign for the state senate (a Goliath-slaying effort against a corrupt political machine) to his single term as governor (the hallmark of which was reorganization of state government), Carter was squarely within the tradition of southern business progressivism.[21]

Fusing populist rhetoric and progressive programs was nothing new in Carter's South, but how would it play on a national stage? Political strategists, like generals, plan for the next war by studying the last one. The 1972 campaign was Jimmy Carter's textbook, and the buzzword that year was populism. Whether the

20. H. C. Nixon, quoted in George B. Tindall, "Business Progressivism: Southern Politics in the Twenties," in Tindall, *Ethnic Southerners*, 148. The analysis of Carter as a business progressive is based on Tindall's development of that political type, here and in *Emergence of the New South*.

21. Bartley, "Jimmy Carter and the Politics of the New South," 5–10; Gary M. Fink, *Prelude to the Presidency: The Political Character and Legislative Leadership Style of Governor Jimmy Carter* (Westport, Conn., 1980). In Fink's view the most apt description for Governor Carter's political philosophy is "temperamental pragmatism" (p. 3). My own assessment of Carter's place in the Bourbon-Populist-Progressive triad was first expressed in Arthur S. Link *et al.*, *The American People: A History* (Arlington Heights, Ill., 1981), 1010–12.

"populism" of 1972 embodied a radical critique of the existing order or was just another name for social backlash, covering as it did
"everyone from Spiro Agnew to Bella Abzug or from George Wallace to George McGovern," it most certainly gave voice to the sense
of estrangement and powerlessness that gripped more and more
Americans as the decade wore on. Populist rhetoric was made to
order for the candidate who could cast himself as the outsider, as
George Wallace had already proved, but it was not without risks.[22]

The Carter presidential campaign strategy for 1976, designed by a small circle of Georgians in 1972, saw Wallace as the
first obstacle. Carter's aide Hamilton Jordan feared that a Wallace
campaign would preempt Carter's candidacy, but as Jordan advised
his boss in his now-famous memorandum of November 4, 1972,
"Hopefully he will not run for President in 1976 and your candi
dacy should be an effort to encompass and expand on the Wallace
constituency and populist philosophy by being a better qualified
and more responsible alternative to George Wallace."[23]

Here was the risk—and the opportunity—of the Carter candidacy: Carter would articulate a "populist philosophy" to attract
Wallace's supporters, northern and southern, while at the same
time conveying an aura of responsibility and competency to those
Democrats for whom the term "southern populist" evoked images
of demagoguery and provincial buffoonery. The trick was to evoke

22. Quotation from George B. Tindall, "Populism: A Semantic Identity Crisis," in
Tindall, *Ethnic Southerners*, 163. Jimmy Carter was not the only claimant for the title
of "populist candidate" in 1976. Former senator Fred Harris of Oklahoma had written a book called *The New Populism*, cultivated his southwestern twang, and mapped
out a "guerrilla" campaign very similar to the one being outlined by Carter and his
aides. Harris' campaign fizzled, leading him to remark that he was the candidate of
the little people and that on election day they had been unable to reach up and pull
the lever on the voting machine. Harris' campaign manager, Jim Hightower, followed the Harris strategy with greater success, winning election in Texas as state
agriculture commissioner. He is arguably the only genuine populist holding state-
wide office in the South in the early 1990s.

23. Quoted in Jules Witcover, *Marathon: The Pursuit of the Presidency, 1972–1976*
(New York, 1977), 110.

the spirit of populism without actually raising its troublesome ghost. Southern progressives had long since mastered this black art by appealing to the "little man" in the style of old-time Populists, but without launching a full-fledged attack on entrenched power.

Jordan's balancing act had another dimension to it, which he described after Carter had secured the Democratic nomination: "Although the Southern states provide us with a rich base of support, it would be a mistake to appear to be overly dependent on the South for victory in November. . . . To the extent that regional bias exists in this country—and it does—there would be a negative reaction to a candidacy that was perceived as being a captive of the Southern states and/or people."[24]

An analysis of voting behavior in New York state (where Carter lost badly in the primary but won in November) confirms the burden of southernness for candidate Carter. Geographer Robert M. Pierce concluded: "Like other social scientists, geographers have reported a marked tendency by northerners to perceive the population of the South as racially biased, provincial, slow moving and generally anti-northern." And, if that were not enough: "The ideal public official in the minds of northern voters is one who, among other things, is not from the South." (The social-scientific evidence to support the first conclusion was a quotation from H. L. Mencken. For the second, survey research had to suffice.) How then to account for Carter's showing? An ingenious survey that Pierce took in May and repeated just before the general election indicated that New Yorkers still had an aversion to southerners, but not to Carter: they did not perceive him as one of the breed![25]

Even allowing for a certain amount of hyperbole in Pierce's startling conclusion (most New Yorkers presumably knew where Georgia was), the fact remains that in 1976 Carter campaigned in the non-South as a scientist and engineer, as a businessman, as an

24. Quoted *ibid.*, 520.
25. Robert M. Pierce, "Jimmy Carter and the New South: The View from New York," in *Perspectives on the American South: An Annual Review of Society, Politics, and Culture,* ed. Merle Black and John Shelton Reed (New York, 1984), II, 184–89.

outsider not tainted by the mess in Washington, and as a good and decent man deserving of the nation's trust. He did not dodge the subject of his roots in the national campaign, but neither did he make an issue of his southernness with nonsouthern audiences.

Witness, for example, the interview with Carter by Bill Moyers, which was broadcast over public television in May, 1976. Fellow Southern Baptist Moyers began with sympathetic questions about family, homeplace, and religion. The two men could even speak in a certain regional code ("BTU" stood for Baptist Training Union). Carter was open, at ease, and enjoying himself. But then Moyers shifted out of the fellow-Southerner role to convey a question from a "New Yorker friend" who had said of Carter, "He strikes me as a decent but provincial and narrow-minded man from the South who's lived most of his life in that environment." The friend, Moyers said, wanted to know if Carter could lead a pluralistic society.[26]

The "southern question" was every bit as important for Carter as the "Catholic question" had been for John Kennedy, and Carter's answer was well rehearsed. He began by acknowledging the rural isolation of his childhood, recalling that he was "a minority member in a predominantly black neighborhood." But rather than telling how this distinctly southern experience had prepared him for leadership in a pluralistic society, Carter proceeded to list all the countries he had visited, the world leaders he had met, and the books he had mastered on America and its government. He had studied, Carter explained, all 435 of the nation's congressional districts and had read the campaign platforms of "every person who's ever run for President."[27]

No more evocation of Sunday evenings in Dixie, no more talk about how the South would lead the nation into a new era in race relations. This is self-improvement with a vengeance. Carter demonstrates mastery, not of his own history, but of the nation's.

26. Interview with Jimmy Carter by Bill Moyers, "USA: People and Politics," May 6, 1976, pp. 163–82.
27. *Ibid.*, 169.

One can acknowledge that "I am a Southerner," yet still be careful to pronounce the postvocalic *r*'s.

Whatever the Candidate might say on national television, in November southerners knew that a homeboy had been elected president. To many in Dixie, the inauguration of a president from the Deep South in 1977 signified sectional reconciliation. "The South and the Nation are Joined," proclaimed the editor of the Anniston *Star.*[28] This time, unlike 1877, black southerners could join the celebration, for they had given Carter his margin of victory in the region.

But once the euphoria of having "sent them a President" wore off, what difference would it make to have a southerner in the White House? Would Carter as president be recognizably southern? With regard to management style and policy agenda, Carter remained true to type, the southern engineer-business progressive. But the public image and personal style that President Carter and his handlers chose to project was, for the most part, surprisingly unsouthern.

Jimmy Carter's administrative style, like that of many other southern progressives, had never fitted the mold of the gregarious, backslapping, storytelling, hard-drinking southern pol. When a reporter asked the president-elect how he would arrive at policy decisions, Carter replied that the "exact procedure is derived to some degree from my scientific or engineering background." He then spelled out a decision-making process that owed more to Admiral Hyman Rickover, his boss in the nuclear submarine program, than to down-home politics.[29]

Before his administration was well launched, the stories of Carter's technocratic style were legion. Even if many of the anec-

---

28. Carter, *Keeping Faith*, 22. Editor Brandt Ayers was a confidant of Carter's and very much an advocate of the New South progressivism that Carter espoused. See Ayers' essay "You Can't Eat Magnolias" in a volume of that same title, ed. Ayers and Thomas H. Naylor (New York, 1972), 3–24.

29. Neal R. Peirce, "The Carter Presidency: Plans and Priorities," in *The Presidency Reappraised*, ed. Thomas E. Cronin and Rexford G. Tugwell (2d ed.; New York, 1977), 44–45.

dotes are apocryphal, the testimony of participants in the Carter White House and the first fragmentary evidence from Carter's presidential papers confirm the image of a hands-on, meticulous engineer's approach to the presidency. Carter *did* master the detail of legislative and policy decisions, double check budget arithmetic, and balance cost-benefit equations on his trusty legal pad.[30]

Many of the domestic policy initiatives Carter put forth were squarely in the tradition of southern progressivism, particularly as it had evolved since World War II. Southern governors like North Carolina's Luther Hodges and Florida's Leroy Collins developed the policy agenda that Carter and his contemporaries elaborated on: within the context of fiscal conservatism they tinkered with government organization and service delivery, promoted economic development while deemphasizing government regulation, and empaneled experts to engineer growth. In addition, southern governors of Carter's cohort had to address environmental and energy crises that threatened the region's new-found prosperity.[31]

In the White House, Jimmy Carter reorganized and deregulated, grappled with energy crises and budget deficits, struggled with the conflicting aims of controlling stagflation and protecting the environment, and launched studies of industrial innovation and goals for the eighties. Evaluation of Carter's domestic policy

30. Not surprisingly, the first sets of White House papers opened for research by the Carter Library reveal relatively little about Carter himself. Much of the material now available consists of copies, the paper flow *to* Carter and his top aides. In many instances the paper trail now open for inspection stops short of the president's desk. More will be learned with the opening of key record sets, including the Presidential Handwriting Files and other sensitive documents now under seal. Nevertheless, some notes from the president and a fair amount of presidential marginalia on memoranda confirm the public impression of Carter's crisp, technocratic style of management. Toward the end of his term, when asked by an Indiana newspaper editor what his pet peeve was, Carter replied, "People being late." Jim Bannon to Jody Powell, June 19, 1980, and marginal notation by "Jimmy C." in WHCF, Box 83, PP-14, "1/20/77–1/20/81."

31. Tom R. Wagy, *Governor LeRoy Collins of Florida: Spokesman of the New South* (University, Ala., 1985); Luther H. Hodges, *Businessman in the Statehouse: Six Years as Governor of North Carolina* (Chapel Hill, 1962).

initiatives is beyond the scope of this essay, but when the critical history of policy making in the Carter years is written, it will be essential to ask how well the venerable tradition of business progressivism served President Carter in dealing with the multifaceted national crises of the 1970s—including the complex and novel economic problems that brought Americans face to face with the prospect of a "quite un-American experience with poverty."[32] Un-American, perhaps, but not un-southern.

Scholars of the Carter presidency will also do well to recall his toast to Deng Xiaoping, with its references to the rural South. A set of values about land—land as inheritance and birthright, land as the object of stewardship—permeates decisions on issues ranging from the Camp David accords to the Panama Canal treaties to Carter's domestic agriculture policies.[33]

32. Instant assessments of Carter's domestic policy initiatives have found them wanting on the grounds that the Carter administration (pick one) tried to do too much all at once, lacked the political and communications skills to enact a legislative agenda, or simply applied the wrong solutions to the problems at hand. Barbara Kellerman, *The Political Presidency: Practice of Leadership* (New York, 1984), chap. 10; James Fallows, "The Passionless Presidency: The Trouble with Jimmy Carter's Administration," *Atlantic*, May, 1979, pp. 33–48, and June, 1979, pp. 75–81. Studies of Carter's environmental policy based on preliminary examination of White House files offer a more balanced view of the Carter White House than either Kellerman or Fallows. See the following graduate seminar papers: Mark L. Demyanek, "The Carter Administration and the Issue of Acid Precipitation," Carol Carmichael Jacobs, "White House Response to the Chemical Emergency at Love Canal, August, 1978–October, 1980," and David E. Jacobs, "Carcinogens: How OSHA Tackled the Problem During the Jimmy Carter Years," all in possession of Robert C. McMath, Jr. Quotation from C. Vann Woodward, *The Burden of Southern History* (Rev. ed.; Baton Rouge, 1968), 17.

33. On the Middle East conflict and Camp David accords as a land issue, see Jimmy Carter, *The Blood of Abraham* (Boston, 1985), 31–48. On the Panama Canal Treaty, see Carter, *Keeping Faith*, 152. On the Carter farm policy, which tried to address the structural problems of family farming and to balance environmental concerns against the demands of agricultural production, see Jimmy Carter, "Department of Agriculture: Remarks and Question and Answer Session with Department Employees, February 6, 1977," in *Public Papers of the Presidents of the United States:*

The story of this southerner in the White House is not just about policy making, however much or little that activity may have been influenced by Carter's southern roots. Candidate Carter had offered *himself* as the solution to the nation's ills, more than any particular policies. What, if anything, would Carter's southernness have to do with his presidential persona?

Six weeks *before* Jimmy Carter was inaugurated, his pollster and political confidant Patrick Caddell delivered to the president-elect a fifty-seven-page memorandum modestly entitled "Initial Working Paper on Political Strategy." Carter read the document, underlined portions of it, and circulated it among top aides and the vice-president-elect with the notation, "Excellent. See me re this."[34] The campaign to define a presidential image and the campaign to reelect Jimmy Carter had begun.

Among the passages Carter underlined was one noting the fragility of his regional base. Dissecting the results of the election just past, Caddell concluded, "In the end, the decline in the South that took place in October because of [conservative] ideology, was reversed only by regional pride." Looking toward the next campaign, the president "must use regional sentiment, regional appointments, and his own personal leadership . . . to maintain the base in the South."[35]

But of course Carter did not hold his southern base in 1980, except for Georgia. That failure had mainly to do with the force of events: no amount of regional pride could have overcome the brutal facts of stagflation, agricultural depression, energy shortages,

---

Jimmy Carter, 1977 (Washington, D.C., 1978), I, 167–71. Carter's approach to land issues is consistent with the interpretation of land as a biblical theme presented in Walter Brueggemann, *The Land: Place as Gift, Promise, and Challenge in Biblical Faith* (Philadelphia, 1977).

34. Patrick H. Caddell, "Initial Working Papers on Political Strategy" (with marginal notations), December 10, 1976, in Jody Powell, 1976 Campaign/Transition File, Box 4, Carter Presidential Library.

35. *Ibid.*, 8, 22, 27.

and the Iran crisis. It is nevertheless amazing to note how seldom President Carter referred in public to his own regional identity and how infrequently he invoked the southern experience in appealing either to regional or national audiences.

Perhaps the Carters were stung by preinaugural barbs from Washington journalists about "the prospective dearth of social grace in the White House and . . . four years of nothing but hillbilly music and ignorant Bible-toting Southerners"—protestations to the contrary notwithstanding.[36] Certainly Carter faced embarrassment from down-home friends and relations. Only a few months into his term, the revelation of Bert Lance's north Georgia banking practices threatened to saddle the administration with a major scandal, while Billy Carter, the epitome of the good ol' boy, steadfastly refused to stay out of sight as other First Brothers had done. One also detects in President Carter a desire to shed the southern image. Roy Blount observed, with a touch of sadness, that Carter wanted to be "National. International. Humanitarian. No Cracker."[37]

Blount based his assessment, in part, on personal observation of Carter at a town meeting in Yazoo City, Mississippi, in July, 1977. Blount was closer to the truth than he knew. The stop in Yazoo City was part of the president's first extended tour of the South after taking office, a trip that began with an address before the Southern Legislative Conference in Charleston. Prior to the trip, the White House speechwriter Jim Fallows had outlined for the president the themes Fallows thought should be covered in the Charleston speech: "This is the chance to give a very personal and philosophical speech about the way your Southern background has shaped your decisions as president. Although it should be delivered frankly as one Southerner speaking to his fellow Southerners, it would be of interest to the rest of the country as well. . . . Southerners—you and your audience—are shaped by special tra-

36. Carter, *Keeping Faith,* 23. In *his* memoirs, Carter's press secretary was more willing to castigate the national news media for their antisouthern bias. Jody Powell, *The Other Side of the Story* (New York, 1984).

37. Blount, *Crackers,* 287.

ditions, experiences, guilt, and wisdom, which will yield lessons that are particularly timely for the country now. Inevitably, you have brought this perspective to much of what you have done or will do as President." [38]

Fallows had read his Woodward, but the president had other ideas. Carter's reply was brief: "Jim—I'd like to review foreign policy—include Panama Canal—emphasis on E[ast]-W[est relations]. J." The speech as delivered dealt almost entirely with U.S.–Soviet relations, specifically arms control. The president opened with just enough reference to the South to show he knew he was in Charleston, South Carolina, not Charleston, Massachusetts. [39] So much for a southern strategy.

Things were a little different that same evening when fourteen hundred people squeezed into the auditorium of Yazoo City's new high school to see the president from Georgia. With television lights adding to the discomfort, Carter joked with his sweltering audience about the use of "southern self-propelled air-conditioners" and praised Yazoo City voters for approving a bond issue to build a new school for a student body two-thirds black and one-third white (roughly the inverse mix of the crowd that night). Then, for an hour and a half, Carter fielded questions on subjects ranging from energy and inflation to abortion and the neutron bomb. His exchanges with members of the audience showed Carter at his best: self-confident and in command of the facts. The engineer-president had done his homework and was giving an impressive account of himself on the issues. Then, toward the end of the session, one question pushed him into the confessional mode that Fallows had urged on him. A Yazoo City housewife, Mrs. Betty Rainey, asked the president: "What aspects of what you con-

38. Jim Fallows, "Memorandum for the President," June 5, 1977, WHCF, Box SP-21 (Sp 3–43), "1/20/77–1/20/81."

39. *Ibid.*, marginal notation; *Public Papers of the Presidents . . . Jimmy Carter, 1977,* II, 1309–15. Two years later Fallows, no longer in the president's employ, wrote a scathing critique of Carter's ability to communicate, published in the *Atlantic* as the two-part "Passionless Presidency" cited above. Hell hath no fury like a speechwriter scorned.

sider to be your southern heritage have led to your concern about human rights in this nation and abroad?"

Carter replied with a list of regional-personal characteristics—carefully qualified so as not to sound exclusively southern or exclusively his—all of which affirmed the worth of individuals and the possibility of progress: religion, rural self-sufficiency, historical preference for local government, and finally guilt and redemption: "In the South we were guilty for many years of the deprivation of human rights to a large portion of our citizens. Now, to look back 20 years, when black people didn't have a right to vote, didn't have a right to go to a decent school . . . is an indictment on us. I think it was with a great deal of courage that the South was able to face up to that change. I personally believe it was the best thing that ever happened to the South in my lifetime."[40]

It was a message—white and black southerners can work together—that Carter had delivered with remarkable effectiveness in black churches during the campaign. It was a theme—praise for the civil rights movement and confession of sin—that had given Carter credibility with liberal Democrats. It was a litany—"The South and the Nation are Joined"—that brought applause (and one rebel yell) from a predominantly white audience in a steamy high school auditorium on the edge of the Mississippi Delta.

Here was a message that Carter could deliver with all the power of a southern preacher, a message which would put his autobiographical southernness to good use: support for human rights, at home and abroad, stems from the recollection of "the good things and the bad things in our [southern] heritage."[41] Wisely used, the phrase "I am a Southerner" could take on the same power as the slogan of another southern Baptist, Jesse Jackson: "I am somebody." No slogan for an unforgetting Old South, this, but an affirmation of change in the New.

Why did this theme not catch on among white southerners?

40. *Public Papers of the Presidents . . . Jimmy Carter, 1977*, II, 1328.
41. *Ibid.*, 1329.

For one thing, it was used very sparingly. Even in Yazoo City it was buried in an impressive but arcane discussion of policy issues. But also, this was just not the message they wanted to hear. When linked to civil rights, such talk raised the specter of racial quotas. When applied to the international scene, it conjured up images of an administration gone soft on communism and intent on giving away the Panama Canal. And when employed in the heat of a re-election campaign, it brought cries of mean-spiritedness and unfair attacks on an opponent more popular in the South than the homeboy.

Carter repeated his Yazoo City appeal for an end to bigotry during the 1980 campaign, when Ronald Reagan seemed to be capitalizing on a "whites only" southern strategy. Carter's remarks, some of them added extemporaneously to prepared texts, evoked the most racially enlightened aspects of southern populism and business progressivism, but that won him few converts.

Carter opened the campaign at a Labor Day picnic in the Tennessee Valley community of Tuscumbia, Alabama. Gospel and country music groups warmed up the crowd. A pantheon of Deep South Democrats ringed the stage—John Stennis, George Wallace, Albert Gore, Sr., and Jim Folsom among them. With Klansmen parading noisily in the background (Tuscumbia was home to one branch of the Ku Klux Klan), Carter blasted the KKK in tones that echoed Big Jim Folsom's blasts at the Invisible Empire. Acknowledging a shared pride in "our region, the Southland," Carter denounced those "who practice cowardice and who counsel fear and hatred. . . . I say that those people in white sheets do not understand our region and what it's been through, they do not understand what our country stands for, they do not understand that the South and all of America must move forward." [42]

Campaigning in Detroit the same day, Ronald Reagan said of Carter: "He's opening his campaign down in the city that gave birth to and is the parent body of the Ku Klux Klan." Democrats,

42. Press Release, September 1, 1980, in WHCF, SP3–1/ST1/80.

sensing that they had Reagan in a bind, rose to defend the honor of the South, at the same time linking *Reagan's* candidacy to the Klan (the leader of another branch of the KKK had already endorsed Governor Reagan): "A callous and opportunistic slap at the South," cried seven southern governors in chorus. "I think it was something that all Southerners will resent," said Jimmy Carter.[43]

Two weeks later Carter addressed a rally at Atlanta's historic Ebenezer Baptist Church. On his way into the church a local reporter whom Carter knew well asked about "this effort to bring the Ku Klux Klan into this presidential race." Carter shot back, "Well, obviously the Ku Klux Klan is an obnoxious blight on the American scene and anyone who injected it into the campaign made a serious mistake."[44]

Ebenezer was packed with black leaders from across the South, among them the father and widow of Martin Luther King, Jr., whose church it was. Carter departed from his text to restate an oft-repeated theme, that he could never have been elected president had it not been for the Kings, father and son.

A year earlier Jim Fallows had intimated that Carter needed public-speaking lessons, and James David Barber, trying to be helpful, had mailed him a copy of William Jennings Bryan's most famous Chautauqua speech.[45] Carter needed no coaching that day

43. New York *Times,* September 2–4, 1980.

44. Press Release, "Informal Question and Answer Session with the President Outside the Ebenezer Baptist Church, September 16, 1980," SP34/SD-10, Carter Presidential Library.

45. Fallows, "Passionless Presidency" (May), 44. Barber's gifts (not only Bryan's "Prince of Peace" speech but also Russell Conwell's "Acres of Diamonds") came during the struggle for Jimmy Carter's soul that preceded his "crisis of confidence" speech. Substantively, they were meant as a counterweight to the arguments being put forth by Patrick Caddell, Christopher Lasch, and others—just in case those advisers "have convinced you all that the citizenry are on their way to hell in a hand basket, wallowing in sloth and narcissism." One may also infer that the gifts were intended as gentle hints on how to communicate with ordinary Americans. James David Barber to Jody Powell, May 29, 1979, in Powell, Box 55 ["Dinner with Bill Moyers, *et al.,*" May 30, 1979], Carter Presidential Library.

at Ebenezer. He slipped naturally into the cadence of preachers who had stood in Ebenezer's pulpit before him: "In this region for too long, politicians who hoped to be elected to the office of county commissioner or mayor or governor or congressman or senator— had to divide blacks from whites. They had to blame the poverty that afflicted our nation among white people on the black people or vice versa." And in another departure from the text others had written for him, Carter said: "You've seen in this campaign the stirrings of hate and the rebirth of code words like 'states' rights'. . . . That is a message that creates a cloud on the political horizon. Hatred has no place in this country. Racism has no place in this country."[46]

Carter's addresses in Tuscumbia and at Ebenezer were remarkable, both in content and in the effectiveness of their delivery, yet they went largely unnoticed, save for mention of the sparring between Carter and Reagan on the subject of the Klan. Perhaps the appeal to southern tradition in opposition to racism simply did not compute. Redneck chic, a mainstay of campaign reporting in 1976, was now out of fashion. What might have been construed as a courageous statement four years earlier was now reported as a mean-spirited political attack.

That is not to say that the press was responsible for Carter's political downfall or that his southernness could have somehow transformed his political liabilities into assets. The end of the 1970s was not a propitious time for hard sayings from a presidential Jer-

46. Press Release, "Remarks of the President at Meeting with Southern Black Leaders, Ebenezer Baptist Church, September 16, 1980," and Press Release, "Text of the President's Remarks at the Ebenezer Baptist Church [advance text], September 15, 1980," both in WHCF, Subject File, Box Sp-19, "1/20/77–1/20/81"; "Remarks at a Meeting with Southern Black Leaders, September 16, 1980, Atlanta," *Public Papers of the Presidents . . . Jimmy Carter, 1980–81*, II, 1750. On the difficulties of tracing the development of Carter's speeches in draft using materials currently available for scholarly research, see David E. Alsobrook, "Resources of the Carter Library in the Study of Recent Georgia History" (Paper presented at the annual meeting of the Georgia Association of Historians, April 18, 1987, copy in possession of Robert C. McMath, Jr.).

emiah or a James the Baptist, even when pronounced with a southern accent or tempered with the technocratic bent of progressivism. The curse of southern populists and prophets is to be branded as "calamity-howlers." The curse of southern business progressives is to be perceived as dull and uninspiring. In 1980 Jimmy Carter experienced both.

Was Jimmy Carter a southerner in the White House? Yes, but of a particular type, or more precisely of the two types just noted: the southern populist as outsider and prophet, and the middle-class southerner as engineer and progressive. For most of his presidency, the latter had the upper hand. As Carter himself acknowledged, this dictated an approach to governance that ran more toward management than charisma, and a style that deemphasized public displays of regionalism. Roy Blount was right: "National. International. Humanitarian. No cracker." When it came time to construct a Presidential Image, Jimmy Carter's autobiographical southernness seemed to disappear like the Cheshire cat, leaving only the smile.

On rare occasions Carter the southern populist *did* use the presidency as a bully pulpit with "The Burden of Southern History" as his text. He was better at it than he has been given credit for. But neither in those moments when he sounded for all the world like Big Jim Folsom, or even Martin Luther King, nor in those long months when he dutifully plugged away at his job like a good progressive, did he find political advantage for 1980.

If we must ask of Carter, "what kind of southerner," we must also ask "which South?" Or more precisely, "which Souths," for Jimmy Carter made his way between two epochs of southern history, and in so doing exemplified the adaptability of southern culture.

Excepting an occasional ceremonial flourish or genealogical aside, one finds in Carter's political and administrative record no trace of the antebellum yeoman or the fire-eating southern nationalist, nor even of the postbellum champion of the Lost Cause. For him localism, states' rights, and white supremacy were gone with the wind. The point of departure for Carter's southernness was the "New" South of approximately the 1880s to 1920—the age of the Bourbons, Populists, and Progressives. By the time of Carter's return to Georgia in the 1950s, *that* New South was being bulldozed into oblivion and a Newer one erected in its place.

In the 1960s and 1970s, Carter and his generation of middle-class white southerners crafted a usable past from the memories of the turn-of-the-century South: variations on a theme by Henry Grady and Hoke Smith and young Richard Russell (with a few notes from Tom Watson thrown in for dramatic effect). To affirm, as candidate Carter did in 1975, that one was a farmer, an engineer, a planner, a businessman—and a southerner—was to signify, in the midst of bewildering change, continuity with an older but not Old South.

Interview with
George Brown Tindall

Conducted by Elizabeth Jacoway, Dan T. Carter, and
Robert C. McMath, Jr.

Jacoway: George, we thought it would be fun to get together and visit a bit, though we're not going to try to capture
George Tindall in two hours. We would like to do that, but we
know we can't ask everything we might want to ask. But we
thought it would enhance the volume tremendously to let our
reader just have a little bit of the flavor of the man.

Tindall: As I suggested a while ago, you could just reprint
that essay "History and the English Language." You may decide to
do that before you're finished.

Carter: George may be apprehensive about this because of
one other experience he and I had in which we were asked to take
part in a panel for Jack Bass on "The American South Comes of
Age." And I don't know whether George remembers it as quite the
nightmarish evening that I do. But if you remember, I was supposed to be moderating and I had that darned microphone in my
ear and that idiot kept talking to me the whole time while we were
supposed to be going back and forth. And he would say, "All right,
now turn to so-and-so and ask him a question." Of course, I didn't

have a foggiest question in my mind at the time. So this works better.

Jacoway: But we have the microphone!

Tindall: I won't have the foggiest answer.

Jacoway: Well, do you guys have an appropriate zinger that you wanted to use?

Carter: No, beauty before age.

Jacoway: All right. I am curious to know about how you chose UNC for your graduate work.

Tindall: I had a professor of English who sort of took me under his wing when I was a freshman at Furman, named C. L. Pittman. He was not a person who ever established a great reputation for publication in the field; in fact, he died fairly young. But he had taken a degree in the English department at Chapel Hill. I think the department had a reputation, and I thought of Chapel Hill because of Frank Graham. And, I knew that Norman Foerster had been there. I was thinking of Chapel Hill as a place where I might major in English. I was in the graduating class of '42 at Furman, and my draft notice came the day before commencement and my parents hid it from me till the day after commencement. I had applied for graduate fellowships and the one place I got one was LSU. Had I not gone into service I might have accepted that and gone there, but by that time Brooks and Warren were already gone anyway. I had majored in English and had a double major in history; but I had fixed in my mind that Chapel Hill was a preferred place.

I don't know where it came from, it may be like the thing that Louis B. Wright said. Louis B. Wright grew up in Greenwood, South Carolina, not Greenville but Greenwood, and in his memoir of his life he tells about going to Greenville when there was some special occasion like a concert or something that was more likely to come to Greenville because it was a little bit bigger place. Anyway, he said, paraphrasing Samuel Johnson about the Scots, "The fairest prospect that faces the South Carolinian is the high road to Chapel Hill." So when I came back from the war I took that high road, fancying myself a major in English. Had I not had a few years out of school and in the military, I don't know, I probably would have gone on and be retiring as a frustrated assistant professor still reading freshman themes on "what I did last summer."

Jacoway: Was it Frank Graham's racial liberalism that attracted you or just his general reputation for liberalism?

Tindall: I think it was just his general reputation for liberalism that I found attractive. And it may have been his—maybe I should be embarrassed to say this—his celebrity status that sort of gave Chapel Hill an identity. Looking back on it now, I realize that a lot of the push that made Chapel Hill what it was in those days had come from Harry Woodburn Chase, who was a New Englander but whose inaugural address as president (he'd been in the South ten years, at Chapel Hill, when he became president in 1919), his inaugural in 1920 was a real New South speech. He was broadening out the idea that had been expressed by his predecessor, Edward Kidder Graham, in developing extension work: the campus of the university extends to the boundaries of the state. And Chase was consciously broadening this to the South. And of course there were people like [Roulhac] Hamilton, who was already gathering the manuscripts for the Southern Historical Collection, and so on. Anyway, it was just that reputation and my having very early, and at an impressionable age, come in contact with somebody from Chapel Hill who touted the place highly.

I don't know whether you all have heard this story but I'll tell it. Furman was such a small place, Pittman came to double as the press bureau, the equivalent of publicity man. And Albert Einstein came to town to visit his son, who was there. (He became a very noted scientist himself, in his own right. He was working for, I don't know who, DuPont or somebody that was stationed in Greenville.) And Pittman had arranged it so that he would come over to visit the Furman campus; this was purely a publicity stunt, the man was being used. And they asked me if I would care to go with him to pick up Einstein and bring him over, so I said yes and I went with such awe and fear and trembling of this famous man.

We came back to the campus and we got out of the car, and there was instant recognition all around the campus, crowds began to gather, they followed us across the campus to the science building, where I had barely set foot myself.

He was ushered in there and—this is getting long-winded, I have to tell this story anyway, even if I am wasting your tape—he went through, and I have never known, I never tried to find out (I didn't really want to know, I guess, how it happened), but somehow a crowd spontaneously gathered in one of these big, tiered, science lecture rooms. And at the end of his tour through the building and meeting the people he was ushered through a door that placed him right in front of that room with those tiers of seats filled with students. He was obviously miffed at this. He stood there and he said, "I had been told that I was coming over here to see the science building and to meet with the people in the sciences. I was not told that I would be expected to give a lecture, but I will answer any question that any of you might have." And so a good friend of mine stood up and said, "Dr. Einstein, your name has been associated with the theory of relativity." I forget exactly how he expressed it, but it went something like this. "In a few words, I wonder if you could explain to us what your theory of relativity is."

Einstein said, "Young man, you're a student here, aren't you?"

"Yes sir."

"What class are you in?"

"I'm a junior."

"Well, then, you should know what the theory of relativity is."

And nobody else had any questions. But anyhow we still had senior superlatives back in those antediluvian days, and I think it was a consequence of that trip and having been seen by so many people getting out of the car with Albert Einstein, I was chosen the most intellectual.

Carter: Proximity.

Tindall: Proximity. In the women's class Blossom was the most intellectual. There is a picture of the two of us coming down the steps together in the yearbook. You can make that a frontispiece. I was thin then.

Carter: George, you later switched from English to history once you got to Chapel Hill; do you think your experiences in the military affected either your interest in southern history or your decision to go to Chapel Hill? I mean, did you have any kind of consciousness of being a southerner more than you were before?

Tindall: Looking back on it, I don't think really that was the influence. I think it came earlier. Somehow, I think it came probably from where we recruit many, if not most, historians, except maybe the antiquarians, true antiquarians. I was a newspaper junkie as far back as I can remember, I still am. You seem to have a discipline in this house, Dan, that we don't have. We get infinite newspapers and magazines and they pile up and they drive Blossom crazy. They drive me crazy too, because I can't get around to reading the *Federalist Papers* or something, for reading the newspapers. And I just had that orientation and it was still there when I got to graduate school; I found if I picked up the *Atlantic* or *Harper's* or something, the things I was reading first were commentaries on current events. (Incidentally the thing that brought Blossom and me together was that we were coeditors of the school magazine. Furman and the Greenville Women's College had just recently been united, and so there were coeditors. Some of my credentials as an early feminist were, the editor from the women's campus was a coeditor until the year we served and I insisted that we both be bracketed as coeditors—my name first of course!) I hadn't really thought of southern history. I didn't have a course in southern history when I was an undergraduate, and in fact because of a conflict in the schedule I didn't even have the course in recent American history, the area in which I have focused most, subsequently. But I got to Chapel Hill and there was a young man there who had been the head librarian at Furman, named J. Isaac Copeland, who was a graduate student in history. I was getting more and more restless and talking with Isaac more and more, and one day he took me over and introduced me to Fletcher Green. And so the more I thought about it the more I was interested. I had written a rather youthful paper as a senior in high school—we had to write a term paper because we would be expected to write term papers—those of us going to college. And my subject was "Negro Education." That was the title. Ten pages.

Jacoway: Do you still have it?

Tindall: No, thank God. I don't think it still exists. I hope it doesn't still exist.

Jacoway: How did it happen that you did a term paper on Negro education?

Tindall: It's hard to figure out what the influences were, but I can remember there were various things. I think the earliest thing I can remember was an incident that occurred that I was not part of and didn't even witness, but there had been a shoving match between some of the kids from the school I went to, Donaldson School on Tindal Avenue—Tindal spelled with a single *l*, however. I had a fourth grade teacher named Laura Butler who gave a little lecture to the class about this, informing us that those black children—she may have said Negro or colored then; she wouldn't have said black—that their parents paid taxes and they owned the sidewalk just as much as we did. And it wasn't appropriate for us to try to push them off the sidewalk, but to share the sidewalk with them. That stuck in my mind and it's still stuck there.

And there must have been some influences from the interracial movement that I was totally unaware existed, but I think some of that filtered through somewhere, and I think this would be surprising, even shocking to some of the young academics, but I think growing up in what was essentially a very conservative Baptist church there were religious influences at work that set me to thinking about that. But I exhausted the subject of Negro education in ten pages.

Carter: Were you fur it or agin' it?

Tindall: I was for it, but I didn't really know how bad it was. I learned only later there hadn't even been a public high school for blacks in Greenville ten years before I entered high school. There was, by then, Sterling. Jesse Jackson was a graduate of Sterling High School later. But there had been some kind of a pathetic effort that maintained a separate academy that the black community had organized.

And then there was the instance, I think an influence: I had taken as an elective a course in state history my senior year in high school. And one thing I remember from that is J. Mauldin Lesesne. He was then a candidate for a doctorate at the University of South Carolina and later president of Erskine. He was one of the three to whom *The Ethnic Southerners* is dedicated. Some of us he put to searching the *Dictionary of American Biography,* for the words *South Carolina* or *South Carolinians;* he was trying to identify every South Carolinian who appeared in there. He put a group of us—to *each* of us, as I recall, about four volumes to go through. We were doing speed reading before Evelyn Wood, skimming the columns looking for the words *South Carolina;* it got kind of tedious after a while. I'm still shocked when students come in, even an occasional graduate student comes in and has never heard of the *Dictionary of American Biography.* It was fairly new at that time—this was 1938, my senior year.

The one thing that led to my dissertation—well, to my thesis topic at first—was a remark Lesesne had made about the South Carolina convention of 1895. In the convention the issue arose of how you define *Negro,* and the committee proposed "one-eighth," and there was a move to make it "any" Negro ancestry. And George Tillman stood up, Ben Tillman's older brother, a former congressman, and said this would embarrass some respectable families who were respected and accepted in the white community. Moreover, he even made the radical statement that there was probably not a single pureblooded Caucasian on the floor of that convention. Well, there were six who were clearly black; but it wasn't necessarily any mixture of black, but some would have American Indian ancestry or some kind of Asian ancestry way back in their family history.

270

And that was something that just stuck in the mind, as I think it would most impressionable seventeen-year-olds in South Carolina in 1938; I'd never heard anything like this, you know. Just something I hadn't really given that much thought to. And that lodged in my mind and it was still there when I decided to switch to history, and so I decided I'd look into that convention of 1895. That made a nice, well-defined topic for a master's thesis. And while I was working on that, Vernon Wharton's *Negro in Mississippi* appeared in print, and Eureka! I had found a topic for this dissertation. So, life is made up of a lot of serendipity, or I could drag in theology and say it was Providence.

McMath: How did Fletcher Green respond to that topic?

Tindall: As I recall, he accepted it immediately as a matter of course. As a matter of fact, a few years before that he had directed a dissertation by a Solomon Breibart, who had a career teaching high school in Charleston after that. I have never met him. It was a thesis on the South Carolina convention of 1868. So I guess that seemed a pretty obvious and natural subject to him at the time.

Jacoway: George, I meant to say at the outset that Les Lamon is with us in spirit today, and he was sorry he couldn't come and be here. But he did send some questions that he wanted us to ask. And one of them was what was the reaction of your family, friends, relatives, whatever to your decision to pursue a racially liberal course of study?

Tindall: I think it was more pride than anything else: that I was concerned about other people. The only question that was raised, my grandfather was a little fearful that I might damage my chances of getting a job. Actually, what he really wasn't aware of was that it enhanced my chances of getting a job.

Jacoway: How would you describe Fletcher Green as a mentor? How active was he in guiding your work?

Tindall: I think my style probably was somewhat unconsciously molded after his, in a way. There was a lot more formality about him, a lot more distance. He frightened a number of students, I think, by this. Looking back on it, I think it may have been a kind of basic reserve on his part, maybe even a certain shyness. It was a rather formal relationship. He was not quite Professor Kingsfield, exactly. I remember one graduate student at that time who said Fletcher Green didn't scare him. He said, "I just go in and tell the old geezer off, and then I just go home and change my drawers."

Frankly, there was never the close personal relationship there that I feel I have had with graduate students. But he set an example. He has a reputation for never having published much, but you start digging around in periodical literature and digging out all the articles he published, and he published more than a lot of people are aware that he did. But he did belong to an old school that put much emphasis on teaching. He was a stickler for—boy, he crammed the bibliography into us. That was the way at that time: you learned reams of bibliography of books that you'd never have the opportunity to read, but you knew what literature was out there if you ever had the need to go for it. And I think there's something to be said for that as against a lot of the theoretical and interpretive stuff that students tend to get now before they get much information about what it is they are theorizing or interpreting about.

But Green's style in your doing the research, I don't think I would describe it as a hands-on thing. I don't know that I ever heard it expressed in quite these terms, but just in the way he went about things, it was the idea that students should find a topic that engages their interest, that you should not try to press a topic too hard on a student. I've had regrets that I ever brought up Scottsboro, for example; I should have saved that for myself! But there, I did; I've always said that I threw out topics and I suggested topics, but it seems to me it's a perfect formula for failure to try to develop a school of thought about history as some people have done. Or maybe they didn't set out to do it, but somehow it's just worked out that they have.

Maybe I have somehow unconsciously done it too, but I didn't set out to do that, because I think I belong to a fairly eclectic school, actually. And I think Fletcher Green did too, because he had students who did a variety of things, and he had a number of students who were quite conservative in their outlook, others who were quite over on (at least what was then) the liberal side in their outlook. And he was pretty even-handed with all of this. One topic he did sort of press on me—but it was not in the sense of "I'm assigning you this topic"—was North Carolina as a progressive state. How did it come about that North Carolina got this reputation? So that's an interesting question, but it just was not a question that grabbed me at that time, and so he didn't insist upon it. And I was already into that thesis at the time, and then when Wharton's book appeared, that's when I realized I was already well on the way to doing for South Carolina what he had done for Mississippi.

Carter: Did you have any sense in the late forties of being in a kind of community of people that maybe shared common ideas—other graduate students, for example?

Tindall: Harry Williams used to like to refer sarcastically to "that brilliant group of young scholars who gathered in Chapel Hill immediately after the war." And you know, that was a good group. I think one reason for that was, of course, that you had a group of veterans from World War II who came in about '45 and '46, and you had sort of compressed there into one group people who had finished college over the previous four years, so that it was a different kind of group from the kind that you get with students coming in from year to year.

I've always thought that when you get right down to it, graduate students do more to educate each other than the faculty does to educate them. I'm going to make a mistake of omitting somebody's name I'm afraid, but Dewey Grantham was part of that group. We had interesting experiences; one was we both went—drove—over to Greensboro together to interview for the same job and were put in rooms across the hall from each other and interviewed in sequence by half the faculty, and Dewey got the job. He also got the job at Vanderbilt that we were competing for. I think he got every job that we ever competed for. And our friendship survived it all, and I think it would have if I had gotten the jobs too. But Dewey was there, Bob Lively was there; Bob, unhappily, died relatively young. I think there was a consensus in both the faculty and among his contemporaries that he was the bright shining light of that generation and would have been the person who would have gone on to be the star of that generation; it didn't work out. Charlie Sellers was there, who was somewhat younger, I believe—as I recall. John Snell, in European history, was part of that group. Bob Lambert, who wound up at Clemson. Whitey Lander was around, though he had been there before the war. Frank Ryan also entered before the war but was still there. Ernest Hooper, who retired from Middle Tennessee in Murfreesboro. Joe Steelman and Lala Steelman were both there. There were still around, just about finished, Mary Elizabeth Massey, Hilda Jane Zimmerman, who died young—Mary Elizabeth did too, fairly young, I think.

More people did dissertations under Fletcher Green than anybody else. He directed far more than I ever did. Of course he was there in the real boom years, the late forties, fifties, sixties. He had come back to stay on the faculty in '36; I guess that's why Vann Woodward was not his student: he didn't get back early enough. But as to members of the faculty, I think Albert Ray Newsome was one of the best-organized lecturers I ever heard. Howard Beale was an interesting character. He was an erratic lecturer—most interesting in a seminar-type situation, I think. I think for our whole generation of southern students there he was a major adventure in culture shock. Howard came from a Yankee background, he came from a background of considerable wealth and style and fashion from the Ivy League; he was the kind of person who had the most generous, liberal impulses, and at the same time was one of the biggest snobs you ever encountered. One unfortunate thing about him was, he had pets, student pets. It turns out that I was one of them, as a matter of fact, but I felt uncomfortable in that role nevertheless.

One interesting thing about Beale, he held a regular Tuesday afternoon tea to which all his students were invited. It was at his Tuesday afternoon tea that I first met Vann Woodward, for example, who was his—I think he's one of only two Ph.D.'s that Beale produced at Chapel Hill. Well, Beale wasn't there very long. As a matter of fact, when you begin to calculate, he came in just—I think—a year before Green returned, and he was away doing war work with the American Foreign Service Committee and had just returned when we arrived after the war and was off to Wisconsin two years later in '48. In fact, we had occupied his house the summer before he left. They were away, and our rent was to help them pack when they got back. And, incidentally he—this was before the age of computers, he could afford this—he had two complete sets of notes on Theodore Roosevelt that he kept in different places. He was drowning in notes; that's why he never wrote the biography of Theodore Roosevelt, I guess, which he was supposed to do.

Anyway, there was Hugh Lefler. I think he would be—clearly he was the most popular lecturer around. Full of good stories, always attacking the administration, and students who didn't know any better thought this was a very courageous thing to be doing, you know. And he was just full of anecdotes, some of which got on the shady side at times. He taught colonial history and he taught state history and he was rather a prolific writer on the subject. Those were the people I guess who made the greatest impression on me. Young Lyle Sitterson at the time was the—he had not yet acquired the patina that he did later—he was the terror of the graduate students on doctoral exams, on oral exams. He would set out in his questioning to entrap you, and usually succeeded. When he began the questioning, people generally were really, really frightened of him. But I found him a very effective teacher. I think, though, Newsome and Green were the best lecturers, the best organized, and Green was—well, he was always right up to date on the literature and was working this material into his lectures. And he was strictly no nonsense about any fooling around or conversations in class. That became very clear very quickly and it was something that just didn't occur in his classes.

Carter: You mean this was a problem even in the 1940s and 1950s, of students sitting there in the room talking while you're trying to lecture?

Tindall: I know it's hard to believe, but sex was also invented a long time ago.

McMath: George, what about influences outside the department? How much interaction was there, for example, with Vance and people in the sociology group, or just sort of climate in the town of Chapel Hill?

Tindall: I think this was more the general climate in the town. I think we were still living, looking back now, sort of in the twilight years of the southern Regionalist movement. Odum was still there, and I knew Odum, and I really didn't get to know Vance until later, but I got to know him very well in later years. As students will do sometimes, I got these great ambitions about going and auditing all these things and broadening my horizons, and as the semester began to close in on me I quit auditing those things because I had assignments to do. I audited a good part of Gordon Blackwell's Southern Regions course, but hadn't had the course; Blossom had the course at Furman. She says it was about kudzu and lespedeza. But Blackwell was one of Odum's students who had taken over a course, the course in Regionalism there.

But actually we were in and out of Odum's house quite a bit because the Odums rented rooms to students, and somehow I think they had a policy of not renting them to students in sociology, that that could lead to problems for obvious reasons. And whether by design or chance, they were renting to graduate students in history. So a number of our friends, Isaac Copeland lived there, Ernest Hooper lived there. Mrs. Odum was a delightful and very proud person about all these graduate students who passed in and out of that house. Howard Odum was always busy all the time so I can't say that I knew him well; I don't know whether he ever knew who I was. We didn't get on very close personal terms.

One of the influences was—except for a brief experience in Officer Candidate School toward the end of the war, which was my first experience with token integration in education. We had one black in our graduating class at of all places, Montgomery, Alabama, better than ten years before the bus boycott. Maxwell Field it was. Except for the room, everything was integrated. We were housed six to a room; we were in two squadrons and he was in the other squadron. A member of the squadron volunteered to room with him and was not permitted to do it. So he had the advantage of having a private room. He had the disadvantage that he had to clean up everything all by himself for inspection. So it all balanced out.

I learned many years later from a reminiscence that John Hope Franklin wrote that he was there at the same time; we'd never heard of each other and didn't meet for several years after that. He was doing research in the Alabama archives right there, just a few miles away, having his first, one of his first, experiences with token integration too. He was right well received there in the Alabama archives; there was no effort to Jim Crow him in the reading room or anything like that. Marie Bankhead Owen brought him into her office for frequent conversations but never invited him to sit down, you see, when he was in her office. But we were there at the same time, I thought that was an interesting fact. And that black officer candidate was named Cecil Poole, damned if it didn't turn out that John Hope Franklin knows Cecil Poole. He became a federal district attorney in San Francisco. He's now a federal circuit judge out there.

But I was going to say I was very much caught up in the activities of the American Veterans Committee, which was sort of a New Dealish liberal answer to the American Legion and the whole line of veterans organizations. We had a rather active chapter. The organization kind of faded, I think it got sort of done in. Well, one of its more famous members at the time was a man named Ronald Reagan. He had fought the battle of Fort Roach during the war— Hal Roach Studios. But he got disillusioned with communism, you see, and he left AVC—which was one of the few liberal groups that fought off and triumphed over the Communist infiltration. We had a long, debilitating battle over that right there in Chapel Hill. Those were the years when Junius Scales was there. We regarded his crowd as being in the "east wing," that is, the east wing which looked to Moscow for guidance.

Carter: Did you know Junius Scales?

Tindall: Yes, I knew him, and I can't say that I disliked him. In fact, we have become firm friends in recent years. He still turns out at historical conventions for the Carolina party and so on. I had a view of him then—and I think it was true—that he was the sort of idealist that, come the revolution, the real Bolsheviks would have had him for breakfast the next day. And there were a number of them who were like that. But it was an interesting experience— in retrospect, I think, a big time-waster. Blossom became a sort of— there was actually this term in the organization—she became an "AVC widow" because I got so caught up in that for a while.

Carter: Was it a political action committee kind of thing?

Tindall: Yeah, and they were always trying to get us to send a delegate to the civil rights congress or some other Communist front organization and striving to take over. And it was the classic pattern of the popular front. And they had the fellow travelers who didn't believe anything that was published in the lying capitalistic press and so on. Most of them became totally, if not all of them by now, became totally disillusioned after Khrushchev's speech on the crimes of Stalin. But there were some really true believers there at that time. But it was also an interesting experience in that it was one of my earliest experiences with integration. Actually, while I was chairman of the group, we invited Dorothy Tilly from Atlanta, who was on Truman's civil rights commission. She and Frank Graham were the two white southerners that were on it.

We invited her and we sponsored her in speaking over in Hill Hall. It turned out a pretty good audience, and we took care that the invitations went out to Shaw and St. Augustine's and North Carolina College for Negroes, now North Carolina Central. We had very much an interracial audience in Hill Hall, and then we staged a reception over at Graham Memorial, which was then the student union. We violated the ultimate taboo of having tea and cookies, breaking bread—or breaking cookies—with the guests. Looking back on it, you know, that could have turned out to be a real disservice to Frank Graham if somebody had gotten a picture of him mingling in that group and Jesse Helms and his crowd had gotten such a picture; I sometimes get chills thinking about what they might have done to him. But it didn't happen.

I remember going to see Fred Weaver, who was dean of students at the time, to tell him what we were planning to do, having this integrated group there. It had been common from the twenties to do that kind of thing on the campus. Of course, as the civil rights issue developed, it became a more delicate question. As long as segregation was not really being challenged, you could do all sorts of things. Odum from 'way back had had black speakers; James Weldon Johnson spoke on the campus on at least one occasion I know about—that is, I've read about it. Fred Weaver said, "You know, sometimes it's best not to ask too many questions."

Carter: In other words, don't come and ask him about it.

Tindall: That's right. So I said I get your message, thank you very much, I won't ask you any more. He didn't say anything. So we went ahead with it without incident. We turned out a good crowd. I was presiding and this black young woman got up and began attacking Dorothy Tilly for not being prepared to go all the way on everything, not being prepared to climb up on the cross and sacrifice herself, I think, at the time. Dorothy Tilly really gave her a put-down. She was not into the white liberal guilt trip. She said, "I don't recall having appointed you the keeper of my conscience." And that was the end of that. It was sort of like Einstein.

279

I never got the attention of the New York *Times* until *The Ethnic Southerners* appeared, and it was subordinated to some potboiler in a joint review even then. I believe that *Emergence of the New South* was the only volume in the History of the South series that the *Times* never reviewed. I was told that the people at LSU understood that a review had been written and had been set up waiting for the appropriate space, but it never got in. I don't know whether their information was correct. I think my timing was so bad that if I had written a book entitled *Emergence of the New South* when I published *South Carolina Negroes*, it would have gotten reviewed. And if I had published one entitled *South Carolina Negroes* when the *Emergence of the New South* came out, it would have gotten reviewed too. Bad timing.

Carter: You said you're not sure exactly how, you thought maybe [Wendell] Stephenson might have had something to do with the recommendation that you be invited to publish that volume.

Tindall: I think so. It was pretty clear that Stephenson was really the more active of the two editors. In fact, he was one of the two original editors, and [Charles] Ramsdell had died and Coulter was his replacement. So I think Stephenson, as the senior editor, really sort of ran the thing and Coulter was somewhat passive. I got through second- or third-hand information the story that Stephenson said that had his eyesight not been failing when that manuscript came in, he would have seen to it that it would have been one-third shorter, and I would have been better off for it.

McMath: Coulter didn't, for example, comment on substantive matters to do with race?

Tindall: The one thing I remember is he did try to get me to tone down the description of a lynching that had occurred in Georgia. And I insisted there ought to be one example. I told him I could give more horrifying examples if I had chosen to. Like this Neal lynching down in Pensacola. The Claude Neal case, that is, I think that's the worst I've ever seen. Although the one I described, this was during the Wilson years, the lynching in which the woman was strung up by her heels and the unborn baby was cut out and—it was terrible. But the Claude Neal thing was as bad or worse. That was just unbelievable.

Carter: Had Vance done any real work on the project? What's the relationship between what he had been doing and what became of the book?

Tindall: There's a good bit of relationship. Incidentally, I have in a jocular sort of way acknowledged Arthur Link as my research assistant there. Actually, he was Vance's research assistant, but I inherited a preliminary bibliography that he had prepared for Vance. This happened about '41, '42, when Vance was just getting started on it. Vance had done some very rough drafts, and in fact there are two chapter titles that were Vance's. I have acknowledged that. "In the House of Their Fathers" is the first chapter, and a later chapter, "The Uneven Places," on welfare. The first two paragraphs of the book are paraphrases of Vance's draft paragraphs. The first paragraph is almost, really, stolen from Vance. Somebody is going to catch me unconsciously tracking somebody else's prose one of these days—that's one of my perennial nightmares.

I also—and Arthur Link has since told me he gathered a lot of this—I inherited a big batch of clippings and old pages taken out of *Time* magazine and so on, and oh, a couple of boxes full of various odds and ends of fugitive pamphlets and mimeographed material and so on. Vance had done a lot of piecemeal work, but he had gotten caught up in other sorts of things. You know, right at the end of the war in '45, he brought out this tremendous book *All These People*, the demographic study of the South. And he was drifting more and more into demography and other commitments, and time's winged chariot was catching up with him, and he decided he had to cut his commitments somewhere, and it was my good fortune that he decided on this.

After my dissertation I had resolved on doing a biography of Wade Hampton III—who had figured in the dissertation, of course. I was getting more and more bored with the old man, to tell you the truth. I've always believed that there was a serendipity or a Providence at work in that. When this was all coming up, Wendell Stephenson was at LSU teaching summer school and I was there. And I had shown him the chapter I had written for *The Southerner as American*, "The Central Theme Revisited," and he seemed to have liked that. So I think all the personal contact there worked out to my advantage.

Carter: In terms of your commitment to spending a lot of time in the sources and working through, is that part of it a chore for you, or do you really enjoy it?

Tindall: It's a chore, yeah, but I think the writing itself can be more of a chore. Often there is the excitement of discovery, but you have to be prepared to accept the inevitability of a lot of tedium in this game. And going through a lot of materials or going down dead-end roads, sinking dry wells, and when you don't find anything but every now and then you, you know, you stumble across a real nugget, a great quotation or bits of information. I don't think, though, I've ever had the—the aging has something to do with it, maybe—I've never had quite the sense of excitement that I felt doing my dissertation and discovering, essentially, what Vernon Wharton had already discovered about the history of segregation, that the world hadn't always been the way it was. When you're very young, I think you're not in a position to see the other possibilities and to look critically so much upon the world. You take it as you see it but assume that's just the way it's always been. And yet I discovered in the course of that dissertation that there had been a world where the segregation practices of the first half of the twentieth century hadn't yet hardened into the form that they did around the turn of the century.

Jacoway: Well, speaking of *The Strange Career of Jim Crow,* would you comment on your relationship with Woodward?

Tindall: I have always had a very friendly relationship with Woodward, and in *The Strange Career of Jim Crow* he gave special acknowledgment to me and to Wharton. Now, I have to say Wharton is the one who made the breakthrough, because if you go back and read, his dissertation was finished in 1939, and it's almost word for word what was published in 1947. It's all there, I think—the basic argument that I developed for South Carolina, that Woodward developed for the *Strange Career,* is there in Wharton's dissertation in 1939. He had found this fluidity in Mississippi that I found in South Carolina and others who've done subsequent state studies in that period have found.

So I have nothing but very friendly feelings toward Vann. Although it has led—I remember very well, I'll have to confess—to a certain feeling of frustration. I was sitting down at LSU, having just recently written this dissertation, and working up piecemeal a proposal for a paper or maybe a session at one of the historical meetings to be titled "Wanted: The History of Segregation." "A History of Racial Segregation," I think I called it. And I mentioned it to somebody, I wish I could remember whom it was I should give credit to, but I don't. Somebody said, "I heard that Vann Woodward recently gave some lectures on that subject." So I wrote Vann and asked him, and by return mail I got page proofs to *Strange Career of Jim Crow.* So I did have a certain feeling of frustration.

But I had a certain eerie feeling thereafter. Shortly after it [*Strange Career*] appeared, there was a little part of the interracial movement which had turned into the Southern Regional Council—a local group in Baton Rouge met in the University Methodist Church in the educational annex. And I heard this earnest young student, I don't know who he was, stand up and cite things from *The Strange Career of Jim Crow* which were things that Woodward had cited from my dissertation about how the world hadn't always been the way it was with respect to segregation. And it was kind of eerie, but it was also kind of gratifying that the word *relevant* hadn't been spoiled then the way it became later. That I had done something—I don't think I even thought of that word at the time—I'd done something that had to do with live issues, it wasn't just the dead past.

Carter: Or that ideas had impact.

Tindall: Just information had impact in that area.

McMath: Is it possible to say how much of your conclusions came from the reading of the historical texts or—did the extra data present themselves to you, as opposed, really, to the *need* for those ideas to be there in 1949 or 1950?

Tindall: That's a good question because there was a whole generation of southern white liberals there who felt, I think, who felt, whether consciously—fully consciously—or not, the need to demonstrate that the South had not always been monolithically conservative, that there was some kind of a liberal tradition in the South, [and they] did pounce upon such materials eagerly. And there was—I do think there's a certain tension, this is not peculiar to that generation—there's a certain tension to want to do good in the world. And who was it who said, "When man sets out to be an angel, he often winds up playing the devil?" Totalitarian regimes have come out of that sort of thing. Bad history has probably killed more people than nuclear science, actually. So historians ought to get more respect, good historians.

McMath: Or be feared more.

Tindall: Or be feared more. The tension between the desire to do good and the desire to tell it like it was, you know. And I don't think that's something anybody can ever sort out, just how his mental processes went. I never thought I could read anybody else's mind because I can't read my own, you know, in so many ways. Or trying to attribute motives to other people is always bad. You can testify to what they say or do but how can you ever know their motives when you're never quite sure what your own motives are? Often I find that young, inexperienced historians will fall into that trap of saying "He thought" when all you can know is "He said this." There's no way you can know what a person is really thinking, it's hard enough to know what you're thinking yourself. And there's that old saying, you know, that I don't know what I think about that because I haven't written it yet. That's a good test to sorting out what you really are thinking. That exercise in writing and revision and trying to state it with clarity and so on. Yeah, I think there was that urge there, and I would be one of the examples of it in that generation, and Vann Woodward would be. I don't think it's peculiar for that generation of historians either by a long shot.

I have felt that where this sort of thing can betray people is where they get so committed to a cause that they begin to preach. And they're apt to carry far less conviction—*I* think, at least—than if one sets out, the best one can, simply to find out the truth of the matter. And I think to try to take the dispassionate view will increase the writer's credibility with the reader. But if you get carried away too much with preaching sermons in writing history, it's apt to put the reader on guard and cautious and make the reader suspicious.

McMath: One place where I read passion into your work is in *Emergence* in the treatment of labor, of mill people.

Tindall: Yeah. I had kind of tenuous connections there. My paternal grandfather moved from the farm when my father was still a child; they moved a pretty short distance actually, into Clifton Mill. And then my father moved on into town and got into retail business. There's not a single whole generation there that was in the mill or in the mill business. Incidentally, Wilbur J. Cash's father had some association with Clifton Mills. I had a great-grandmother named Cash. I'm going to do this—I didn't used to be interested in genealogy, I'm getting very curious—I'm going to have to establish that Wilbur Cash and I are cousins.

Jacoway: Do you suppose that familial connection is why you have a kind of tendency to come down on the side of continuity as opposed to change?

Tindall: I would say I have a tendency to come down on the side of both continuity *and* change. There's a clever new title for you! Squarely on both sides because I think that's the way it is. I don't believe there's any revolution in human history that has involved total change and total destruction of the old, except for maybe where there has been total genocide, something like that. But short of that there's going to be a continuity. Certainly we're seeing that there are surprising continuities in Eastern Europe and Russia. Certainly there was never the kind of totalitarian control to wipe out that continuity in our society. Perhaps more as it affected blacks than as it affected whites, but even there there are a lot of cultural continuities and a lot of drastic change both. I think after so long a time the debate over continuity and discontinuity becomes kind of fruitless because I don't see how you can come down totally on the side of one to the exclusion of the other. They're both there. History is a complex thing. It's not simple like the sciences where there is a clear-cut answer, like solving an equation. You're dealing with human beings.

Carter: Have you ever thought self-consciously about the methodology that you adopted, or that your students ought to adopt?

Tindall: Well, I guess a simple answer would be no, but that would be too simple. I think there's such a thing as getting so involved in methodology—or what is spoken of as methodology now. One of which has to do with simply the sheer mechanics and techniques of research: quantification and that sort of thing. But then there's a kind of thing that many refer to as methodology, which I would regard as theory or ideology, actually. I get even more concerned about that, particularly since it is already the danger that it will turn into dogmatism and intolerance of different ideas. It has happened of course.

And I also think of the constant fascination with the "new history." The date of the book of that title was 1913. I can show you a quotation—which is posted on my office door right now, as a matter of fact—I think I may have sent you a copy. I've got it headed *"Fin-de-Siècle* Cutting Edge," and it's a review-essay that appeared in the *American Historical Review* about Karl Lamprecht's *Deutsche Geschichte,* or *German History,* in which—it's not a review, but an essay about the general reception of it. And that it's being well received because there is a new perception that history is not just past politics. And that accounts for the great reception this book has had. Well, the date of that essay is 1898. David Moltke-

Hansen says he can produce an address to the South Carolina Historical Society in which the speaker is saying, "We know a lot about
our politics and our officeholders and so on; we need to know
about the life of the people." The date of that is 1856. So "new" may
be a misnomer.

 Carter: So it's not the "new" social history. Then what is
different?

 Tindall: In the years since I first got into the history dodge,
there've been real contributions. Vernon Wharton and I and others
were working in black history at that time; that was in large part
something new. Of course, Carter Woodson had been in there
working on that for years and years. The kind of new discoveries
that I suggested a while ago created such excitement about finding
these things. They are old hat now. I don't think any of us talked
about doing the "new history" then. There have been successive
waves of things, and I think all of them have gone through a kind
of aggressive phase of trying to get established. The new economic
history—that was quantification, to a considerable degree. But
those quantifiers finally reached the point where, as Robert Higgs
said, the new economic historians had to recognize that English is
a language too. They began to discover that things that they were
finding through using methods of quantification often were similar
to the things that had been found through traditional methods of
research. They might have confirmed them a bit more. This is also
a field in which Greene's law applies. Jack Greene's law is: "The
more susceptible to proof, the more trivial the question." And I
think there's a lot of truth in that. Though that's not susceptible to
proof, maybe, itself. And over time the new economic history has
sort of become assimilated, it's part of the profession. We went
through the new political history. Then we come to the new social
history, and women's history. And those are both, I think, still kind
of in the aggressive stage of not feeling that they have quite become
established, and needing to fight the battles for acceptance. I think
to many of the old-timers it looks like they're—as I guess these
other things did earlier—it looks like they're just moving in and

taking over the whole field. And there are people who are trying to do that, I think.

Jacoway: That's where your mug fits in.

Tindall: My mug?

Jacoway: "Save the males."

Tindall: Save the males. Not all social history is about women, but men enter into it too. The field *has* become so diverse, and I think it's something to welcome, but it's that continuity and change applies to the *field* of history, too. You don't have to reject all the old in order to introduce the new. I got quite a start when I attended a session on historical publication at a meeting in Dallas of the AHA when a noted historian got up—I won't mention any names, but his initials were Gordon Wood—and he gave us a discourse on how the single-author textbook had become impossible because of the proliferation of techniques and approaches and methodologies. This was in the late seventies, when I was already involved in writing my single-author text, and that gave me some bad moments. I have some comments in the front of the second edition about that. Bernard Bailyn has put it that only a besotted Faust would think that he could keep up with even a major part of all this stuff. But the more I thought about it, the more I thought, "Now, am I supposed to get freshmen and sophomores on top of all of this? Or a general reader who might buy that trade edition?" I found it something of a relief when I realized that you give them some basic outline of American history, you open some doors on some of these things, but you don't have to go through those doors. You give them a glimpse, and if they're interested they may pursue it at some time in the future.

That's what the survey course is about, I think, and if you get too much into some specialized methodology or interpretation you're likely to have some kind of a trendy book that won't last too long, because trends have a way of changing, like fashions. I've seen them change so much in academia, and it's just like in clothing and other things. So you try to make people aware that these things are there, you try to open doors and give them a glimpse, but no one person can give even himself a thorough course in all this—we've just gotten beyond that. I'm not sure there's ever been a point at which anybody could be on top of all of it. But it does trouble me when the new-new-new does become so vaunted.

Recently I've been having a kind of a block. It is not a writer's block, but a kind of rites-of-passage problem. I guess my first realization of it came several years ago when I was coming down the steps of Saunders Hall and I passed one of my younger colleagues and he said, "How are you, Sir?" and I realized then that that was a rite of passage. And then, April 20, there's going to be a retirement reception for me and George Taylor. I dread that. And then there's this *festschrift*. I get the sense of time's winged chariot—everything seems to have piled up on me. I thought in the last semester things would start tapering off. But now I've got to go have a retirement picture or portrait made. I've been stalling on that one, and then George Taylor came to my rescue. It's been customary at these retirement parties to unveil them, but George said he didn't want his unveiled until after he had formally retired, June 30, and then it would just be sneaked in some night and appear on the wall. So *I* can't very well insist that *mine* be unveiled! I recently discovered that the best portrait over there was done by a man named Frank Rosenthal, so I think I'm going to call Rosenthal, and I might take some of the younger colleagues by surprise by looking real mod and hip and all.

Carter: George, are you also concerned about the theme of southern adaptability that we're pursuing in this volume? In my essay I'm going to say that this is *not* a way of explaining or categorizing what has taken place in the South—as either being a South which is traditional and that has been adapted a little bit, or a South which has adapted or changed so much that there's not much of it left—but simply as a way of looking at the *process* by which that "other South"—that South that was—is becoming different, or changing.

Tindall: It *is* a theme of continuity *and* change, and that point should be made explicitly; maybe that phrase, hackneyed though it is, should be thrown in there. Sometimes there's a reason for having clichés: they're there because they express things that are true. But there *are* people who will interpret this as a mossback defense of continuity versus change—which would be to my mind a futile effort, doomed to failure. Although *we* all know better, there are people who wouldn't, so we'll have to be armed against that.

McMath: George, has the cracker crumbled? Is southern history over?

Tindall: I've managed to make a pretty good living out of this for a good many years, and if you all will just keep your mouths shut, you can too. Just stop talking about "the vanishing South"!

THE PRINCIPAL WRITINGS OF
GEORGE BROWN TINDALL

BOOKS

South Carolina Negroes, 1877–1900. Columbia, S.C., 1952. Paperback rpr. Baton Rouge, 1966.

Ed., *The Pursuit of Southern History: Presidential Addresses of the Southern Historical Association, 1935–1963.* Baton Rouge, 1964.

Ed., *A Populist Reader.* New York, 1964. Rpr. Magnolia, Mass., 1975.

The Emergence of the New South, 1913–1945. Baton Rouge, 1967. Paperback rpr. 1970. Volume X of *A History of the South,* edited by E. Merton Coulter and Wendell H. Stephenson. 10 vols.

The Disruption of the Solid South. The Eugenia Dorothy Blount Lamar Memorial Lectures, Mercer University. Athens, Ga., 1972. Paperback rpr. New York, 1972.

The Persistent Tradition in New South Politics. The Walter Lynwood Fleming Lectures, Louisiana State University. Baton Rouge, 1975.

The Ethnic Southerners. Baton Rouge, 1976. Paperback rpr. 1977.

America: A Narrative History. New York, 1984. Published in one-volume hardback, two-volume paperback, and two-volume boxed trade edition. Rev. ed. 1988. Brief Edition, with David Shi, 1989.

Ed. and comp., *Education, Environment, and Culture: The Quality of Life in the South.* Research Triangle Park, N.C., 1986.

ARTICLES AND ESSAYS

"The Campaign for the Disfranchisement of Negroes in South Carolina." *Journal of Southern History,* XV (1949), 212–34.

"The Liberian Exodus of 1878." *South Carolina Historical Magazine,* LIII (1952), 133–45.

"The Question of Race in the South Carolina Constitutional Convention of 1895." *Journal of Negro History,* XXXVII (1952), 277–303.

"Problems of the Southern Schools." *Current History,* XXXII (1957), 272–77.

"John Milliken Parker" and "Arsene Paulin Pujo." In *Dictionary of American Biography,* Supplement Two. New York, 1958.

"The Significance of Howard W. Odum to Southern History: A Preliminary Estimate." *Journal of Southern History,* XXIV (1958), 285–307.

"The Economics of the New South." *Current History,* XXV (1960), 277–81.

"The Central Theme Revisited." In *The Southerner as American,* edited by Charles G. Sellers. Chapel Hill, 1960.

Introduction to "The Status and Future of Regionalism: A Symposium." *Journal of Southern History,* XXVI (1960), 22–24.

"The South: Into the Mainstream." *Current History,* XL (1961), 269–73, 290.

"Business Progressivism: Southern Politics in the Twenties." *South Atlantic Quarterly,* LXII (1963), 92–106.

"Mythology: A New Frontier in Southern History." In *The Idea of the South: Pursuit of a Central Theme,* edited by Frank E. Vandiver. Chicago, 1964.

"The Benighted South: Origins of a Modern Image." *Virginia Quarterly Review,* LX (1964), 281–94.

"Southern Negroes Since Reconstruction: Dissolving the Static Image." In *Writing Southern History: Essays in Historiography in Honor of Fletcher M. Green.* Baton Rouge, 1965.

"The Bubble in the Sun." *American Heritage,* XIV (1965), 76–83, 109–11.

Commentary on David M. Potter's "Depletion and Renewal in Southern History." In *Perspectives on the South: Agenda for Research,* edited by Edgar T. Thompson. Durham, N.C., 1967.

"The Colonial Economy and the Growth Psychology: The South in the 1930s." *South Atlantic Quarterly,* LXIV (1968), 478–95.

"The Burden of Change." *Furman University Magazine,* May, 1968, pp. 10–17.

"The Southern Strategy: A Historical Perspective." *North Carolina Historical Review,* XLVIII (1971), 126–42.

"Populism: A Semantic Identity Crisis." *Virginia Quarterly Review,* XLVIII (1972), 501–18.

"The People's Party." In *History of the U. S. Political Parties,* edited by Arthur M. Schlesinger, Jr. Vol. II (1707–1807) of 4 vols. New York, 1973.

"Beyond the Mainstream: The Ethnic Southerners." *Journal of Southern History,* XL (1974), 3–18.

Commentary on Yoshimitsu Ide's "The Image of the South and the West." *American Review*, VIII (1974), 147–50.

"The Burden of Change in the American South," in *Americana-Austriaca: Beiträge zur Amerikakunde*, III. Vienna-Stuttgart, 1975.

Contributor to panel discussion. In *Southern Literary Study: Problems and Possibilities*, edited by Louis D. Rubin, Jr., and C. Hugh Holman. Chapel Hill, 1975.

"Onward and Upward with the Rising South." In *The Rising South*, edited by Joab Thomas and Donald Noble. Tuscaloosa, 1976.

"Politics." In *The People of the South: Heritages and Futures*. A Regional Conference on the Humanities and Public Policy, May, 1976. Pp. 10–24.

"The New South." In *Reconstruction and the American Negro*, New York, 1976. Vol. VIII of *The American Destiny: A Bicentennial History of the United States*, edited by Henry Steele Commager *et al.*

"The Changing South and World Southernization." Interview by Nagayo Homma. In *The Study of Current English*. Tokyo, 1977.

"A Surfeit of Southern Fried Chic." *Wall Street Journal*, February 9, 1977.

"The Cost of Segregation." In *The Age of Segregation: Race Relations in the South, 1890–1945*, edited by Robert D. Haws. University, Miss., 1978.

"V. O. Key, Revised and New Directions." Commentary on symposium, "The Legacy of V. O. Key's *Southern Politics*," edited by Jack R. Censer, in *South Atlantic Urban Studies*, III (1979), 289–92.

"Georgia: History." In *Collier's Encyclopedia*, 1979.

"Louisiana: A History," In *Collier's Encyclopedia*, 1979.

"The Sunbelt Snow Job." *Houston Review*, I (1979), 3–13.

"The Resurgence of Southern Identity." In *The American South: Portrait of a Culture*, edited by Louis D. Rubin, Jr. Baton Rouge, 1980.

"History and the English Language." *Perspectives* (October, 1984), 7–8, 10–11.

"The South." In *Franklin D. Roosevelt, His Life and Times: An Encyclopedia*, edited by Otis L. Graham, Jr., and Megham Robinson Wander. Boston, 1985.

"North Carolina: From Lubberland to Megastate," Raleigh *News and Observer*, July 14, 1985, pp. 2, 21. Special 400th anniversary edition, Roanoke colony.

"The South's Double Centennial." In *Developing Dixie: Modernization and Traditional Society*, edited by Winfred B. Moore *et al.* New York, 1989.

"Mythic South." In *Encyclopedia of Southern Culture*, edited by Charles Reagan Wilson and William Ferris. Chapel Hill, 1989.

CONTRIBUTORS

DAN T. CARTER is Andrew W. Mellon Professor of Southern History at Emory University. His first book, *Scottsboro: A Tragedy of the American South*, won the Bancroft Prize in History for 1969. His latest book is *When the War Was Over: The Failure of Self-Reconstruction in the South, 1865–1867*.

CHARLES W. EAGLES is associate professor of history at the University of Mississippi. He is the author of *Jonathan Daniels and Race Relations: The Evolution of a Southern Liberal* and *Democracy Delayed: Congressional Reapportionment and Urban-Rural Conflict in the 1920s*.

GARY FREEZE is assistant professor of history and government at Erskine College. His dissertation is now being revised as "The Model Mill Men: The Paternalistic Ethic in a Southern Cotton Mill, 1877–1908."

JERROLD HIRSCH is assistant professor of history at Northeast Missouri State University. He is the author of "Folklore in the Making: B. A. Botkin," published in *Journal of American Folklore*, and of the foreword to the reprint of B. A. Botkin, ed., *Lay My Burden Down: A Folk History of Slavery*.

ELIZABETH JACOWAY is visiting associate professor of history at Arkansas College. She is the author of *Yankee Missionaries in the South: The Penn School Experiment*. She also edited, with David Colburn, *Southern Businessmen and Desegregation*.

LESTER C. LAMON is professor of history and vice-chancellor for Academic Affairs at Indiana University. He is the author of *Black Tennesseans, 1900–1930* and *Blacks in Tennessee, 1791–1970*.

JACK MADDEX is professor of history at the University of Oregon. He is the author of *The Virginia Conservatives, 1867–1879: A Study of Reconstruction*

Politics and *The Reconstruction of Edward A. Pollard: A Rebel's Conversion to Postbellum Unionism.*

Robert C. McMath, Jr., is professor of history at the Georgia Institute of Technology. He is the author of *Populist Vanguard: A History of the Southern Farmers' Alliance* among other works. His next book, *Toward the Cooperative Commonwealth: A Social History of American Populism,* is forthcoming.

Wayne Mixon is professor of history at Mercer University. He is the author of *Southern Writers and the New South Movement, 1865–1913* and the editor of a new edition of Opie Read's 1896 novel, *My Young Master.*

Julian Pleasants is associate professor of history at the University of Florida. He is the author, with Augustus M. Burns III, of *Frank Porter Graham and the North Carolina Senate Election of 1950.*

Walter B. Weare is associate professor of history at the University of Wisconsin–Milwaukee. He is the author of *Black Business in the New South: A Social History of the North Carolina Mutual Life Insurance Company* and "Charles Clinton Spaulding and the Black Bourgeoisie," in *Black Leadership in the Twentieth Century,* edited by John Hope Franklin and August Meier.

INDEX

Abernathy, Milton A., 184
ACLU. *See* American Civil Liberties
  Union (ACLU)
Addams, Jane, 140
Adger, John B., 21, 24, 41
African Americans. *See* Blacks
Agee, James, 243
Agrarians (Nashville), 153, 158–60,
  163
Agriculture, 213, 216–17, 243–44,
  244*n*
Alabama. *See* Lowndes County, Ala.
Alabama Christian Movement for Hu-
  man Rights, 221*n*
Alsberg, Henry, 156
American Civil Liberties Union
  (ACLU), 230
Anderson, Charles W., 115
Anderson, Isaac, 64, 65, 65–66*n*3,
  67–68
Ashby, Warren, 178
Ashmore, Harry, 191
Astor, John Jacob, 127
Atlanta Compromise, 107, 112, 119,
  121
Atlanta University, 121

Bacon, Alice, 109
Bagby, George W., 138
Bailyn, Bernard, 288
Baker, Ray Stannard, 169
Baldwin, John C., 72, 73

Baptist church, 60, 61
Barber, James David, 239, 260
Bartlett, Alexander, 77, 83
Bartlett, Peter Mason, 79, 83, 84–85
Bartley, Numan, 209
Bass, Jack, 198, 264
Beal, Fred, 179
Beale, Howard, 274–75
Bean, William S., 43
Beck, John J., 48
Bendix, Reinhard, 62
Berea College, 83, 89
Bevel, James, 220
Bierbaum, Theodore, 55
Bingham, Barry, 191–92
Black Panther party, 233
Blacks: Tindall on, 2–3, 5–9; Presbyte-
  rians' view of, 12, 82–83; decision
  of Maryville College to admit, 13,
  64, 70–72, 75–76; and exposition
  movement, 13–14, 99–123; bour-
  geois black society, 13–14, 93–95,
  97–98, 100, 105; in Lowndes
  County, Ala., 15–16, 212–36; membership in Presbyterian church, 24–
  26, 75, 76, 82–83; education of, 64,
  65–66, 73–74, 76–79, 86, 186, 187,
  204–206, 219, 231, 232, 269–70; attendance at Maryville College, 76–
  77, 80, 83, 84, 84*n*, 88–89; opposition to, at Maryville College, 77–81,
  83, 84–86; and civil rights, 78, 194–

96, 197, 212–13, 220–36; in Tennessee, 81–82; and Republicans, 82; and New South Creed, 90–94, 91*n*, 110–11; and genocide, 92; disfranchisement of, 93, 214, 218; fairs and festivals for, 95–97, 104; discrimination against, 117, 120–21, 186, 187–88, 214, 218–19, 227–28; and race riots, 118, 121, 122, 229; as writers in Federal Writers' Project, 150; FWP life histories of, 165–67; portrayal in FWP southern guidebooks, 167–74; and Graham, 182–88, 194–209; in North Carolina, 182–88, 194–209; as elected officials, 212, 233, 235–36; violence against, 214–16, 219, 222, 230; lynching of, 215–16; poverty of, 218, 234; voter registration of, 220–24, 226–29, 231. *See also* Slavery

Blackwell, Gordon, 276
Blount, Roy, Jr., 240, 256, 262
Boardman, Samuel W., 84
Boas, Franz, 157
Boggs, William E., 23, 33
Botkin, B. A., 15, 148, 149, 153–61, 165, 166, 167, 174–75
Bourbonism, 7, 16, 246, 247, 263
Breibart, Solomon, 271
Brooks, Cleanth, 265
Broughton, J. Melville, 197
Brown decision, 218
Bryan, William Jennings, 115, 260
Business progressivism, 16, 54, 61–62, 248, 254, 262
Butler, Laura, 4, 269
Byrd, William, 136

Cabell, James Branch, 146
Caddell, Patrick, 255
Caldwell, Erskine, 162–63
Carmichael, Stokely, 223, 232
Carnegie, Andrew, 114

Carter, Billy, 256
Carter, Earl, 239, 247
Carter, Jimmy: and business progressivism, 16, 248, 254, 262; political tradition of, 16, 246–50, 262; as southerner, 237–41, 245–46, 251–52, 255–56, 258, 261–63; biographical information on, 238, 244–45, 246, 248; and *Playboy* interview, 239; as middle-class southerner, 240–43; religion of, 242–43; and technology, 243–45, 244*n*; as president, 244, 252–59, 262; and race relations, 245, 258–61; as governor, 247, 248; first presidential campaign of, 247–51; administrative style of, 252–53, 253*n*, 262; domestic policy of, 253–54, 254–55*nn*; tour of South during presidency, 256–59; and human rights, 257–58; second presidential campaign of, 259–62
Carter, Lillian, 247
Carter, Rosalynn, 238*n*, 241, 243
Cash, Wilbur J., 124, 176, 285
Cather, Willa, 139, 139*n*
Centennial Exhibition (Philadelphia), 101
Chamberlain, Hope Summerall, 50, 53
Chase, Harry Woodburn, 266
Chopin, Kate, 135, 139*n*
Churches. *See* names of specific churches
Civil rights: under Truman, 194–96, 197; in Lowndes County, Ala., 212–13, 220–36; and Jimmy Carter, 245, 258–61; political beneficiaries of, 245–46*n*. *See also* Blacks
Civil Rights Act (1964), 219
Civil Rights Bill (1874), 78
Civil Rights Committee/Commission, 194–96, 200–201, 278
Coleman, Tom L., 230, 233
Colleges. *See* Maryville College; and

names of other colleges and universities
Collins, Leroy, 253
Columbia Seminary, 32, 34
Communist party, 177, 179, 180, 182–83, 191, 192–94, 200, 225, 278
Confederacy. *See* Presbyterian Church in the Confederate States of America (PCCSA)
Conner, R. D. W., 4
Connor, Eugene "Bull," 189
Conwell, Russell, 54
Copeland, J. Isaac, 2, 268–69, 276
Cotton mills: in Salisbury, N.C., 13, 44, 48–49, 54–55, 57–59, 61–62; and philanthropic impulse, 44–45, 50, 54–56, 58–59, 61–62; as commercial venture, 45–46; before the Civil War, 56–57
Cotton States Exposition (Atlanta), 105, 107–11
Couch, W. T., 153, 156, 173
Craig, John Sawyers, 69
Crawford, G. S. W., 77
Crum, William D., 117
Crummell, Alexander, 102, 105

Dabney, Robert L., 20, 24, 25, 27, 33–43
Daniels, Jonathan (newspaper editor), 183, 197, 198
Daniels, Jonathan Myrick (civil rights worker), 15–16, 229–30
Darwinism, 92, 93, 98, 110
Davis, O. D., 60
Degler, Carl N., 133
Deng Xiaoping, 244, 245, 254
DeVries, Walter, 198
Dickson, Andrew F., 33
Dodge, William E., 72, 73
Douglas, R. D., Jr., 192
Douglass, Charles Remond, 109
Douglass, Frederick, 96, 101, 104, 107, 109

Du Bois, W. E. B., 90, 92, 100, 104, 109, 117, 120–23
Durr, Virginia, 5

East Tennessee Wesleyan College, 74
Edmonds, Richard Hathaway, 53
Education. *See* Blacks; Maryville College; and names of other colleges and universities
Edwards, Jonathan, 65n2
Einstein, Albert, 266–67
Ellison, Ralph, 109
Engerman, Stanley, 91n
Ericson, E. E., 182–83
Erskine, George M., 65–66
Escott, Paul D., 45–46, 48, 62
Evans, Walker, 243
Exposition movement: rationale for blacks' involvement in, 13–14, 99–101; origins of, 94–97; and world's fairs, 97–99, 105; Centennial Exhibition (1876) in Philadelphia, 101; separate black expositions, 101–102, 111–12; Woman's Building at expositions, 101, 106; Cotton States Exposition (1895) in Atlanta, 105, 107–11; Jamestown Tercentennial Exposition (1907), 105, 117–21; South Carolina Interstate and West Indian Exposition (1902) in Charleston, 105, 112, 115–17; Tennessee Centennial Exposition (1897) in Nashville, 105, 112–15; Negro Buildings at expositions, 106–108, 111, 113, 115, 117, 118, 119–20; World's Industrial and Cotton Centennial (1885) in New Orleans, 106–107

Factories. *See* Cotton mills
Fair Employment Practices Commission (FEPC), 195, 197, 199, 200, 201, 202, 203, 207
Fallows, Jim, 256–57, 260
Federal Writers' Project: significance

of, 14–15; and Botkin, 148, 153–61, 165, 166, 167, 174–75; folklore studies and, 148–50, 154–60; black writers in, 150; cultural politics of, 150–53, 172–75; national perspectives on, 150–53, 161, 172–75; views of local southern Federal Writers, 152–53, 161, 165–75; and Lomax, 154–55; and Couch, 160–65, 173; southern life-history project of, 160–65; publication of *These Are Our Lives*, 164–65; interviews of blacks for life histories, 165–67; former slaves' narratives for, 166–67, 174; guidebooks to the southern states, 167–71; plantation tradition in southern guidebooks, 167–72; portrayal of blacks in southern guidebooks, 167–74

Feminism, 135–41, 145
FEPC. *See* Fair Employment Practices Commission (FEPC)
Fisher, Charles S., 55
Fisk, Clinton B., 95
Fisk University, 74, 119
Fogel, Robert, 91*n*
Folklore: definition of, 14–15; Botkin's views on, 148, 153–61, 165, 166, 167, 174–75; relationship with history, 148–50, 164–65; and Federal Writers' Project, 154–60; Lomax's views on, 154–55; and southern life-history project, 160–61; in FWP southern guidebooks, 167–71
Folsom, Jim, 259, 262
Ford, James W., 182, 183
Foust, I. Henry, 52, 57–58, 60, 61
Franklin, John Hope, 277
Franklin, William Henderson, 76–77, 81, 88
Frazier, E. Franklin, 94
Free-Soil controversy, 20
Freedmen's Bureau, 70, 73, 74
Freedmen's Normal School, 78

Friedman, Jean E., 135
FWP. *See* Federal Writers' Project

Gaines, Francis Pendelton, 171
Gamble, Arthur, 225
Garveyism, 100, 122
Gaston, Paul, 113
Gay, Peter, 132, 147
Gender discrimination, 135–41, 145
Genovese, Eugene, 91*n*
Girardeau, John L., 21, 23, 24, 25, 41
Glasgow, Ellen, 140, 146
Golson, Carl, 220, 221
Gordy, Jim Jack, 247
Gore, Albert, Sr., 259
Grady, Henry, 53, 104, 244, 263
Graham, Edward Kidder, 266
Graham, Frank Porter: defeat for U.S. Senate seat, 15, 208–11; significance of, 176–177, 210–11; as university president, 177, 181–85, 266; early life and education of, 177–78; membership in liberal and radical organizations, 177, 193–94; values of, 178–79, 181, 183, 191, 201, 209; and improvement of working conditions, 179–80; and race relations, 179, 182–88, 194–210; defense of Lawrence, 180–81; and academic freedom, 182–83; and Southern Conference for Human Welfare, 189–93, 194; on Civil Rights Committee/Commission, 194–96, 197, 200–201, 278; on National War Labor Board, 194; appointment as U.S. senator, 196–97; campaign for U.S. Senate, 199–208; as U.S. senator, 200, 203; influence on Tindall, 265, 266
Graham, Hugh, 209
Grantham, Dewey, 273–74
Green, Fletcher, 2, 269, 271–73, 274, 275–76
Greene, Jack, 287

Haller, John, 133
Haller, Robin, 133
Hamilton, Joseph G. de Roulhac, 4, 266
Hampton, Wade, III, 281
Hampton Institute, 114
Hardy, Thomas, 129
Harlan, Louis, 109
Harlem Renaissance, 100
Harris, Fred, 249n
Harrison, William Henry, 238
Hauser, William, 205
Haywood, William Dallas, 103
Helms, Jesse, 279
Higgs, Robert, 287
Hightower, Jim, 249n
Hill, Richard, 113
Hodges, Luther, 253
Hoey, Clyde, 203
Hoge, Moses Drury, 22, 29, 34, 35
Holden, W. W., 33
Hooper, Ernest, 274, 276
Hoover, Herbert, 245
Hopkins, Samuel, 65, 65n2
Horah, Rowan, 52
Horney, Karen, 140
Howard, O. O., 70, 72, 73
Howard University, 119
Hughes, Langston, 122, 184
Hulett, John, 16, 221, 232, 233, 235–36
Hunt, Jason, 52
Hunt, Martha C., 52
Hunter, Charles Norfleet, 102–105, 111, 118, 119
Hunter, Osborne, Jr., 102
Hunter, Osborne, Sr., 103

Industrialization. *See* Cotton mills

Jackson, Jesse, 258, 270
Jackson, Stonewall, 22
Jamestown Tercentennial Exposition (1907), 105, 117–21

Johnson, Andrew, 73
Johnson, Frank M., 232
Johnson, Gerald, 183
Johnson, James Weldon, 279
Johnson, Jeff, 201, 208
Johnson, Samuel, 265
Johnson Normal School, 104
Johnston, Mary, 146
Jones, Anne Goodwyn, 134–35
Jones, Charles, 188–89
Jones, Charles Colcock, 21
Jones, Leroy, 204–207
Jordan, Hamilton, 249, 250

Kellogg, John H., 132
Kennedy, John, 251
Key, V. O., Jr., 176, 198
Khrushchev, Nikita, 278
King, Martin Luther, Jr., 220–21, 222, 260, 262
Kittrell College, 104
Kluttz, Theodore, 50, 52, 59
Knox, John M., 52, 61
Knoxville College, 78
Ku Klux Klan, 200, 222, 224, 225, 259–60, 261

Lamar, Thomas Jefferson, 68–70, 72, 73, 75, 77, 79, 83, 88
Lambert, Bob, 274
Lamprecht, Karl, 286
Lance, Bert, 256
Lander, Whitey, 274
Lane, Edward, 37
Langston, John Mercer, 95
Lawrence, Alton, 180–81, 188
Lawrence, D. H., 128
Lawrence, Job, 81–82
LCCMHR. *See* Lowndes County Christian Movement for Human Rights (LCCMHR)
LCFO. *See* Lowndes County Freedom Organization (LCFO)

Lee, Robert E., 125
Lefler, Hugh, 275
Lesesne, J. Mauldin, 270
Lewis, Kemp P., 184
Link, Arthur, 281
Liuzzo, Viola, 15–16, 222–23, 224–25
Lively, Bob, 274
Lomax, John, 154–55, 156
Long, Huey, 247, 247*n*, 248
Lowndes County, Ala.: civil rights movement in, 15–16, 212–13, 220–36; black elected officials in, 212, 233, 235–36; violence in, 212, 214–16, 219, 222, 230; agriculture in, 213, 216–17; economic conditions in, 213, 216–18, 233–35; history of, 213–17; population of, 213, 215, 216–17, 235; slavery in, 213; black voter registration in, 220–24, 226–29, 231; education in, 227–28, 231, 232; blacks' independent political party in, 231–33; improvements in, 233–36
Lowndes County Christian Movement for Human Rights (LCCMHR), 221–24, 231, 234
Lowndes County Freedom Organization (LCFO), 231, 232–33
Lowndes County Private School Foundation, 228
Luckey, Seth J. W., 69*n*14
Lutheran church, 60
Lynchings, 215–16

McCorkle, James M., 50
McCulloch, George D., 85–86
MacDonald, Edgar E., 146
McIlwaine, Richard, 36
McKinley, William, 115
Makepeace, George, 57, 58
Mallard, Robert Q., 34
Martin, Charles, 190
Martin, Joel, 53, 54
Maryville College: decision to admit blacks, 13, 64, 70–72, 75–76, 88; during Civil War, 64, 68–69; founding of, 64–65; reopening after Civil War, 64, 69, 69*n*14, 88; before Civil War, 67–68, 88; fund-raising efforts of, 69–70, 72–75, 84; blacks' attendance at, 76–77, 80, 83, 84, 84*n*, 88–89; opposition to admission of blacks, 77–81, 83, 84–86; decision to educate whites only, 86–88, 89
Massey, Mary Elizabeth, 274
Maynard, Horace, 69*n*14
Maynor, Dorothy, 187–88
Meier, August, 94
Mencken, H. L., 146, 250
Methodist church, 13, 58–59, 60–61, 74, 78
Miller, Thomas Ezekiel, 116
Miller, William Lee, 238*n*
Mills. *See* Cotton mills
Mitchell, Broadus, 44–45, 46, 48, 49, 50, 56, 57, 62
Mitchell, Margaret, 140
Moltke-Hansen, David, 286–87
Moody, Dwight, 51
Moore, Fred R., 119–20
Morrisroe, Richard, 229–30
Morristown College, 78, 83*n*
Morse, Wayne, 194
Morton, G. Nash, 37
Moses, Wilson, 109
Mossell, Nathan F., 120–21
Moton, Leroy, 222
Moyers, Bill, 239, 251
Murdoch, Francis J., 54–55, 57, 58, 59, 60–61
Murfree, Mary Noailles, 137
Murphy, Matt, 225
Murphy Law, 86, 89
Murray, Chalmers S., 166
Murray, Pauli, 186, 187
Myrdal, Gunnar, 190

NAACP, 103, 122, 187, 204, 221*n*
National Council of Colored People, 94

National Democratic Party of Alabama (NDPA), 233
NCIA. *See* North Carolina Industrial Association (NCIA)
NDPA. *See* National Democratic Party of Alabama (NDPA)
Neal, Claude, 280–81
Negro Convention Movement, 94
New Negro movement, 122
New School Presbyterians, 19, 21, 22, 72, 73, 74
New South Creed: and blacks, 90–94, 91*n*; Grady and, 104–105; and exposition movement, 105–106; and race relations, 110; blacks' response to, 110–11; in FWP southern guidebooks, 168; and Jimmy Carter, 262–63
Newman, Frances, 140
Newsome, Albert Ray, 274
Niagara Movement, 118, 121
Niebuhr, Reinhold, 243
Nixon, Richard, 247
North Carolina. *See* Salisbury, N.C.
North Carolina Industrial Association (NCIA), 104–105
Northern Presbyterian Church. *See* Presbyterian Church in the United States of America (PCUSA)

Odell, Ann Cox, 60
Odell, John L., 60, 60*n*
Odell, John Milton, 58–59, 60
Odum, Howard, 276–77, 279
Owen, Marie Bankhead, 277

Page, Thomas Nelson, 167
Palmer, Benjamin M., 20, 26, 35, 41
Paton, Alan, 123
PCCSA. *See* Presbyterian Church in the Confederate States of America (PCCSA)
PCUS. *See* Presbyterian Church in the United States (PCUS)

PCUSA. *See* Presbyterian Church in the United States of America (PCUSA)
Pearson, Drew, 201
Pearson, Robert Gamaliel, 50–55, 58, 61
Peck, Thomas E., 34
Phillips, Charles, 33
Phillips, U. B., 3*n*
Pierce, Robert M., 250
Pittman, C. L., 265, 266
Pittman, William Sidney, 119
Plantation tradition: in southern guidebooks, 167–72
Plessy v. *Ferguson*, 107, 206
Plumer, William S., 34
Poole, Cecil, 277
Populism, 7, 16, 246, 247–50, 247*n*, 249*n*, 262, 263
Potter, David, 6, 8
Presbyterian Church in the Confederate States of America (PCCSA), 19, 22–23, 26, 27, 28, 30, 32, 39–40, 43
Presbyterian Church in the United States (PCUS): changes in attitude toward blacks, 12; and reunion with northern counterparts, 18, 40–42; membership of, 19, 31–32; views on slavery, 19–22, 24, 29, 35–37, 40, 41–42; founding of, 23–24; blacks in, 24–26; conflicts with PCUSA, 24, 26–28, 37, 38, 39, 41; apolitical stance of, 27–28; interchurch relations of, 29–30, 37–39; redefinition based on southern identity, 30–31, 42–43; New South agenda of, 32–35, 42–43; recovery of sense of American patriotism, 34–35; foreign missions of, 36–37, 42; in Salisbury, N.C., 60
Presbyterian Church in the United States of America (PCUSA): and Maryville College, 13, 64, 65, 71; and reunion with PCUS, 18, 30, 31, 40–42, 82; conflicts with PCUS, 24,

26–28, 37, 38, 39, 41; and blacks, 25, 82–83; views on slavery, 65–67
Progressivism, 7, 16, 246, 247, 248, 253–54, 262, 263

Quakers, 78

Rabinowitz, Howard, 101
Race relations. *See* Blacks
Race riots, 118, 121, 122, 229
Rainey, Betty, 257–58
Ramsdell, Charles, 280
Ramsey, Hiden, 202
RCA. *See* Reformed Church in America (RCA)
Reagan, Ronald, 259–60, 261, 278
Reed, John Shelton, 145, 240–41, 242
Reformed Church in America (RCA), 38
Regionalists (Chapel Hill), 153, 159, 276
Religion. *See* names of specific churches
Religious revivals, 44–45, 49–55
Reuther, Walter, 209
Revivals. *See* Religious revivals
Rives, Amélie: significance of, 14, 126, 145–47; biographical information on, 125–27, 142–43, 144–45; sexuality in works of, 127–35; criticism of works of, 129, 131, 134; poor whites in works of, 129–31, 136–37; critique of gender discrimination in works of, 135–41, 145; blacks in works of, 136*n*; upper-class southern women in works of, 137–39; male characters in works of, 141–44; and love of place, 142–45. Works: *World's-End*, 14, 131–32, 141–44; *The Quick or the Dead?* 127–29, 134, 135, 142; *Barbara Dering*, 129, 134, 138–39, 140; *Virginia of Virginia*, 129–30, 131, 134, 136–37; *Tanis, the Sang-Digger*, 130–31, 136–37; *Shadows of Flames*, 144

Robinson, Stuart, 27, 31
Roosevelt, Eleanor, 197
Roosevelt, Franklin, 189
Roosevelt, Theodore, 117, 275
Rosenthal, Frank, 289
Ruffner, William Henry, 33
Rumple, Jethro, 60
Russell, Richard, 247, 247*n*, 263
Ryan, Frank, 274
Rydell, Robert, 98, 99

Salisbury, N.C.: cotton mill in, 13, 44, 49–50, 59, 61–62; religious revival in, 44, 46–47, 49–50, 52, 52*n*15; as trade center, 47–48; during Civil War, 47; interest in new cotton mill for, 48–49, 57–59; churches in, 59–63
Sanford, Terry, 211
Scales, Junius, 278
SCHW. *See* Southern Conference for Human Welfare (SCHW)
SCLC. *See* Southern Christian Leadership Conference (SCLC)
Scott, Kerr, 196–97, 203, 209
Segregation: in education, 86, 186–88, 206, 219, 227–28, 232; elimination of, 195–96, 206; in Lowndes County, Ala., 214, 218–19, 232. *See also* Blacks
Sellers, Charlie, 274
Sexuality, 127–35
Shuttlesworth, Fred L., 221*n*
Simkins, Francis Butler, 177
Singal, Daniel J., 62, 159
Sitterson, Lyle, 275
Skaggs, Merrill Maguire, 137
Slavery: Presbyterians' views on, 19–22, 24, 29, 35–37, 40, 41–42, 65–67, 73; and abolitionism, 22, 66–67; FWP former slaves' narratives, 166–67, 174; in Lowndes County, Ala., 213. *See also* Blacks
Smith, Benjamin M., 32
Smith, Hoke, 263

Smith, Preserved, 72, 73
Smith, Willis, 200–202
Smithsonian Institution, 99, 102
SNCC. *See* Student Nonviolent Coordinating Committee (SNCC)
Snell, John, 274
Social Purity Movement, 132–33
Socialist party, 180, 181, 183, 194
South Carolina Interstate and West Indian Exposition (1902) at Charleston, 105, 112, 115–17
Southern and Western Seminary, 75
Southern Christian Leadership Conference (SCLC), 220, 221, 229
Southern Conference for Human Welfare (SCHW), 189–93, 194
Southern Presbyterian Church. *See* Presbyterian Church in the United States (PCUS)
Southern Regional Council, 191, 283
Spencer, Cornelia Phillips, 33
Steelman, Joe, 274
Steelman, Lala, 274
Stennis, John, 246*n*, 259
Stephenson, Wendell, 280, 282
Stevenson, Adlai E., 47, 108
Student Nonviolent Coordinating Committee (SNCC), 220, 223–24, 226–27, 229, 231
Sumner, Charles, 78, 103
Sweatt, Heman, 206
Sweatt v. *Painter*, 206
Swift Memorial Institute, 81, 87

Talmadge, Herman, 246*n*
Tate, Allen, 159, 164–65
Taylor, Alrutheus Ambush, 95
Taylor, George, 289
Tennessee Centennial Exposition (1897) in Nashville, 105, 112–15
Textile industry. *See* Cotton mills
Thaw, William, 72, 73, 79–81, 84, 89
Thomas, John W., 113
Thompson, Holland, 56

Thornwell, James H., 20–21, 22, 27, 28
Thurmond, Strom, 246*n*
Tillman, Ben, 270
Tillman, George, 270
Tilly, Dorothy, 278–79
Tindall, Blossom McGarrity, 2, 4, 10*n*18, 267–68, 276, 278
Tindall, George Brown: career of, 1–8; lectures of, 1, 7–8, 11; education of, 2, 3–4, 265–79; writings of, 2–3, 5–7, 280, 291–93; opposition to racial discrimination, 3–5, 269–70; humor of, 7–8; on the writing of history, 9–11, 284–90; on variety of styles in the South, 125, 246, 289–90; and business progressivism, 248; on research techniques, 282; relationship with Woodward, 282–83; retirement of, 289. Works: *South Carolina Negroes*, 3, 280; *The Emergence of the New South*, 5–7, 280–81, 285; "History and the English Language," 9–10, 264; *America: A Narrative History*, 11; *Ethnic Southerners*, 280
Troubetzkoy, Pierre, 127
Truman, Harry, 194, 195, 197, 200, 278
Turner, Henry M., 104, 106–107
Tuskegee Institute, 109, 114

Union Seminary, 32, 42
United Presbyterian Church in North America, 78
Universities. *See* names of specific universities
University of North Carolina, 177, 181–85, 186, 187, 265, 266
University of Texas, 206

Vance, Rupert, 5, 281
Voter registration, 220–24, 226–29
Voting Rights Act (1965), 229

Waddel, John N., 32
Wallace, Anthony F. C., 46
Wallace, George, 246*n*, 249, 259
Wallace, Paris A., 84, 89
WARC. *See* World Alliance of Reformed Churches (WARC)
Ward, Lester Frank, 140
Warren, Robert Penn, 265
Washington, Booker T., 92, 93, 100, 102–12, 114, 116, 117, 119, 121, 122
Watson, Tom, 247, 263
WCTU. *See* Women's Christian Temperance Union (WCTU)
Weaver, Fred, 279
Webb, Walter Prescott, 10
Welty, Eudora, 143
Wharton, Edith, 139
Wharton, Vernon Lane, 3, 271, 273, 282–83, 287
White, Theodore, 245
White, Walter, 187, 204
White Cross Society, 133
White v. *Crook*, 231–32
Wiebe, Robert, 98

Wilde, Oscar, 127
Wiley, Samuel H., 57–58, 59, 60, 61
Wilkins, Collie Leroy, 224–26
Williams, T. Harry, 273
Williamson, Joel, 82, 92
Wilson, Samuel Tyndale, 89
Wilson, Woodrow, 280
Women's Christian Temperance Union (WCTU), 132
Wood, Gordon, 288
Woodrow, James, 22
Woodson, Carter, 287
Woodward, C. Vann, 3, 6, 45, 46, 91*n*, 106, 113, 237, 243, 257, 274, 275, 282–83, 285
World Alliance of Reformed Churches (WARC), 38, 40
World's fairs, 97–99, 105, 106–107
World's Industrial and Cotton Centennial (1885) in New Orleans, 106–107
Wright, Louis B., 265

Zimmerman, Hilda Jane, 274